Dreams of Prevention and Control

Policing and Public Health in Colonial Asia

Dreams of Prevention and Control

Policing and Public Health in Colonial Asia

Edited by
Takeshi Onimaru

Kyoto University Press

TRANS PACIFIC PRESS

First published in 2025 jointly by:

Kyoto University Press
69 Yoshida Konoe-cho
Sakyo-ku, Kyoto 606-8315, Japan
Telephone: +81-75-761-6182
Fax: +81-75-761-6190
Email: sales@kyoto-up.or.jp
Web: http://www.kyoto-up.or.jp

Trans Pacific Press Co., Ltd.
[Editorial Office]
2-2-15-2F, Hamamatsu-cho, Minato-ku,
Tokyo, 1050013, JAPAN
[Reistered Office]
PO Box 8547 #19682
Boston, MA, 02114, United States
Email: info@transpacificpress.com
Web: http://www.transpacificpress.com

Copyedited by Dr Karl E. Smith, Melbourne, Australia
Layout designed and set by Ryo Kuroda, Tsukuba-city, Ibaraki, Japan

Cover photo: The corner of Robinson Road and Market Street, Singapore, c. 1928. Source: National Museum of Singapore.
Back cover photo (left): Police in Shanghai, c. 1924. Source: Smith Archive / Alamy Stock Photo.
Back cover photo (right): A group of people being inoculated against the plague in a bazaar in Mandalay, c. 1906. Source: Wellcome Collection / CC BY 4.0.

Distributors

World
Independent Publishers Group (IPG)
814 N. Franklin Street
Chicago, IL 60610, USA
Telephone inquiries: +1-312-337-0747
Order placement: 800-888-4741 (domestic only)
Fax: +1-312-337-5985
Email: frontdesk@ipgbook.com
Web: http://www.ipgbook.com

Japan
For purchase orders in Japan, please contact any distributor in Japan.

China
China Publishers Services Ltd.
718, 7/F., Fortune Commercial Building,
362 Sha Tsui Road, Tsuen Wan, N.T.
Hong Kong
Telephone: +852-2491-1436
Email: edwin@cps-hk.com

Southeast Asia
Alkem Company Pte Ltd.
1, Sunview Road #01-27, Eco-Tech@Sunview
Singapore 627615
Telephone: +65 6265 6666
Email: enquiry@alkem.com.sg

Library of Congress Control Number: 2025901724

ISBN: 978-1-920850-54-8 (paperback)
ISBN: 978-1-920850-55-5 (eBook)

Table of Contents

List of Figures

List of Tables

Acknowledgment

This edited volume originated from the panel, 'State and Surveillance: Comparative Colonial State Formation in Southeast Asia,' at the Inaugural Conference of the Consortium for Southeast Asian Studies in Asia, held in Kyoto in December 2015. The contents of this volume have subsequently been discussed at several workshops sponsored by research grants from the Japan Society for the Promotion Science (JSPS) and the Ministry of Education, Culture, Sports, Science and Technology (MEXT), Japan. These grants are Grand-in-Aid for Scientific Research on Innovative Areas No. 25101004, Grant-in-Aid for Scientific Research (B) No. 17H02239 and No. 20H04406, and Grant-in-Aid for Scientific Research (A) No. 23H00017. The research for Chapters 1, 2, and 8 was also supported by Wellcome Trust Funding.

The conference and workshops provided valuable and constructive comments, suggestions, and advice especially from Robert Cribb, Akihito Kudo, Chris Baker, Pasuk Phongpaichit, Yusuke Takagi, Tetsushi Sonobe, and Geoffrey Wade. I would like to thank Geoffrey Wade, for introducing me to a member of the Wellcome Unit for the History of Medicine at the University of Oxford. Khoo Boo Teik and Caroline Hau read the original manuscripts of all chapters and offered suggestions and comments. Without their help, I could not have realized this project.

About Authors

Takeshi Onimaru is a Professor at the Faculty of Social and Cultural Studies, Kyushu University. His research interests cover political history and modern state formation processes in East and Southeast Asia, mainly focusing on colonial surveillance and policing. His major publications include 'Itinerary, Revolution, and Port Cities: Comparative Study on Maritime Port Cities as Arenas for Asian Revolutionary Movements', in Shigeru Akita, Hong Liu, and Shiro Momoki (eds.), *Changing Dynamics and Mechanisms of Maritime Asia in Comparative Perspectives* (Palgrave Macmillan, 2021), 'Financing Colonial State Building: A Comparative Study of the 19th Century Singapore and Hong Kong', in Takashi Shiraishi and Tetsushi Sonobe (eds.), *Emerging States and Economies: Their Origins, Drivers, and Challenges Ahead* (Springer, 2018), and 'Living "Underground" in Shanghai: Noulens and the Shanghai Comintern Network', in Caroline S. Hau and Kasian Tejapira (eds.), *Traveling Nation-Makers: Transnational Flows and Movements in the Making of Modern Southeast Asia* (Kyoto University Press and National University of Singapore Press, 2011).

Mark Harrison is a Professor of the History of Medicine at the Faculty of History & Pandemic Sciences Institute, University of Oxford. His research interests cover the history of disease and medicine in relation to British imperialism, the military and globalisation. His publications include *Contagion: How Commerce has Spread Disease* (Yale University Press, 2012); *The Medical War: British Military Medicine in the First World War* (Oxford University Press, 2010) and *Medicine and Victory: British Military Medicine in the Second World War* (Oxford University Press, 2004).

Atsuko Naono is a Research Associate at the Oxford Centre for the History of Science, Medicine, and Technology, University of Oxford. Her research interests cover the history of epidemics and public health in Southeast Asia and the history of medicine and conflict. Her major publications include 'Going "the Last Mile" to eliminate malaria in Myanmar?' in *Centaurus-Journal of the European Society for the History of Science*, 64(1), 2022, 'Rural Health in Modern Southeast Asia' in Tim Harper and Sunil Amrith (eds.), *Histories of Health in Southeast Asia: Perspectives on the Long Twentieth Century* (Indiana University Press, 2014), and *State of Vaccination: The Fight Against Smallpox in Colonial Burma* (Orient BlackSwan, 2009).

Noriyuki Osada is an Associate Professor at the Faculty of Social and Cultural Studies, Kyushu University. His research interests cover the history of Burma and the political and social issues in contemporary Myanmar. His major publications include 'Partitioned lives: Myanmar-born Indians in the Manipur borderland', in Mayumi Murayama, Sanjoy Hazarika, and Preeti Gill (eds.), *Northeast India and Japan: Engagement through Connectivity* (Routledge, 2022), *Taidō suru kokkyō: Eiryō Biruma no imin-mondai to toshi-tōchi* (The border in embryo: Immigration and urban governance in colonial Rangoon), (Yamakawa Shuppan-sha, 2016), and 'An embryonic border: Racial discourses and compulsory vaccination for Indian immigrants at ports in colonial Burma, 1870–1937', *Moussons: Recherche en sciences humaines sur l'Asie du Sud-Est,* Vol. 17 (2011).

Tomokazu Okada is an Associate Professor at the Graduate School of Humanities, Osaka University. His research interests cover the French colonial history in Indochina and the history of Vietnam. His major publications include '1936–37 nen Hanoi ni okeru rōdōsha storaiki undō (The labour strike movement in Hanoi 1936–37)', *Tōnan Asia Kenkyū* (Southeast Asian studies), Vol. 52(2) (2015), *Les villes vietnamiennes au contact de la colonisation. Structuration et restructuration de la société urbaine en Indochine française (1887–1945): le cas de Hanoi, Haiphong et Saigon* (Vietnamese cities in contact with colonization. Structuring and restructuring of urban society in French Indochina (1887–1945): The case of Hanoi, Haiphong and Saigon), Thèse de doctorat, Aix-Marseille Université (2013), and 'Furansu shokuminchi teikoku ni okeru gentijin kanri seido – Indosina wo jirei ni (The French colonial empire's native civil service system: The case of Indochina)', *Shigaku-Zasshi* (Journal of historical science), 119(6), 2010.

Takashi Shiraishi is a Distinguished Professor Emeritus, Kumamoto Prefectural University. His research interests cover politics and history in Southeast Asia, international relations in the Asia Pacific, and economic security policies. His major publications include *Standing Firm For Indonesia's Democracy: An Oral History Of President Susilo Bambang Yudhoyono* (edited with Nobuhiro Aizawa, Jun Honna, and Wahyu Prasetyawan, World Scientific, 2024), *The Phantom World of Digul: Policing as Politics in Colonial Indonesia, 1926–1941* (National University of Singapore Press in association with Kyoto University Press, 2021), and *Maritime Asia vs. Continental Asia: National Strategies in a Region of Change* (Boulder, 2021).

Ma. Mercedes G. Planta is a Professor of History at the University of the Philippines, Diliman. Her research interests cover the history of medicine in colonial Southeast Asia and traditional medicine in the Philippines. Her major publications include *Traditional Medicine in the Colonial Philippines, 16th to 19th Century* (University of the Philippines Press, 2017), 'Hansen's Disease and International Public Health in the Philippines, 1900–1930s', in Ma. Serena I. Diokno (ed.), *Hidden Lives, Concealed Narratives: A History of Leprosy in the Philippines* (National Historical Commission of the Philippines, 2016), and 'Spanish Enlightenment, Alessandro Malaspina and the Asian Mediterranean', in National Historical Commission of the Philippines, *Reexamining the History of Philippine-Spanish Relations* (National Historical Commission of the Philippines, 2016).

Jeong-Ran Kim is a Research Associate at the Oxford Centre for the History of Science, Medicine, and Technology, University of Oxford. Her research interests cover the history of disease, medicine and war in modern East Asia in a wide context of the Japanese Empire and the Cold War. Her major publications include 'Medicine in the Korean War (1), (2)', *Korean Journal of Medical History,* 32(2 and 3), 2023, 'Malaria and Colonialism in Korea, *c.*1876–*c.*1945', *Social History of Medicine,* 29(2), 2016, and 'The Borderline of "Empire": Japanese maritime quarantine in Busan c.1876–1910', *Medical History,* 57(2), 2013.

Introduction

Dreams of Prevention and Control: Policing and Public Health in Colonial Asia

Takeshi Onimaru

The nineteenth and early twentieth centuries were a time of political, economic, and social changes that led to the modern era in which we now live. These changes included the formation of the modern state, the rise of political movements such as nationalism and communism, economic development through industrialisation and the formation of national economies, advances in science and technology, urbanisation, the development of transport and communication technologies like railroad, steamship, and the telegraph, all of which stimulated and expanded the movement of people, goods, and information on a global scale. Most of these changes, often called 'modernisation,' occurred first in Western countries, especially Europe. However, the impact of these changes was not limited to the Western world but extended to the non-Western world under the rubrics of 'modernisation' and 'Westernization.'

When we consider the impact of modernisation and Westernization in the non-Western world, we need to recognise the primary method of expansion of the West to the world during the same period: colonisation. Most regions of Asia and Africa were colonised or semi-colonised in the nineteenth and early twentieth centuries. Although there were places where colonial rule had begun earlier, such as the Dutch East Indies and the Spanish Philippines, most Asian and African regions were colonised in the nineteenth century by the British, French,

Dutch, Americans, Japanese, Italians, Germans, Belgians, Portuguese, and Spanish.

The purposes of colonisation ranged from economic – such as exploitation of natural resources, cultivating commodity crops on plantations, and establishing regional trading centres – to political, such as securing strategic bases or dividing Asian and African regions into colonies as part of the struggle for power in Europe. To achieve their diverse purposes, colonising states introduced modern institutions, technology, and infrastructure that were being developed in the West. For example, to export commercial crops or natural resources from plantations or mines inland, they had to be connected to maritime ports by road or rail. Military garrisons with modern weaponry were constructed if a colony was geopolitically important. These modern technologies and weaponry were 'the tools of empire' that enabled the Western powers to colonise Asian and African regions in the nineteenth century (Headrick 1981). Thus, colonial expansion was strongly connected to developing science and scientific knowledge.

Another important tool introduced by colonising states was colonial rule and the colonial state. Colonies were places where people of different languages, cultures, religions, and customs lived. Under these circumstances, effective colonial governance was required to develop and advance the colonies and protect the safety of the colonisers. Colonial states were built to achieve these tasks.

In *Imagined Communities*, Benedict Anderson identifies three institutions that shaped the policies and ideologies of colonial states in Southeast Asia from the mid-nineteenth century: censuses, maps, and museums. According to Anderson, these were all invented by the mid-nineteenth century, when colonial states sought to 'imagine and grasp' their populations through censuses, their governing spaces through maps, and the historical genealogy and legitimacy of their states through museums. Consider how these institutions were used in colonial rule, taking the example of the census. The census was conducted to grasp the number of inhabitants to be governed by assigning them to each ethnic category set by the rulers, such as 'Chinese,' 'Indians,' 'Malays,' and so on. The colonial state then established administrative structures in charge of education, justice, public health, public order maintenance, and immigration control based on the ethnic categories used in the census and governed the people through these administrative structures. In other words, the census was not only a framework for how the colonial state 'imagined' the population to be governed but also a framework for governance. Anderson notes that the framework of censuses, maps, and museums was taken over and utilised by the post-independence states (Anderson 2006: Chap. 10).

Anderson's argument that the institutions introduced by colonial states laid the foundations for the post-independence state and nationalism highlights the need to examine the colonial era as a prelude for understanding contemporary politics and societies, not only in the Southeast Asian region but wherever colonial rule was experienced. By focusing on censuses, maps, and museums, Anderson shed light on another crucial aspect of the colonial state and rule: the importance of surveys, science, and technology. The census was conducted to obtain information on the demographics of the population, and geographic and spatial information obtained through land surveys was essential to create accurate maps. Museum exhibits are based on information and knowledge obtained through research on history, customs, and culture, as well as natural and ecological environments. Scientific methods and techniques, supported by 'native' collectors, informants, guides, and clerks, were applied to the colonial rule and were deployed to analyse and process data, information, and knowledge obtained through censuses, land surveys, academic research, statistics, cartography, reports and museum displays. The 'invention' of the census, the map, and the museum by the mid-nineteenth century was possible because surveys utilising scientific methods and technologies had been developed by this time. The colonial state was a 'survey state' built on science and technology.

In the last section of the chapter in *Imagined Communities*, which discusses censuses, maps, and museums, Anderson introduces *The Glass House* by Indonesian novelist Pramoedya Ananta Toer, which describes life and politics in colonial Indonesia. Anderson argues that *The Glass House*, like Bentham's 'Panopticon,' connotes the colonial state's attempt to achieve 'total surveyability' of its subjects (Anderson 2006: 184–185). However, although Anderson does not discuss the total surveyability of colonial states further in *Imagined Communities*, there were certain aspects of colonial administration where this total surveyability was more necessary than censuses, maps, and museums: policing, medicine, and public health.

Total surveyability was necessary for policing, medicine, and public health because, for the colonial state, the threats to colonial policing, medicine, and public health were mainly hidden in the local society and people. To identify and control these threats, it was essential to make the potential threats in the local society and people 'visible' and sometimes to intervene with and penetrate the local society and people directly to prevent disorder caused by these threats. Policing, medicine, and public health were machines in charge of these missions and embodied the total surveyability of the colonial state. Policing, medicine, and public health were the 'eyes' and 'hands' of colonial states.

Whatever the purpose of colonization in Asia and Africa, order and security had to be maintained in the colonies. It was not easy, however, to maintain order and security in a territory and environment unfamiliar to most of the colonisers, with a population whose language, culture, and customs were different. In addition, colonisation often expanded from city bases. As economic activity in cities increased, people flocked to them in search of jobs and opportunities. To sustain economic development in cities, it was essential to maintain security and order by cracking down on crimes such as theft, robbery, and murder, which increased as the urban population grew. Furthermore, as colonial rule began to expand from the urban areas to the suburban and local areas, opportunities for contact between the colonisers and the local people increased, sometimes leading to a growing backlash against colonial rule. This opposition sometimes developed into rebellions and uprisings, such as the Great Indian Mutiny. From the late nineteenth century onward, opposition against colonial rule was linked to political and religious movements, such as nationalist, communist, and pan-Islamist movements, leading to anti-colonial movements aiming at liberation from colonial rule. To maintain security and order in the colonies and to keep the colonies themselves stable, it was necessary not only to crack down on ordinary crimes but also to properly control political movements that sought to disrupt and liberate the colonies so that they would not lead to actual rebellions, disturbances, and revolutions. To this end, the colonial state had developed a modern police force in its attempt to monitor and control crime and anti-colonial movements.

Another challenge that needed to be addressed in developing the colonies and ensuring the colonisers' safety and life was how to maintain health and control the spread of infectious diseases and illnesses. Most colonies in the Asian and African regions were in tropical and subtropical areas, where colonists coming from temperate zones sometimes had difficulty maintaining their good physical condition. Infectious diseases such as cholera, plague, smallpox, malaria, and dengue fever were prevalent in these areas, threatening the lives of not only the colonists but also the local people. Outbreaks of infectious diseases also affected the politics and economy of the colonies. For example, when cholera or the plague broke out, quarantine was tightened to prevent the spread of infection, and the movement of infected people and the distribution of goods from the epidemic area were restricted. These restrictions on the movement of people and goods affected economic activities such as trade and commerce. They sometimes created political, social, and religious conflicts with the locals suffering from restrictions (Harrison 1994: 117–138). Furthermore, the spread of venereal diseases in military garrisons was a problem for military operations and the maintenance of security and order. In response to these problems, the colonial state established a medical and sanitation system that included hospitals, clinics, and water and sewage systems and attempted to monitor and control outbreaks of infectious diseases and illnesses.

There are several similarities between policing and medical and public health and the censuses, maps, and museums discussed by Anderson. First is the importance of science and technology. Although there were various organisations and schemes for maintaining order, curing diseases, and helping the poor before colonisation, it was not until after colonisation – or more precisely, after the mid-nineteenth century when colonial state-building started in earnest in many important colonial territories – that science and technology began to be deployed to address these issues in the colonies. In policing, since the end of the nineteenth century, fingerprints and photographs have been used to conduct scientific investigations of crimes. In medicine and public health, knowledge of pathogens such as bacteria, which was the result of medical research in the West led by Koch and Pasteur, and treatment methods that applied this knowledge came to be used. In other words, the police and the medical and public health services introduced in the colonial period were 'modern' in the sense that they utilized science and technology, just like censuses, maps, and museums, and were the prototype for policing, medical, and public health activities by the state after independence.

Another similarity is that the information obtained through surveys was compiled into statistics and other forms of quantification in an effort to grasp the overall picture. The police compiled the number of crimes and arrests by crime types, such as robbery, murder, and theft, to grasp the conditions of order and security. Medicine and public health also attempted to grasp the health status of the population and the prevalence of infectious diseases and illnesses by compiling vital statistics, such as the number of births and deaths, and the number of infected persons and patients. These attempts were much like Anderson's discussion of censuses, maps, and museums, where the colonial states attempted to grasp and visualise the subject through quantification. However, there is a big difference when we focus on visualisation, or what Anderson calls total surveyability.

First, the census was intended to count all inhabitants under colonial rule, categorise them, and create a demographic topography for use by the colonial administration. This demographic topography was unique in that it was created from above, and the targeted population was unaware of its gaze (Anderson 2006: 168–169). In other words, the visualization and total surveyability required by the census were sufficient for the colonial state to quantify all inhabitants and place them within a framework of ethnic categories. Therefore, the 'gaze' of the census was a one-way beam of light from the colonial state toward the local people, and it was not necessary to constantly update the data; it was sufficient to conduct periodic censuses and obtain snapshots of the population from time-to-time. This one-sided gaze from the colonial state and the lack of need for constant updating also apply to maps and museums. In other words, the visualisation and total surveyability required for censuses, maps, and museums were sufficient to quantify and visualise the information and knowledge obtained from the colonial state's gaze (survey) from above, and did not require constant attention and constant updating of the target.

In contrast, the mission of policing was to maintain security and order in the colony, while that of medical and public health was to protect the people's health and keep the colony in a sanitary condition. To accomplish these missions, it was not enough to distance themselves from the local people and project their gaze from above, as in the case of the censuses. To crack down on crime, prevent disturbances, rebellions, and revolutions, improve the sanitary conditions of the colonies, and prevent the spread of infectious diseases, it was necessary to penetrate the local society, which comprised the majority of the population, with different languages, customs, religions, and so on. In particular, to 'prevent' disturbances, uprisings, revolutions, and outbreaks of infectious diseases, it was necessary to constantly monitor the movements of activists and outbreaks of contagious diseases, detect 'signs,' and intervene appropriately. In other words, the colonial state had to become a 'surveillance state' in policing, medicine, and public health, where it was required to constantly 'monitor' its targets.

However, the construction of this 'surveillance state' was not easy. With its limited human and financial resources, the colonial state had great difficulty in monitoring the movements of the local population. In particular, it was difficult, and sometimes impossible, for the colonial state to expand its surveillance beyond urban areas where its resources were relatively concentrated. Of course, the colonial state made efforts to have its administrators and police officers learn the local language, customs, manners, culture, and religion, as well as to overcome differences and enter the world of the local people. However, the direct intervention of the colonial state in the form of police, medical care, and public health services itself generated opposition and resistance. In the field of medicine and public health, for instance, the intrusion of the colonial state's 'eyes' and 'hands' into women's bodies and into the home for childbirth and childcare generated significant cultural and religious opposition.

To avoid such difficulties, resistance, and opposition, colonial states needed local collaborators incorporated into their police, medical, and public health activities. Taking the Dutch East Indies and the British Straits Settlements as examples, Takashi Shiraishi argues that when these colonial states penetrated local society, they found themselves in a 'twilight zone,' a place astride the official and the unofficial as well as in-between the legal and the illegal. To manage the twilight zone, he argues, the colonial state had to embed itself in the zone, incorporating not only the local authorities but also outlaws, including gangsters, thugs, and local toughs (Shiraishi 2021b: 55–63). The success or failure of policing and medical and public health activities depended precisely on the colonial state's ability to monitor and control the twilight zone through various means. In this sense, the focus on policing and medical and public health activities not only embodies Anderson's notion of the total surveyability of the colonial state, as per Pramoedya's *The Glass House* and Bentham's Panopticon, but also reflects the essence of colonialism. It is also an excellent resource for understanding the nature and limits of the colonial state and colonial governance, as well as the relationship between the colonial state and local society and its inhabitants.

Based on the above background, this edited volume aims to clarify the realities and limitations of policing and medical and public health activities from the nineteenth to the early twentieth centuries, which are essential in considering the colonial state and governance in Asia. To maintain and develop the colonies, it was necessary to properly manage 'threats' to the colonial order and security, such as crime, disturbances, rebellions, and revolutions, as well as threats to the life and health of the population, such as infectious diseases and illnesses. This book examines how this was done from the perspectives of surveillance and prevention, the relationship with the 'twilight zone,' and the opposition and resistance of the local people.

The subject of this edited volume, policing, medicine, and public health in Asian colonies, has been studied in the history of colonial police and colonial medicine and public health. In particular, research on the history of colonial medicine and public health has been accumulating.

Since the 1990s, various studies have been published on medicine and public health in Asian colonies. This book draws heavily on these results, but among them, the work most relevant to the theme of this volume is David Arnold's *Colonizing the Body: State Medicine and Epidemic Disease in Nineteenth-Century India*, which describes the development of medical administration by the colonial government in British India in the nineteenth century. Arnold describes the process by which Western medicine, in the form of colonial medicine, penetrated Indian society, using the treatment of infectious diseases such as smallpox, cholera, and the plague as cases. The most important point of the book is that the penetration of Western medicine did not proceed smoothly, and it was not until the 1890s that its dominance was established. The reasons include the colonial government's limited human and financial resources for medical care and public health, as well as the local people's cultural, religious, and psychological resistance and opposition to unfamiliar Western medicine and hygiene interventions. It is also important to point out that Indians were not passive to Western medicine's demands but played an active role in adapting Western medicine to Indian culture and customs.

Another important work on British India is Mark Harrison's *Public Health in British India: Anglo-Indian Preventive Medicine 1859–1914*. Harrison describes the development of preventive medicine and public health policies in British India from the mid-nineteenth century to the early twentieth century. He first points out the importance of examining the political aspects of the various tactics and conflicts between administrators and physicians, central government and local municipalities, and British and local elites over policy formulation and implementation for understanding preventive medicine and public health in British India. He also points out that there were limits to implementing interventionist sanitary measures in local communities. The reasons for this were the strong cultural and religious opposition of local communities to intervention, especially in the areas of women and the family, even though this opposition gradually faded. The colonial government was also concerned that interventionist sanitary measures would generate a backlash after the Great Indian Rebellion of 1857 and that there were significant financial constraints on implementing sanitary measures.

Outside of British India, Lenore Manderson's *Sickness and the State: Health and Illness in Colonial Malaya, 1870–1940* is an enlightening study. Manderson begins with a description of how the colonial state tried to grasp the overall picture of medical care and public health in British Malaya using medical statistics, etc., and then examines the reality of medical and public health measures formulated based on biological and medical findings, including the improvement of urban dwellings and the health of plantation workers and prostitutes, and the care of women's births and children in the home. The book is also important because it discusses the surveillance that the colonial state conducted of cities, plantations, prostitutes, and mothers with children, using staff from the police and departments in charge of medical care and labour.

Another study in Southeast Asia is Warwick Anderson's *Colonial Pathologies: American Tropical Medicine, Race, and Hygiene in the Philippines*. Anderson describes the process by which the US colonial government in the Philippines sought to remake the local sanitation environment and the bodies of the local people to be more 'hygienic and healthy' by introducing tropical medicine and public health measures and how issues such as race and Americanization became intertwined in this process. Anderson notes that the process of American 'sanitization' of the Philippines was a process of 'civilization and Americanization' and that it was inextricably linked to the movement for civil and political rights for the local people. Anderson also argues that the Philippine experience was brought back to the United States and influenced public health policies there.

In previous studies,[1] including those mentioned above, research on medicine and public health issues in Asian colonies

1 Other important works in the history of colonial medicine and public health in Asia are as follows: in the British India, Ramanna (2002), Wakimura (2002), Pande (2010), Pati and Harrison (eds.) (2018), in Southeast Asia, Bevoise (1995), Naono (2009), Au (2011), Hesselink (2011), Monnais and Cook (eds.) (2012), Harper and Amrith (eds.) (2014), Pols, Thompson, and Warner (eds.) (2017), Pols (2018), Monnais (2019), in East Asia, Sinn ([1989] 2003), Rogaski (2004), Iijima (2005), Yip (ed.) (2009), Fukushi (2010), Peckham and Pomfret (eds.) (2013), Ho (2017), Yip, Wong, and Leung (eds.) (2018), Moira (2018).

has been conducted and accumulated from various perspectives, including the development of medical administration, hospitals, and clinics; the way Western medicine and public health measures were introduced; the acceptance and opposition of local people; the relationship with local conventional medical practices; control and management of the body in the Foucauldian sense and resistance to it; and measures against infectious diseases such as smallpox, cholera, plague, malaria, and venereal disease.

In contrast, there has been relatively little research on colonial policing compared with that on colonial medicine and public health. Why is this the case, given that, like medicine and public health, policing was a fundamental activity of the colonial state? One reason is that, as a fundamental activity of the colonial state, it is difficult to obtain sources on key aspects, such as those related to the monitoring and policing of local political movements. Just as medical and public health activities contributed to the health and safety of both the local people and the colonisers, police activities also provided security to the local people through crime control. However, from the end of the nineteenth century onward, when anti-colonial movements by the local people became more active, the colonial state developed political police to strengthen surveillance and policing. The activities of the political police were indispensable for maintaining the colony, but at the same time, they symbolised the 'dark side' of the colonial state, and to this day, the sources have not been fully disclosed to the public.[2] Nevertheless, some important research has been published.

2 In many cases, police records, especially those that reveal the 'dark side' of police activities, were intentionally destroyed. For example, most political and military police records from Imperial Japan were destroyed in August 1945 before the American occupying forces landed in Japan.

The first major work is Alfred W. McCoy's *Policing America's Empire: The United States, the Philippines, and the Rise of the Surveillance State*, which describes the history of policing in the Philippines from the early twentieth century, when the US took control of the Philippines from Spain, through its independence and into the twenty-first century. The greatest challenge when the US assumed colonial rule of the Philippines at the beginning of the twentieth century was how to 'pacify' the Filipino independence movement. To this end, McCoy points out that the United States introduced technologies such as photo identification systems, fingerprints, and telephone networks to the police, stored information about radicals on file cards, and used this information to conduct surveillance and policing. Another interesting aspect of McCoy's argument is that this police surveillance also turned its attention to the political leaders of the Philippines, and that the United States was trying to control them by using the information about their scandals obtained by the police, and that this legacy was not only carried over to the post-independence Philippines, but was also brought back to the American homeland, including surveillance techniques and practices that influenced the way surveillance was conducted in the United States.

Another important study is Takashi Shiraishi's *The Phantom World of Digul: Policing as Politics in Colonial Indonesia, 1926–1941*. Shiraishi describes the policing of political movements in the Dutch East Indies in the 1920s and 1930s. One of the important points of the book is that a system of self-policing was established to prevent the local population from approaching radical political movements in the eyes of the colonial state, such as communism. The concentration camp set up in Digul, an outpost of the colony, played a crucial role in this system. The policy of the colonial state regarding the nationalist movement, which had been allowed to operate legally, changed drastically in 1926 and again in the early 1930s, and those who were deemed to have exceeded the permissible limits set by the colonial state were rounded up and sent to Digul. Shiraishi argues that policing was an essential part of this colonial government policy.

David Arnold, who wrote the previously mentioned *Colonizing the Body*, also published a study of the police in British India: *Police Power and Colonial Rule: Madras 1859–1947*. Arnold describes the development of policing in colonial Madras, noting that the police were an essential tool of colonial rule. He argues that the police force started to be developed in response to the Great Indian Mutiny of 1857, but little progress was made until the 1890s, especially in monitoring and policing political movements. Policing political movements intensified in the 1920s and 1930s, mainly through the political intelligence police. He also argues that the police did not draw a clear line between ordinary crime and anti-colonial movements, and police activities themselves sometimes deviated from the 'rule of law.' The police provided protection not only to the colonizers but also to local influential figures, which was an important factor in the colonial police structure surviving after independence without major reorganization.

Ban Kah Choon's *Absent History: The Untold Story of Special Branch Operations in Singapore 1915–1942* describes the activities of the political police in Singapore during the inter-war period. Ban traces the targets of the Singapore political police as they shifted from Indian nationalist movements to communist movements and then to Japanese activities from the mid-1930s. Ban reveals the exchange of information in and outside the colony, as well as the use of censorship of letters and other means to gather information and monitor and contain communist movements.

Finally, Frederick Wakeman Jr.'s *Policing Shanghai 1927–1937* depicts Shanghai as a kind of semi-colony and a major strategic centre for colonial powers in China with the International Settlements and French Concession. Wakeman reveals that the activists who were targets of surveillance and policing were aware that they were being watched. He also argues that the police not only used gangsters and thugs to monitor and police targets but sometimes transformed outlaws into regular police officers. These points suggest how the colonial state used the police to monitor and control the twilight zone.

With regard to police activities in Asian colonies, previous studies,[3] including those mentioned above, are beginning to shed light on how police structures developed, how they policed ordinary crimes, as well as played a role in defining something as a 'crime' in the first place, how they monitored disturbances, rebellions, revolutions, and other situations that could threaten the colonial order, and how surveillance was conducted against political movements and the like.

With reference to the results of the previous studies mentioned above, this book will study the conditions on the grounds and limitations of policing and medical and public health activities in specific Asian colonies, which have been studied separately. It also attempts to clarify the nature of the

3 Other works on the history of policing in colonial Asia include: the establishment and development of colonial police in the British India (Madan 1980), the policing of Indian revolutionaries through surveillance and intelligence (Popplewell 1995), the colonial state's attempt to prevent crimes through the surveillance against 'dangerousness' (Singha 2015), the policing of communal violence after the Indian Mutiny (Doyle 2017), the history of police in British Burma (Hanwong 2015), the history of police in British Malaya (Morrah 1968), the control and suppression of the communist movement in British Malaya (Yong 1997), the daily operations of the political police in Shanghai in the 1920s and 1930s (Bickers 2003), the historical overview of policing and police reforms in Hong Kong (Wong 2015), the crime and police activities in the Spanish Philippine in the nineteenth century (Bankoff 1996), the police activities and the assimilation policy in French Indochina (Anderson 2017), and the policing and control of strikes and labour movements in French Indochina and British Malaya (Thomas 2012).

colonial state and its limitations, as seen through the activities of the police, medical care, and public health.

In considering policing, medicine, and public health in the Asian colonies of the nineteenth and early twentieth centuries, the first point this volume focuses on is survey and surveillance, or in other words, the 'gaze' of the colonial state toward the local society. Like Anderson's three institutions, censuses, maps, and museums, the survey is an attempt to quantify and visualize the subject by collecting information and data and compiling them into statistics and reports to grasp the overall picture. The points to be examined are what information and data were collected on policing, medicine, and public health, who was in charge of collecting them, what means and mechanisms were used to collect them, and how the collected information and data were processed and used. Surveillance differs from investigation in that it is the constant gaze of the colonial state on what it considered a threat to security and order, medicine, and public health. What did the colonial state perceive as threats? In other words, where did the colonial state draw the line between dangerous and safe, abnormal and normal, unhealthy and healthy, illegal and legal, and intolerable and tolerable? What information and data were collected through surveillance, who was responsible for collecting it, what means and mechanisms were used, and how was the collected information and data utilised? By focusing on surveys and surveillance, it is possible to clarify where the colonial state's gaze was directed, what it saw, and what it did not see.

A critical perspective related to this survey and surveillance is the use of science and technology. In policing, medicine, and public health, the most advanced science and technology were used not only for surveillance but also to suppress crimes and political movements and to implement medical and public health measures. In policing, this science and technology was significant in target profiling and identification. For example, as McCoy notes, in the American Philippines, police used fingerprint and photographic profiling, scientific investigation, telephone networks, and other information and communication technologies to monitor, identify, and control their targets (McCoy 2009). In medicine and public health, since the mid-nineteenth century, there have been continuous efforts to develop vital statistics on births and deaths. The discoveries of Pasteur and Koch were applied to analysing medical and public health conditions and identifying, monitoring, and controlling 'breeding beds' for infectious diseases and illnesses. The relationship between science and technology and colonial policing, medicine, and public health is one of the central themes of this book.

Another perspective that all chapters in this book share is the reaction and response of local societies and peoples to colonial policing, medicine, and public health. In other words, how did those who were exposed to the colonial state's gaze respond to it? Policing, medicine, and public health were the contact zones between the colonial state and the local society and people and where the local society and people could feel the presence of the colonial state and its activities. Maintaining order and security and improving medical and sanitary conditions were welcomed by many local peoples, and some locals chose to actively participate in colonial policing, medicine, and public health by studying Western medicine and becoming doctors or becoming police officers or administrators. However, there was also strong opposition and resistance because surveillance and control in policing, medicine, and public health were primarily targeted at the local people. People opposed the colonial state's arbitrary determination of what constituted a threat. Many distrusted foreign medicine, science, and technology. Some resented the sense that their local customs, cultures, and religious practices were being denied. Opposition and resistance took various forms: going underground or moving out of sight of surveillance, refusing police and medical inspections into their dwellings, concealing patients or their bodies, and refusing to administer medicines or vaccines. Moreover, some of those subjected to surveillance and control 'knew' that they were being 'monitored' by the colonial state and acted on the assumption that they were being watched. Thus, when considering colonial policing, medicine, and public health, it is essential to examine both the surveillance from above (the colonial state) and reactions from below, such as local demands, opposition, and resistance.

Another important factor in thinking about colonial policing, medicine, and public health is that the colonial states had limitations. Many Asian colonies did not have sufficient human and financial resources to manage their territories and populations. Therefore, the colonial state's power of surveillance and control diminished further away from the urban centres of political and economic activity. Although the situation gradually improved as colonial and economic development progressed and transportation and communications infrastructure such as roads, railroads, and telegraphs were constructed, this limitation could not be overcome during the colonial period. In addition, the increased movement of people due to the development of railroads and roads and the opening of regular steamship routes, as well as increased economic activity, posed a major challenge to the surveillance and control of the colonial state. Although control of people's movement through passport and visa systems had begun to be introduced, this scheme did not cover many Asian people, and surveillance and control of people on the move was not easy at this time when surveillance cameras did not exist. Although the colonial state tried to overcome this challenge through on-site inspections at ports and stations and the exchange of information within the colony and between neighbouring colonies, the problematic situation did not improve during the colonial period.

With these limitations, it was essential for the colonial state to obtain cooperation from the local people to increase the effectiveness of its policing, medical, and public health activities. The colonial state could, for example, incorporate local people into its security and order maintenance and medical and public health activities as police officers, administrators, and doctors. In the Foucauldian sense, the colonial state taught and showed them what to do and what not to do through education and other means, so that local people would voluntarily cooperate with the colonial state's activities. In addition, acquiring spies and informants was an essential part of incorporation. However, the use of education, especially education in the language of the colonisers, sometimes had the opposite effect to that intended by the colonial state. In this regard, Shiraishi points out that education in the Dutch language in the Dutch East Indies was an important means for the colonial state to 'visualise' the local society and its inhabitants. However, when people started to think in Dutch, to learn political thoughts and concepts, to translate these thoughts and concepts into their mother tongue, and finally to begin their own political movements, this education in Dutch created a new threat to the legitimacy of colonial rule. And the colonial state was forced to transform itself into a 'police state' in response (Shiraishi 2021b: 94–99). The inclusion and education of the local people also worked both for and against. This point in colonial medicine and public health is discussed by Mercedes Planta in Chapter 7 of this book, which describes medical and public health activities in the American Philippines.

Thus, colonial policing, medicine, and public health were not simply or unilaterally imposed from above by the colonial state but were also shaped by the acceptance, cooperation, resistance, and opposition of locals. This volume seeks to elucidate a multifaceted picture of policing, medical, and public health activities in Asian colonies as a two-way and intertwined process between the colonial state and local societies.

This book sheds light on how colonial states attempted to deal with threats to order and security, and to life and health in the colonies during the nineteenth and early twentieth centuries in Asia, from Aden in the west to the Korean Peninsula in the east. Each chapter deals with either the police or medical and public health, but while they differ in their focus, they share the perspectives outlined above as the core of their analyses. The book is organised as follows.

This book starts from Aden, an outpost at the west end of British India on the south edge of the Arabian Peninsula. Britain established a naval base in Aden in the early nineteenth century, which was strategically important for protecting the sea routes to British India. In Chapter 1, Mark Harrison focuses on colonial regulation and surveillance of local prostitutes. The medical regulation of prostitution was implemented in the late nineteenth century to control venereal diseases, which led to the systemic surveillance of prostitutes. The main targets of surveillance soon expanded beyond registered prostitutes to identify unofficial and private sex workers who had remained beyond the reach of colonial control. Although ostensibly a public health measure, the primary purpose of the surveillance was to detect women who might disturb the peace and social order. Harrison explains why this scheme was introduced, how it worked, how locals reacted and resisted, and how policing and medical measures overlapped in colonial surveillance. He provides a vivid picture of the lives of sex workers and a complex scheme of control in colonial Aden.

Collecting data and statistical analyses were essential components of colonial surveillance and control. In Chapter 2,

Atsuko Naono describes how the colonial government collected vital statistics as a part of medical surveillance in British Burma. The basis of vital statistics was the registration of births and deaths by indigenous village headmen, which the colonial state analysed as it tried to identify and control diseases among the indigenous population. However, this scheme frequently suffered from chronic delays in submitting vital statistics, failures in reporting the outbreak of epidemics, and inadequate sharing of critical information. The authorities distrusted information provided by village headmen, and rightly so, as the village headmen were continuously confused by the colonial medical establishment's frequent and complicated changes in the classifications of diseases. Naono reveals these processes and problems in colonial Burma through careful examination of several key epidemics and highlights both the importance and challenges of relying on local people for colonial surveillance and control.

Keeping order and providing security in the colonial urban centres was essential for the colonial state to develop the colonial economy and maintain colonial rule. In Chapter 3, Noriyuki Osada analyzes the urban security problem in Rangoon, the political and commercial centre of British Burma, which attracted both domestic and international migrants. The constant flow of migrants into Rangoon posed a challenge to maintaining law and order. Two target populations were regarded as 'problematic' by the colonial government. The first was Chinese immigrants. The colonial government in Burma developed measures against unlawful Chinese under the Foreigners Act, which authorised the expulsion of undesirable non-British subjects from the territory of British India, which included British Burma at the time. The second target was Indian immigrants. The Foreigners Act did not apply to them because they were British subjects, so the colonial government of Burma enacted the Expulsion of Offenders Act in 1926, authorising the government to expel illegal Indian migrants from British Burma. Osada explores the legal and administrative difficulties faced by the colonial government in Burma, and argues this Act was epochal; it enhanced the territoriality of the province of Burma and was an important contributor to the state-making process of the provincial administrators which finally led to Burma's separation from India.

In the 1920s and '30s, communist movements were regarded as highly problematic and dangerous by the colonial states and were placed under strict surveillance and suppression. Policing and control against communist movements in French Indochina and British Malaya are examined in Chapters 4 and 5, respectively. In Chapter 4, Tomokazu Okada examines how the colonial police monitored, controlled, and suppressed communists in French Indochina in the 1930s. Okada reveals the success and failure of colonial police surveillance and control against the communist movement by focusing on two cases: the surveillance and control of the activities of the Indochinese Communist Party local committee in the border region with China in northern Vietnam in 1935 and that of the communist involvement in organisations and movement of the general strike in Hanoi from 1936 to 1937. In these cases, the police tried to trace the movement and activity of the unidentified communist 'suspect' by utilising informants and spies, and information obtained from interrogations of arrested communists. However, this police surveillance faced obstacles because there were many supporters and collaborators in the villages and cities, and they concealed the communists' movements, whereabouts, and activities from the eyes of colonial surveillance. In this chapter, Okada clearly shows the game between colonial policing and the resistance and reaction of local people to it.

In Chapter 5, Takeshi Onimaru focuses on colonial policing and control in Singapore from the nineteenth to the early twentieth century. Singapore was the political and commercial centre of the British Straits Settlements and British Malaya. Singapore was an immigrant frontier port city, and most of its population was immigrant Chinese from mainland China. These immigrant Chinese provided an essential labour force for the economic development of British Malaya but, at the same time, were regarded by the colonial government as a source of disturbance. There were two main targets of policing in Singapore: the Chinese 'secret societies' and the Chinese communist movements. To maintain commercial development, security and order, the colonial government had to control these targets and prevent riots, disturbances, and strikes organised by the secret societies and communists. Onimaru traces policing and preventive measures against secret societies and communists by focusing on surveillance against them. The key activities to prevent mass disturbances caused by secret societies and communists were to detect and identify their members, monitor them, arrest them, and finally deport them from Singapore to mainland China. Onimaru shows the vital parts of these measures were detection and identification by surveillance and deportation, developed through policing and control against secret societies in the nineteenth century. He points out that the policing and control measures in Singapore were effective in the sense that they prevented mass riots, disturbances, and revolutions, but this did not mean that the colonial state could see everything it wanted.

The communist underground activities were a headache for the colonial government, but the nationalist 'aboveground' movements were also problematic for colonial rule. The nationalist 'aboveground' movements expanded their activities openly and legally, demanded political rights and equality, and finally claimed national liberation from colonial rule. In Chapter 6, Takashi Shiraishi describes how the colonial government policed and controlled the aboveground nationalist movements in the Dutch East Indies after the attempted revolution by the Indonesian Communist Party in 1926 and 1927. The key components of policing and controlling measures were the 'no-trespass sign' and internment in Boven-Digul, Dutch New Guinea. The 'no-trespass sign' was deployed to tell people what they could and could not do and to 'encourage' self-policing in the Foucauldian sense. Internment was the highly visible deterrent to violating the 'no-trespass sign.' Shiraishi explores in detail the Dutch colonial government's policing and controlling measures against nationalist politicians and activists and how the colonial government shaped the political terrain of local politicians and people. He describes how and why the colonial policy against the nationalist politicians changed from tolerance to suppression (arrest and internment) over time and highlights the difficulties and limits of the colonial state in controlling indigenous political movements.

In Chapter 7, Ma. Mercedes Planta examines public health measures in the Philippines by the American colonial government from the 1900s to 1930s. After the Republic of the Philippines declared independence from Spanish colonial rule in 1898, the American colonial rulers guaranteed the future independence of the Philippines. They justified their rule by preparing and improving the conditions for independence in the Philippines. Improving public health conditions was one of the essential components of this American 'civilising' mission. Planta describes how the American colonial government tried to improve public health conditions, especially hygiene, nutrition, and sanitation. She emphasises the importance of primary education, through which school children became collaborators and promoters of American government public health measures and campaigns. She also focuses on the role of local doctors and sanitary officers who cooperated with the American health and hygiene projects. Planta points out that the cooperation from these indigenous doctors was crucial for the American colonial government to achieve their missions, but the American doctors and medical officers did not appreciate the abilities of local doctors and did not promote them to higher and more important positions. The indigenous doctors were frustrated and started thinking that only independence could change this situation. Planta clearly shows the importance of cooperation and collaboration of local people in promoting public health measures, and how the lack of cooperation and collaboration generates frustration that can fuel an independence movement.

The last chapter of this volume is on the control and surveillance of the massive flow of people into and out of Busan, an important port city at the southern tip of the Korean peninsula. Busan has been the gateway of communication and transportation between Korea and Japan since long before Japanese colonial rule. At the end of the Japanese empire in 1945, Busan became the primary port for repatriating both Japanese and Koreans. Jeong-Ran Kim, in Chapter 8, describes how the American occupation forces controlled these human flows in and out of Busan in 1945 and 1946. The American occupation forces aimed to evacuate 4,000 people from Busan to Japan each day. The major problem in these mass human movements was maintaining public health, especially preventing infectious diseases. The American military government imposed a quarantine on Busan to try to detect infected persons. Another problem related to repatriation was the illegal human flow between Korea and Japan. There were restrictions on the number of people who could evacuate and the number of goods that they could bring in authorised repatriation. Many Japanese and Koreans who wanted to skip these restrictions took illegal shipping between Korea and Japan. These illegal evacuators did not undergo medical checks and were regarded as threats to maintaining public health and preventing the outbreak of infectious diseases. These illegal human movements also enhanced the illegal trafficking of goods and money and the activities of pirates. The American military government tried to suppress this illegal trafficking between Korea and Japan by strengthening surveillance and naval patrols together with the Korean Coast Guard, Japanese police, and the British Navy, but it was impossible to stop illegal trafficking completely. In this chapter, Kim shows the procedure of the public health measures against massive flows of people at the entry and exit points and, at the same time, the difficulties of implementing effective control and surveillance against illegal cross-border trafficking.

Through these discussions, we hope to clarify the realities and limitations of policing, medicine, and public health conducted by the colonial states in Asia from the nineteenth to the early twentieth century, especially how they tried to control and prevent threats to public order, medical care, and public health through surveillance and other means, to what extent this was achieved, and to what extent it was only a daydream. Finally, this book deals with the colonial period more than 100 years ago. But in the twenty-first century, especially after the 9/11 terrorist attacks in 2001 and the Covid-19 pandemic from 2019, surveillance in the name of safety and security has been intensified. This modern surveillance, as typified by China's claim of being a 'smart surveillance state,' makes use of science and technology that was not available 100 years ago, including miniaturised surveillance cameras, biometric technology, GPS, AI, and mass data and information of people on the Internet. Does such modern surveillance using the latest science and technology make possible the 'glass house,' which was only a dream for the state 100 years ago? It is our hope that the discussions in this volume will help shed light on the problems of modern surveillance and the logic behind the twenty-first-century surveillance system from a historical perspective.

References

Anderson, Benedict (2006), *Imagined Communities,* London and New York: Verso.

Anderson, Melissa L. (2017), 'Race, Violence, and White Crime: French Assimilationism and its limits in the Saigon Colonial Police,' in Emmanuel Blanchard, Marieke Bloembergen and Amandine Lauro (eds.), *Policing in Colonial Empires: Cases, Connections, Boundaries (ca. 1850–1970),* Bruxelles: P.I.E. Peter Lang, pp. 105–118.

Anderson, Warwick (2006), *Colonial Pathologies: American Tropical Medicine, Race, and Hygiene in the Philippines,* Durham and London: Duke University Press.

Arnold, David (1986), *Police Power and Colonial Rule: Madras 1859–1947,* Bombay, Calcutta, and Madras: Oxford University Press.

Arnold, David (1993), *Colonizing the Body: State Medicine and Epidemic Disease in Nineteenth-Century India,* Berkeley and Los Angeles: University of California Press.

Au Sokhieng (2011), *Mixed Medicines: Health and Cultures in French Colonial Cambodia,* Chicago and London: University of Chicago Press.

Ban, Kah Choon (2001), *Absent History: The Untold Story of Special Branch Operations in Singapore 1915–1942,* Singapore: Raffles.

Bankoff, Greg (1996), *Crime, Society, and the State in the Nineteenth Century Philippines,* Manila: Ateneo de Manila University Press.

Bevoise, Ken De (1995), *Agents of Apocalypse: Epidemic Disease in the Colonial Philippines,* Princeton and New York: Princeton University Press.

Bickers, Robert (2003), *Empire Made Me: An Englishman Adrift in Shanghai,* London: Allen Lane.

Doyle, Mark (2017), 'The Perils of Impartiality: Policing Communal Violence in Victorian India, 1858–1900,' in Emmanuel Blanchard, Marieke Bloembergen and Amandine Lauro (eds.), *Policing in Colonial Empires: Cases, Connections, Boundaries (ca. 1850–1970),* Bruxelles: P.I.E. Peter Lang, pp. 63–79.

Fukushi, Yuki (2010), *Kindai Syanhai to kousyu eisei: Boueki no toshi syakaishi* (Public health in modern Shanghai: Urban social history of preventive medicine), Tokyo: Otchanomizu Syobou.

Hanwong, Lalita Hingkanonta (2015), *Policing in Colonial Burma,* Chiang Mai: Center for ASEAN Studies.

Harper, Tim and Amrith, Sunil S. (eds.) (2014), *Histories of Health in Southeast Asia: Perspectives on the Long Twentieth Century,* Bloomington and Indianapolis: Indiana University Press.

Harrison, Mark (1994), *Public Health in British India: Anglo-Indian Preventive Medicine 1859–1914,* Cambridge: Cambridge University Press.

Headrick, Daniel R. (1981), *The Tools of Empire: Technology and European Imperialism in the Nineteenth Century,* New York: Oxford University Press.

Hesselink, Liesbeth (2011), *Healers on the Colonial Market: Native Doctors and Midwives in the Dutch East Indies,* Leiden: KITLV Press.

Ho, Faith C. S. (2017), *Western Medicine for Chinese: How the Hong Kong College of Medicine Achieved a Breakthrough,* Hong Kong: Hong Kong University Press.

Iijima, Wataru (2005), *Mararia to teikoku: Syokuminchi igaku to teikoku* (The hidden history of Malaria: Colonial/imperial medicine and an integrated regional order in 20th-century East Asia), Tokyo: University of Tokyo Press.

Madan, J. C. (1980), *Indian Police: Its development up to 1905. An Historical Analysis,* New Delhi: Uppal Publishing House.

Manderson, Lenore (1996), *Sickness and the State: Health and Illness in Colonial Malaya, 1870–1940,* Cambridge: Cambridge University Press.

McCoy, W. Alfred (2009), *Policing America's Empire: The United States, the Philippines, and the Rise of the Surveillance State,* Wisconsin: The University of Wisconsin Press.

Moira, M. W. Chan-Yeung (2018), *A Medical History of Hong Kong 1842–1941,* Hong Kong: The Chinese University of Hong Kong Press.

Monnais, Laurence (2019), *The Colonial Life of Pharmaceuticals: Medicines and Modernity in Vietnam,* Cambridge: Cambridge University Press.

Monnais, Laurence, and Cook, Harold J. (eds.) (2012), *Global Movements, Local Concerns: Medicine and Health in Southeast Asia,* Singapore: National University of Singapore Press.

Morrah, Patrick (1968), *The History of the Malayan Police,* Kuala Lumpur: Journal of the Malayan Branch of the Royal Asiatic Society.

Naono, Atsuko (2009), *State of Vaccination: The Fight Against Smallpox in Colonial Burma,* Hyderabad: Orient Black Swan.

Pande, Ishita (2010), *Medicine, Race and Liberalism in British Bengal: Symptoms of Empire,* London and New York: Routledge.

Pati, Biswamoy and Harrison, Mark (eds.) (2018), *Society, Medicine and Politics in Colonial India,* London and New York: Routledge.

Peckham, Robert and Pomfret, David M. (2013), *Colonialism, and the State: Malaria in Modern East Asian History,* Hong Kong: Hong Kong University Press.

Pols, Hans (2018), *Nurturing Indonesia: Medicine and Decolonisation in the Dutch East Indies,* Cambridge: Cambridge University Press.

Pols, Hans, Thompson, C. Michele and Warner, John Harley (eds.) (2017), *Translating the Body: Medical Education in Southeast Asia,* Singapore: National University of Singapore Press.

Popplewell, Richard J. (1995), *Intelligence and Imperial Defence: British Intelligence and the Defence of the Indian Empire 1904–1924,* London and New York: Routledge.

Ramanna, Mridula (2002), *Western Medicine and Public Health in Colonial Bombay 1845–1895,* Hyderabad: Sangam Books.

Rogaski, Ruth (2004), *Hygienic Modernity: Meanings of Health and Disease in Treaty-Port China,* Berkeley, Los Angeles, and London: University of California Press.

Shiraishi, Takashi (2021a) *The Phantom World of Digul: Policing as Politics in Colonial Indonesia, 1926–1941,* Singapore and Kyoto: National University of Singapore Press and Kyoto University Press.

Shiraishi, Takashi (2021b), *Empire of the Seas: Thinking about Asia,* Tokyo: Japan Publishing Industry Foundation for Culture.

Singha, Radhika (2015), 'Punished by Surveillance: Policing "dangerousness" in colonial India, 1872–1918,' *Modern Asian Studies*, 49(2), pp. 241–269.

Sinn, Elizabeth ([1989] 2003), *Power and Charity: A Chinese Merchant Elite in Colonial Hong Kong*, Hong Kong: Hong Kong University Press.

Thomas, Martin (2012), *Violence and Colonial Order: Police, Workers and Protest in the European Colonial Empires, 1918–1940*, Cambridge: Cambridge University Press.

Wakeman, Frederic Jr. (1995), *Policing Shanghai 1927–1937*, Berkeley, Los Angeles and London: University of California Press.

Wakimura, Kohei (2002), *Kikin, sippei, syokuminchi touchi: Kaihatu no nakano Eiryou Indo* (Famine, illness and colonial rule: Development in British India), Nagoya: Nagoya University Press.

Wong, Kam C. (2015), *Policing in Hong Kong: History and Reform*, Boca Raton, London, and New York: CRC Press.

Yip, Ka-che (ed.) (2009), *Colonialism, and the State: Malaria in Modern East Asian History*, Hong Kong: Hong Kong University Press.

Yip, Ka-che, Wong, Man-kong and Leung, Yuen-sang (eds.) (2018), *A Documentary History of Public Health in Hong Kong*, Hong Kong: The Chinese University of Hong Kong Press.

Yong, Ching Fatt (1997), 'Law and Order: British Management of Malayan Communism during Interwar Years, 1919–1942,' in Brook Barrington (ed.), *Empires, Imperialism and Southeast Asia: Essays in Honour of Nicholas Tarling*, Clayton: Monash Asia Institute, pp. 126–148.

Zurbrigg, Sheila (2020), *Malaria in Colonial South Asia: Uncoupling Disease and Destitution*, London and New York: Routledge.

Chapter 1

A System of Sanitary Surveillance: Disease, Prostitution, and Public Order in the Settlement of Aden, 1872–1932

Mark Harrison[1]

From the 1870s, the Settlement of Aden joined other parts of the British empire in implementing measures designed to prevent the spread of sexually transmitted diseases (then known as 'venereal diseases'), the object being to preserve the health of soldiers and sailors. The system which operated there was reminiscent of – and derived from – that in British India and not so different from that which existed briefly in Britain itself: a system of licenced, medically regulated prostitution, based on a register of women who sold sex in officially sanctioned brothels. However, in 1908, Aden introduced a surveillance system without parallel or precedent. Its purpose was to document the lives of women who were said to be 'unauthorised' or 'unregistered' prostitutes rather than 'official' ones, as was normally the case (Levine 2003; Wald 2014; Harrison 2018). This was because the aim of surveillance and control measures was not simply, or even chiefly, to control disease but to maintain public order. The new system of surveillance also recorded information that was not usually required of women who sold sex in Britain's territories: their ethnicity, place of origin and duration of residence, as well as their marital status, other occupations, place of residence and 'character'. Most colonial territories kept

1 The author generously acknowledges the support of the Wellcome Trust for research underpinning this chapter (grant 203132/Z/16/Z).

registers of women who were officially classed as prostitutes, but these were limited in scope and referred chiefly to their disease status and treatment in 'lock hospitals' for venereal infection. In Aden the situation was different. Medical, criminal, and political concerns were tightly intertwined and control over women varied in accordance with which of these concerns was paramount at any given time.

Aden's unique system of surveillance emerged from the confluence of several problems highlighted in the introduction to this volume: migration, nationalism and the protection of imperial manpower. Intensive surveillance was seen as an antidote to all three, although the system changed over time, reflecting the changing political landscape and the slightly different concerns of the military and civil authorities. Whereas the military was primarily concerned with preventing venereal disease among soldiers and sailors, the police had a broader range of concerns including public order and the activities of nationalists and Islamists. By the twentieth century, both these groups were exploiting unease about prostitution and venereal infection in their opposition to British rule. In the end, none of the various modes of surveillance employed in Aden worked. The situation was too fluid and too volatile, illustrating many of the challenges faced in colonies destabilised by nationalism and intra-imperial migration.

Prostitution and regulation in Aden Settlement

Aden Settlement (the area immediately around the port of Aden) was a dependency of the Bombay presidency of India from 1839. In 1932, it was placed under the jurisdiction of the (British) Government of India, before becoming a Crown Colony in its own right, in 1937 (Kour 1981). Aden's importance lay primarily in its location on shipping lanes to India and points further east.

It was a coaling station for the Royal Navy and a regular port of call for passenger steamers. In view of its strategic importance, the settlement grew rapidly and became home to a large garrison of British and Indian troops, as well as a substantial number of sailors (King 1964; Gavin 1975). As in other port cities of the empire, there was increasing concern in military circles about sexually transmitted diseases, which had a major impact on the labour force every year. At the same time, numerous military and naval personnel were discharged on account of serious disability arising from syphilis. At a time of mounting competition between imperial powers, venereal disease (VD) became a matter of national and imperial importance.

Prior to 1909, the regulation of VD in Aden focused on controlling the prostitutes, along similar lines to efforts in Britain following the passage of the first Contagious Diseases (CD) Act in 1864. This legislation provided for the establishment of licensed brothels in garrison towns and naval ports and for the medical inspection of prostitutes. Typically, this was done by an experienced medical practitioner – usually a military or naval surgeon – and could lead to the forcible treatment of women in what were referred to as 'lock hospitals' (Walkowitz 1980). In continental European countries, these measures were relatively uncontroversial and provisions were far more extensive than in Britain. In continental Europe, legalised brothels were tolerated because they kept prostitutes off the streets and away from 'respectable' people (Corbin 1990). In Britain, there were objections to the CD Acts on the grounds that they violated civil liberties and the rights of women in particular. The Acts were said to enshrine a 'double standard' of morality between the sexes and condone immoral practices (Smith 1971, 1990).

Despite these protests, there was a strong appetite for CD legislation in Britain's colonial territories. In British India, such legislation was enacted in 1866 and was more extensive and oppressive than that in Britain. Although both the British and Indian CD Acts were enforced by local police, in India these powers were often abused by corrupt officials (Levine 2003: 87–95; Harrison 1994: 72–75). Nevertheless, most senior military and naval officers recommended the system and their commitment to it was often ardent. In Aden, there was a strong desire to extend the Indian CD Acts to cover the entire settlement. Legislation was first suggested in 1868, shortly after the passage of the CD Act in Bombay and was endorsed by the political resident (a military officer). However, the government of Bombay was reluctant to grant this request and stated that the powers of existing cantonment legislation (1867) were sufficient to introduce a system of medically regulated prostitution.[2] This suggests that the CD Acts offered few powers over and above general legislation that provided for the sanitary policing of military cantonments. While sympathetic to the perceived need to curb VD, the Bombay government was wary of attracting criticism through the extension of the Acts, as they had already aroused controversy in Britain and in India. Undeterred, the authorities in Aden submitted another request in October 1871.[3] This time, the Bombay government asked the Aden authorities to draw up a more detailed proposal containing a plan for how and where the scheme would be introduced.[4] The most likely reason for this change was that the Aden authorities stipulated that it was necessary to have legislative powers that extended across the whole settlement, as most of the 'public prostitutes'

---

2 Sec., General Dept., Govt. of Bombay, to Gen. Dept., Aden, 25 June 1869, General Dept., 1871 and 1872, No.9, Correspondence re. introduction of Contagious Diseases Act into the Aden Settlement, A/398, Asia Pacific and Africa Collection [APAC], British Library [BL].

3 Sec., General Dept., Aden to General Dept., Govt. of Bombay, 17 October 1871, A/398.

4 Sec., General Dept., Govt. of Bombay, to Gen. Dept., Aden, 9 November 1871, A/398.

resided outside the military cantonment.[5] The largest item of expenditure was the proposed lock hospital, which required the services of a surgeon, a matron and various domestic staff, all of which entailed an annual expenditure of Rs. 3,090. It was stipulated that this establishment should be distinct from the civil hospital, possibly to avoid attracting stigma to the latter and to allow the lock hospital to keep a low profile.[6]

However, the government of Bombay still refused to countenance an extension of the CD Act. There was mounting criticism of the Act in India and the legislation was becoming unworkable. Indeed, the Bombay municipal corporation had withdrawn funding for its operation (Harrison 1994: 74). These considerations probably influenced the government's decision with respect to Aden. But the Bombay government argued that wider protection against VD could be afforded by extending Aden's cantonment legislation to cover the whole settlement rather than just the military area. On these grounds, the Bombay government agreed to a revised budget and the erection of a lock hospital under the auspices of existing regulations.[7] The only issue remaining was whether this hospital should be staffed by a military or civilian surgeon. In other cities in which the British established medically regulated prostitution, the control of lock hospitals was normally vested in military or naval surgeons and the military authorities in Aden and the political resident appear to have contemplated a similar arrangement. However, this was resisted by the civil surgeon of Aden, Surgeon-Major R.W. James, because he believed that military officers had no legal authority

5 Sec., General Dept., Aden to General Dept., Govt. of Bombay, 17 October 1871, A/398.

6 Medical Dept., Aden, to Resident, Aden, 31 January 1872; Resident, Aden to General Dept. Bombay, 8 February 1872, A/398.

7 Actg. Chief Sec. to Govt., General Dept., Bombay to Political Resident, Bombay, 14 September 1872, A/398.

outside the military cantonment.[8] James got his way and control of the lock hospital was given to the civil surgeon and remained under his charge. The medical staff of the lock hospital was also augmented from time to time with staff from the civil general hospital.[9]

The blacklists

The system of prostitution established in Aden in the 1870s persisted into the following century. There were no regulated brothels but 'lines' for prostitutes were permitted in some areas of the settlement. In this respect, Aden differed from many British territories and treaty ports, but the Bombay government later chose to adopt measures similar to those in Aden. After the Indian CD Acts were repealed in 1886, medical inspection was performed covertly under powers conferred by the Military Cantonments Acts of 1889 and 1895. These acts became progressively more liberal in their operation but this trend was reversed by the Cantonments Act of 1897, which reinstated the right of cantonment authorities to expel women if they refused treatment and returned VD to the list of 'contagious diseases' over which control could be exercised. The act also allowed brothels to be closed, disorderly persons to be excluded from cantonments, and forbade public soliciting (Levine 2003: 116–119). The 1897 legislation may have been what some officers in Aden had in mind when they proposed a new system of surveillance in the early 1900s. However, their main concern was

8 Surgeon-Major. R.W. James to Brigade Major, Aden, 23 December 1872; James to Resident, Aden, 29 January 1873, R/20/A/612, APAC, BL.

9 Political Resident, Aden to Sec., General Dept., Bombay, 27 February 1883; L.S. Bruce, Deputy Surgeon General, Bombay, to Medical Officer in Charge, Lock Hospital, Aden, 3 February 1882; Resolution No.1996, Financial Dept., Govt. of Bombay, 31 May 1883, R/20/A/580, APAC, BL.

not so much VD control but the conduct of women who were believed to practise prostitution without official authorisation. There were allegations that such women harassed 'respectable' neighbours and made a nuisance of themselves on the streets; some were also suspected of involvement in political disturbances. In 1906, for example, one woman was questioned for her part in a riot, although she was subsequently discharged for lack of evidence.[10]

At the beginning of the scheme's first year of operation, in 1908, Captain Hancock, chief of police for Sheik Othman, one of the settlement's four divisions, noted that there were about twenty women who worked 'more or less clandestinely' as prostitutes, in addition to thirty-three officially registered as public prostitutes, i.e. who were subject to occasional treatment at the lock hospital. Whereas the latter lived in two blocks of houses, the former were scattered throughout the division. Hancock ordered his men to keep a confidential list of such women and to send a return to him quarterly, 'with recommendations for such action as may be considered necessary'. Cases of 'bad behaviour' were also to be recorded as and when they occurred. He hoped that similar actions might be taken in the other three divisions: The Crater, Tawahi and Maala, noting that the latter was a 'great place for prostitutes'.[11] A memorandum the following year for Maala division stated that the lists of prostitutes had been compiled with a view to providing quarters for them, which suggests that the authorities were concerned to contain such women within prescribed boundaries. The emphasis on the behaviour of 'illicit' prostitutes also indicates that public order issues, rather than medical concerns, were paramount

10 List of women carrying on private prostitution at Tawahi, first quarter 1908, R/20/A/1284, APAC, BL

11 Extract from Capt. Hancock's notebook, 1 January 1908, Aden Residency, Prostitutes – List of Private Prostitutes, R/20/A/1284.

as far as the police were concerned.[12] Indeed, some references were made subsequently to the housing of prostitutes on land provided by the settlement authorities. These houses were constructed by private landlords who let the rooms. But such establishments were recorded in Tawahi and Maala divisions only and the vast majority of prostitutes remained scattered throughout the settlement.[13]

While efforts to house prostitutes indicate the primacy of public order, the purpose of the new surveillance system is revealed more clearly in a memorandum of 1911, which declared that 'the object of maintaining these lists is to reduce the number of the prostitutes by deporting the worst of them'.[14] Although some mention was made of venereal infection among the women, the overriding concern at this time was with their character. Other aspects of their life – their marital status, place of origin, etc – were of significance only in so far as they enabled the police to ascertain how these women operated, whom they associated with, whom they were likely to upset, and, most importantly, whether or not they could be deported. If they were not natives of the settlement and had no significant family ties, deportation was feasible.

One of the great difficulties in maintaining order in Aden was its multinational characteristics, sitting as it did at the crossroads of Asia and Africa (Reese 2018). The issues arising in Aden exemplified the difficulties colonial authorities faced in policing increasingly complex and diverse populations. Before considering the process of deportation, it is necessary to determine what kind of information was recorded in the police registers and what type of conduct was regarded as obnoxious.

12 Anon. memo, 16 May 1908, quarter ending 30 June 1908, R/20/A/1284.

13 Anon. memo, 1 August 1908, quarter ending, R/20/A/1284.

14 Anon. memo, 18 October, quarter ending 30 September, R/20/A/1284.

The four divisions began to record information in slightly different ways, but collection was increasingly standardised and typically included the women's name, race, country of origin, length of stay in Aden, occupation (other than prostitution) character and other general remarks. In the third quarter of 1908, for example, the police in Sheik Othman recorded thirty-eight women who were said to be 'private' prostitutes. As in other divisions, this information was obtained by informants (e.g. neighbours) and street-level surveillance by police.[15] Women from the Arabian Peninsula were well represented, as might be expected, but many were from further afield; for instance, from Malaya, India, Somalia, Sudan and Ethiopia. They included Muslims, Christians, Jews and Hindus, religion and 'caste' often being recorded alongside or instead of race. Slippage between these various categories makes it difficult to state the ethnicity of women on the lists with certainty. Yet, it is possible to get a sense of the ethnic composition of clandestine prostitutes and the places from which they came.

Throughout the period in which this surveillance scheme operated (1908–13), the most prominent ethnic group were Somalis (see Figure 1.1). Between 1908 and 1910, during which time surveillance was at its height, they comprised 38.2% of women recorded on the lists. Most seem to have come from Somalia as opposed to being born in Aden and were composed of several clans and sub-clans. The next most numerous were Arabs (26.6%); some from within Aden and other parts of the Yemen and some from surrounding countries, for example Oman and what is now Saudi Arabia. The third largest group were Indians or women of Indian heritage (22.8%), born either within the settlement or in East Africa. Most appear to have

15 Anon memo, 24 October 1908, quarter ending 31 December 1908, R/20/A/1284.

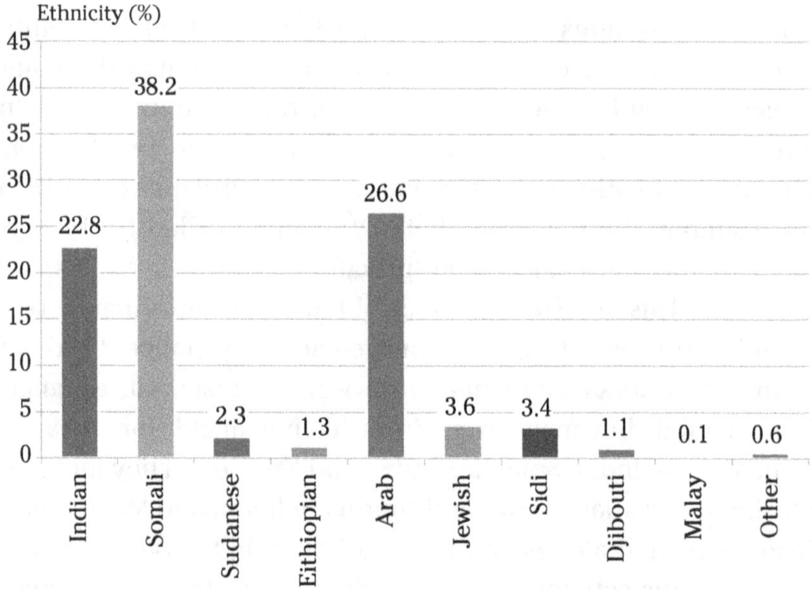

Figure 1.1: Ethnicity of 'private' prostitutes, 1908–9 Source: R/20/A/1284, APAC, BL.

been Hindus but they included a significant minority of Muslims and a few Christians.[16]

None of the other ethnic groups comprised more than 4% of the total but their diversity demonstrates that Aden was a melting pot, drawing migrants from across Asia and East Africa.

The recording of prostitutes' domestic circumstances was less than rigorous and varied from one quarter to another, as well as over time, depending on the whim of individual police commanders. Indeed, the occupation of women designated as unlicensed prostitutes is one of the least consistent aspects of the new surveillance system. A snapshot from the years 1908–9 (Figure 1.2) provides a rough indication of their means of financial support other than prostitution. These figures have been obtained from divisions that listed occupation and other

16 R/20/A/1284, APAC, BL.

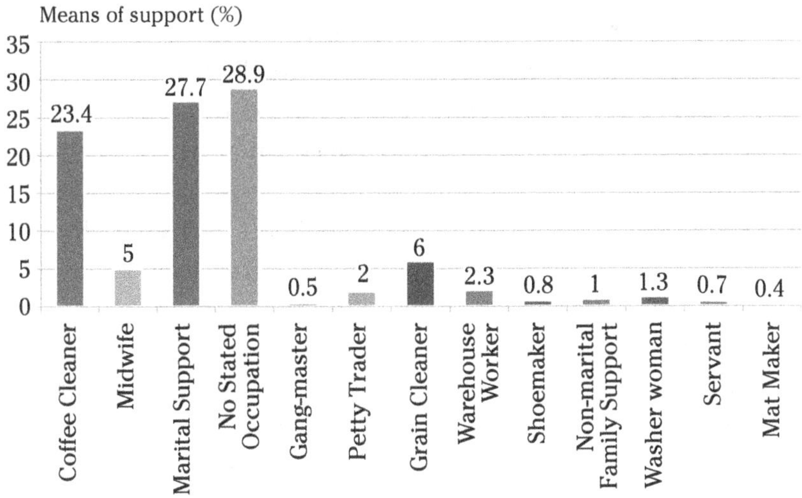

Figure 1.2: Other means of financial support, 1908–9 Source: R/20/A/1284, APAC, BL.

financial circumstances in the years in question and constitute the average of both years combined.[17]

The single largest group (28.9%) consisted of women for whom no alternative occupation was listed. Most were apparently single, some were widowed or divorced. The second largest group (27.7%) were married and their spouse appears to have been their sole or main source of financial support other than prostitution. A few others (1%) received income from siblings, sons or daughters, or from men who 'kept' them as mistresses. Some were recorded as having married recently, sometimes leaving the settlement or moving to another division as a result. Those who did marry sometimes ceased to sell sex but just as many continued to do so or worked as 'procuresses'. Many women appear to have turned to prostitution to supplement meagre household incomes or to support themselves and their dependents after divorce or the death of a husband or father.

17 R/20/A/1284, APAC, BL.

However, one register recorded that a woman, the daughter of an Arab butcher, was married to a man who lived on her earnings as a prostitute. Another woman, divorced from her husband, continued to live with him and carry on prostitution 'under his eyes'.[18]

Of the other occupations they engaged in, by far the most common (23.4%) was coffee cleaning. After that came grain cleaning (6%), midwifery (5%), warehouse work (2.3%) and various other jobs that would have provided a low and unstable income. A few women were formerly 'public prostitutes' (i.e. official, registered prostitutes) but now lived as the mistresses of men working as pimps or who at least tolerated their wives' involvement in prostitution.[19] Of those women who worked long-term as prostitutes, a few – usually no more than one or two per quarterly register – were also listed as 'procuresses', i.e. women who recruited other women into prostitution. We can get some insight into their circumstances from the remarks of police officers. For example, one such woman, recorded in Tawahi in the last quarter of 1908, was said to be the housekeeper of a Parsi businessman. She was once apparently 'famous' as a prostitute but became a procuress as she aged and her popularity waned.[20]

Disturbing the peace

Although the surveillance registers illuminate the domestic and economic circumstances which brought women into unlicensed sex-work, they are, of course, structured according to colonial preoccupations and may therefore distort the situation in which

18 Confidential Register [hereafter, CR] (Tawahi), quarter ending 30 December 1908, R/20/A/1284

19 CR (Sheik Othman), quarter ending 30 September 1911, No.26, R/A/1284.

20 CR (Tawahi), quarter ending 30 December 1908, R/20/A/1284

many women found themselves. Their chief purpose becomes clear from an analysis of their content and structure. The 'character' and 'remarks' sections of the lists reveal the types of behaviour of most concern to the police and these may be divided into several categories. One of the most numerous complaints made against women on the list was that they disturbed the peace in some way. We can see this clearly in the register for The Crater in the third quarter of 1908. One woman, an Indian, married to a washer-man, was said 'to give a lot of trouble' and was recommended for deportation. At the other end of the scale, two Jewish sisters who lived with their mother belonged to a 'respectable' family and sold sex to wealthy people only. They did not constitute any kind of threat.[21] But in the same quarter of 1908, in Maala, one woman (a Somali) was said to be 'Always causing a disturbance… Undesirable character to have in Maala. May be deported.' Another woman, also a Somali, but from a different clan, was said to be 'always quarrelling with all neighbours'. Yet another Somali woman was said to loiter on the streets at night causing 'scenes' with passers-by.[22] Some of these women were targeted for deportation or moved on to other quarters or left the settlement.

Reports of severely disruptive behaviour were rare, however, and on the whole, women in all quarters were said to carry on prostitution quietly and discretely. Even some of those consistently described as 'rowdy' were allowed to remain provided their behaviour did not become too disruptive. For example, three Somali women in Maala division, who were reported as 'rowdy' in several successive quarters, were not deported. Although two of the women had lived in Aden for at least twenty years, the most likely reason they were allowed to

21 CR (Crater), quarter ending 30 September 1908, R/20/A/1284.

22 CR (Maala), quarter ending 30 September 1908, R/20/A/1284.

remain was because they were married; two for some time and one recently (to an Arab merchant).[23] Closely related to the issue of disruptive behaviour was that of sobriety. In Sheik Othman, an Arab woman described as a 'procuress' was said to be both rowdy and a heavy drinker.[24] However, most of those said to be heavy drinkers were Indians, principally Hindus and Christians but also a few Muslims.[25] Yet heavy consumption of alcohol was not regarded as a sufficient cause for deportation or even alarm. In the second quarter of 1909, police in The Crater noted that three women (all Indians) were heavy drinkers but 'quiet'.[26]

In the period 1908–13, in which the surveillance system operated without interruption, the vast majority of women listed as 'private' prostitutes were allowed to continue their activities. Most did not draw attention to themselves and even some of those who did were allowed to remain. Considering that deportation seems to have been the main purpose of compiling the lists, the number recommended for expulsion is remarkably low. Most deportations occurred in the first year of the scheme's operation, when seven women appear to have been targeted: two from The Crater (one Indian, one Somali), four from Maala (all Somali, one of whom was born in Aden); one from Sheik Othman (Somali).[27] After that, there are occasional recommendations for deportation but the reasons are often unclear, as is the outcome. In 1911, for example, there is mention of five women (all Somalis) who were recommended for deportation but it seems likely either that these were earlier cases on which no action had yet been taken or that they were

23 CR (Maala), quarter ending 31 December 1909, R/20/A/1284.

24 CR (Sheik Othman), quarter ending 30 June 1911, R/20/A/1284.

25 CR (Tawahi), quarter ending 30 June 1913, R/20/A/1284.

26 CR (Crater), quarter ending 30 June 1909, R/20/A/1284.

27 Particulars of women under orders for deportation, 15 March 1909, R/20/A/1284.

reported for reasons other than public order, such as refusing medical inspection (see below).[28]

Two of the women recommended for deportation during the first year of the scheme were Kulsom bint Hossain Bux and Shukara bint Abdi, both of whom had been highlighted on lists for The Crater in the second quarter of 1908. Their deportation was ordered in October,[29] but both were still present in February the following year, as the Inspector of Police in that division had apparently 'forgot[ten] all about them'.[30] Abdi was not arrested until 25 February, when she was taken before the inspector of police for her division and told that she should sell all her furniture within four days pending deportation to Berbera, on the coast of Somaliland. Abdi wrote a letter to one of the magistrates protesting that no reason for her deportation had been given and asked to be allowed to remain. She stressed that she had an official pass, means of financial support (from trading) and that she had committed no wrong during her 40-year stay in Aden. Having lived there for so long, she regarded Aden as her home and knew no other place.[31] Towards the end of March, Abdi wrote to the political resident of Aden petitioning him to prevent her deportation. By this time, she had been told of the reasons for her deportation and protested that she had never engaged in prostitution or procurement, nor committed any other misdemeanours. She insisted that she was a cloth-seller and often entered the houses of respectable persons, who would not have allowed her to gain access to their homes if she

28 Anon. memo, 26 July 1911, R/20/A/1284.

29 W.H. Marston, Deputy Superintendent of Police, to Inspector of Police, Crater Division, 24 February 1909, R/20/A/1284.

30 Note by W.H. Marston, 2 March 1909, R/20/A/1284.

31 Shukra bint Abdi to Capt. W.L.P. Wood, Asst. Resident Magistrate First Class, Aden, 3 March 1909, R/20/A/1284.

were disreputable. She added that she would furnish a letter written by her neighbours attesting to her good character.[32]

W.H. Marston, the deputy superintendent of police for Aden, was unsympathetic. Having made further inquiries into Abdi's circumstances, he alleged that she was a 'well-known procuress' who was indebted to prostitutes from whom she borrowed jewellery. Marston considered her continued presence in Aden to be against the public interest.[33] A few days later, he added that 'The petitioner has not put forth sufficient grounds to warrant a reconsideration of the order for her deportation.'[34] However, the day before she was due to leave, Abdi petitioned the first assistant resident, Maj. W. Merewether, pointing out that she had several law-suits pending, which were intended to extract money from persons indebted to her.[35] Marston countered that all her suits had been settled and that there was no reason for clemency.[36] She was deported forthwith.[37]

Although it had taken over six months to deport Abdi, her case was one of the easiest to resolve. Others, in which women were recommended for deportation on grounds of bad character, proved far more difficult and revealed the deficiencies of surveillance based predominantly on hearsay. One such case was Kulsom Hossain Bux, an Indian, who had several family members living in the settlement, including a policeman, Havildar (Sergeant) Ahmed Hossain Bux. On 26 February, the havildar dictated a letter to the Deputy Superintendent of Police describing how another police sergeant arrived at his house to

32 Shukra Abdi to Political Resident, Aden, 25 March 1909, R/20/A/1284.
33 Note by W.H. Marston, 3 April 1909, R/20/A/1284.
34 Note by W.H. Marston, 5 April 1909, R/20/A/1284.
35 Shakani bint Abdu to Maj. W. Merewether, 27 March 1909, R/20/A/1284.
36 Note by W.H. Marston, 10 April 1909, R/20/A/1284.
37 Note by W.H. Marston, 19 April 1909, R/20/A/1284.

summon his younger sister, Kulsom, to the police station. On arrival, she was told to leave Aden within twenty-four hours. On discovering this, their elder brother, Ali, went to the station to request the reason. He was told nothing but his sister was given leave to remain for a few more days. When he dictated his letter to the deputy superintendent, Havildar Hossain Bux had not been informed of the detailed reasons for the deportation order but he had some idea of the charge. He protested that his whole family had been born in Aden and that his sister was married. He also pointed out that there was another woman of the same name as his sister, who led a 'flaunting life' and was well known to the police. It was a case of mistaken identity.[38]

On this occasion, the appeal was successful. After reading documentation on the case, Merewether declared that, 'I do not like this business at all. The form of recommending persons, especially women, puts an enormous power into the hands of the Police which is very liable to abuse unless a careful inquiry into each case is made.' He went on to explain that while men found it easy to prove they were in employment or had not been convicted of any crime, it was practically impossible for a woman to disprove a charge of prostitution. Writing of Hossain Bux, Merewether added that 'It is evident that no proper enquiry was made into this particular case until Lt. Meek [the officer subsequently appointed by Merewether to investigate it] did so.' From that point on, he insisted that Meek should investigate all allegations of procurement and keeping a disorderly house. Merewether declared that he would far rather see a woman escape justice than an innocent one be punished.[39]

38 Havildar Hossain Bux to Deputy Supt. of Police, Aden, 26 February 1909, R/20/A/1284.

39 Note by Merewether 15 May 1909, R/20/A/1284.

Earlier, Marston had denied that there was any merit to Hossain Bux's petition as well as petitions from several Somali women – Awalla Awady, Fatima bint Yasim, Sabho Mohammed – who were scheduled for deportation at that time. But these cases, too, were presenting problems to the authorities. Marston had failed to produce detailed reports on any of the women recommended for deportation, including whether they held property or not. Merewether suspected that at least two or three of the seven women recommended for deportation in October might own property.[40] A further note on this file – probably made by the resident – stated, 'It is all very unsatisfactory. I am looking for an improvement in the Police under Mr. Marston.'[41]

Investigations into the status of women recommended for deportation were time consuming, as were the legal proceedings associated with them. This took momentum out of the system and, although surveillance continued for a few years after 1909, it lacked clarity of purpose. Appraising the scheme in 1913, one official wrote: 'In 1909, a number of them [private prostitutes] were deported at the recommendation of the Police... No recommendations have since been made by the Police and original object with which the lists were introduced therefore fails in effect.'[42] Another memorandum, from the chief of police, declared likewise. It noted that the police had been dissuaded from recommending deportations of prostitutes on grounds of their bad character and stated that this was a 'dangerous power' as well as one that wasted hours of time for them and other officials. Having taken over in 1911, the chief of police had very little use for the 'Black Lists', as he described them, and felt that

40 Note by Merewether 3 March 1909, R/20/A/1284.

41 Anon. note, 3 March 1909, R/20/A/1284.

42 Anon. memo, 23 July 1913, R/20/A/1284.

if the conduct of any woman overstepped the mark, it could be dealt with by means other than deportation.[43]

Military requirements

The system of surveillance devised and executed by the police in Aden from 1908 to 1913 initially had little to do with the suppression of VD but such concerns came increasingly to the fore. As the impetus behind deportation for public order offences ebbed, the surveillance scheme was buttressed by a parallel system which had VD control as its primary objective. As with earlier attempts to regulate VD, this scheme developed in response to military rather than civilian requirements, even though it relied to some extent on civilian personnel. It originated in the observation that rates of VD among civilians in two divisions of Aden – The Crater and Sheik Othman – were particularly high and that this posed a danger to British and Indian servicemen garrisoned nearby. Although troops were then forbidden from visiting Sheik Othman, it was thought that the women who inhabited this division were a reservoir of infection that might spread to other areas. In 1910, it was proposed to extend the system of medical inspections then in force for so-called public – i.e. registered – prostitutes to those who were not registered. If the latter were suspected of being infected, they were to be examined by the civil surgeon and then registered as a prostitute by the police.[44] The primary means of surveillance in this case was contact-tracing. Unlike the blacklists, this information came from soldiers who had presented for treatment for venereal infection, at which time

43 Anon memo, 24 July 1913, R/20/A/1284.

44 Political Resident to Col. N. Denny, Indian Medical Service, 20 November 1910, R/20/A/1285, APAC, BL.

they were required to state the name and address of the woman they believed had infected them.[45]

Lt. Wightwick of the Sheik Othman police was asked to send a report on the extent of VD in his division and undertook to do this shortly, concurring with the opinion that there were many unofficial prostitutes in his division and that they were probably 'well infected'. He also endorsed the proposed system of contact tracing, inspection and registration of women as public prostitutes if found to be infected. He added that if they refused to be inspected and registered, they should be deported.[46] At this point, there were thought to be only fourteen public prostitutes in Sheik Othman but many more private ones.[47] Government dispensaries recorded a fairly high rate of venereal disease, although it was thought that this greatly underestimated the true number of infections because few women cared to visit such institutions.[48] Wightwick's investigations revealed that private prostitution was very extensive and he advocated that such women should be prevented from entering the area of the cantonment, except on special passes for one day only, on the same terms as public prostitutes. In other words, he recommended that all women suspected of prostitution should be registered.[49]

There was scepticism about whether this proposal would work because it was very difficult to accurately identify women as prostitutes and because it would probably entail

45 Col. N. Denny to Political Resident, 27 November 1910, No. 9: Prostitutes – Venereal Disease, R/20/A/1285.

46 Lt. Wightwick to Col. Denny, 24 November 1910, No.9, R/20/A/1285.

47 Memo from Inspector of Police, Sheik Othman to Civil Surgeon, Aden, 24 November 1910, No. 9, R/20/A/1285.

48 3rd Sub-Asst. Surgeon, Sheik Othman Dispensary, 24 November, to Senior Medical Officer, Indian Troops, No.9, R/20/A/1285.

49 Memo from Lt. Wightwick, 1 December 1910, No.9, R/20/A/1285.

much disruption of ordinary business in the settlement.[50] Nevertheless, in 1911, the civil surgeon recommended that all women designated as public prostitutes be compelled to present themselves for inspection on pain of deportation. He deemed this necessary because the power of compulsion had recently been removed by the Government of India. From 1907, inspection of prostitutes of any description had to be performed on a voluntary basis and issuing deportation orders to women who were not born in Aden provided a way round the problem. The civil surgeon recommended that such measures be used in the cantonment area and in Sheik Othman and that all women named by soldiers should be required to present for inspection.[51] The general officer commanding (GOC) the Aden Brigade approved of this proposal, as did the cantonment magistrate and political resident.[52] The magistrate added that the bazaar in the cantonment should also be placed out of bounds to troops, as this was where they would find private prostitutes. However, the GOC thought this impracticable and that troops should be discouraged from visiting certain parts of the bazaar only.[53]

This system went into operation in May 1911, almost as soon as it was approved. It relied on both contact tracing and reports from hospitals which women visited for treatment for venereal disease. Each case was reported by the hospital to the military authorities, regardless of whether women were designated public or private prostitutes. For example, on 10 May, the civil hospital in The Crater reported a Somali woman as being infected, giving her place of residence as a brothel. Another woman, who

---

50 Note from 'J.B.', 3 December 1910, R/20/A/1285.

51 Note from Lt. Wightwick, forwarding report of Civil Surgeon, 4 May 1911, No.9, R/20/A/1285.

52 Note from General Officer Commanding Aden Brigade and Note from Cantonment Magistrate, 15 May 1911, No.9, R/20/A/1285.

53 Note from Cantonment Magistrate, 22 May 1911, No.9, R/20/A/1285.

was not recorded as a public prostitute, was said to reside at House 189, Steamer Point; an area notorious for unofficial prostitution.[54] These cases appear to have been women already under treatment but in the following weeks it became more difficult to obtain such information as some women declined to be inspected and faced deportation as a result.

The first such case appeared at the end of May, when a woman named Hadia Jama was blamed for infecting three persons.[55] At this point, the issue of whether deportation was permissible under the Government of India's rules of 1907 came up for discussion and the deputy adjutant of the Aden Brigade decided that it was.[56] Following this decision, deportation of women designated public and private prostitutes for refusing medical inspection and or treatment became relatively common.[57] At the end of 1912, the first assistant resident, Lt.-Col. H.F. Jacob declared that deportation of every unmarried woman who had VD was the only solution, adding that the police should be vigorous in examining all prostitutes.[58] It is worth noting that the military impetus for deportation on the grounds of venereal infection came at a time when police powers of arbitrary deportation were being criticised and curtailed. It seems that military concerns now outweighed those of the police. However, it is likely that the confidential lists kept by the police were used in identifying women as likely suspects of prostitution

54 Venereal Reports, Civil Hospital, The Crater, 5 May and 13 May 1911, No.12: Prostitutes – Examination and deportation of, suffering from Venereal Disease, R/20/A/1285.

55 Note by C.M., 29 May 1911, No.12, R/20/A/1285.

56 Notes by R.A.R. and Capt. B. Higham, Deputy Adjutant and Quarter Master General, 3 June 1911, No.12, R/20/A/1285.

57 Note from Cantonment Magistrate, 4 June 1911, No.12, R/20/A/1285.

58 Note from First Asst. Resident, 12 December 1912, No.38: Prostitutes – Venereal Disease in Aden – Appointment of a Committee to Inquire into the Question of the Sources of Infection, R/20/A/1285.

and that the two systems worked together to some extent. Deportation on the grounds of refusing inspection had a legal basis in cantonment legislation and did not present problems of mistaken identity, as in the case of allegations of disturbance.

Although deportation increased at this time it was not regarded as a sufficient answer to the problem of venereal infection, which showed no sign of abating. It seemed necessary to augment existing arrangements, and the political resident appointed a committee to consider the options available. This committee comprised Col. R.F. Cleveland, the assistant director of medical services (president) and three other members: J.B.S. Thubron, the chairman of Aden Settlement, Capt. B.R. Reilly, the assistant resident in charge of police and Lt. J. de la Gordon, the cantonment magistrate.[59] The committee made a number of observations, the most important of which was that the number of public prostitutes was negligible and that addressing the problem of venereal disease meant focusing on so-called private prostitutes. It concluded that a multi-pronged strategy was required for dealing with this problem, including ordering soldiers to not consort with private prostitutes, placing Steamer Point out of bounds, strict supervision of areas frequented by troops to prevent women from loitering, continued use of deportation and greater watchfulness to prevent women from returning (as some recently expelled women had) and re-establishing a lock hospital to treat venereal infection.[60]

The demise of the lock hospital in 1912 may seem surprising in view of mounting concern over the spread of venereal diseases. However, the Government of India was looking to economise and had been under the false impression that the problem in

59 Lt.-Col. H.F. Jacob, memo, 13 December 1913, No.38, R/20/A/1285.

60 Report of the Committee appointed by the Political Resident, Aden, to inquire into the question of the sources of infection from venereal diseases in Aden and Sheik Othman, 24 February 1924, No.38, R/20/A/1285.

Aden was easing.[61] The military authorities proposed to not re-open the old hospital but instead have a ward of the civil hospital designated as a venereal ward, with the civil surgeon in attendance. The government in Bombay accepted these proposals but stipulated that the amount paid to the surgeon for these services should be reduced, as he would have less responsibility than before.[62]

Although the measures recommended by the committee were broadly supported by the authorities in Aden – and in Bombay – a few notes of caution were sounded. Even before the committee reported, the political resident and cantonment magistrate indicated their unease with mass deportation. They feared that the innocent would be expelled along with the guilty and that women who had been in Aden over twenty years could suddenly be labelled as 'vicious' and suitable for deportation.[63] A certain amount of caution was therefore exercised but more effort was put into discouraging loitering among women suspected of being prostitutes, especially in the vicinity of cantonments.[64] These measures changed little over the next few years but the declaration of war in 1914 saw more servicemen arrive in Aden and an intensification of concerns about the spread of disease. Another change was the movement, for the first time, of troops into Sheik Othman, which placed them in close proximity to women practicing prostitution privately.

---

61 Lt.-Col. S.E. Praill, IMS, First Asst. Resident, 30 December 1913, No.38, R/20/A/1285.

62 J.L. Riue, Sec. to the Govt. of Bombay, to Secretary of the Govt. of India, Home Dept. (Medical), 28 July 1913, No.38, R/20/A/1285.

63 H.F. Jacob, Circular, 18 January 1914, No.38, R/20/A/1285.

64 First Asst. Resident, Aden, to Asst. Resident in Charge of Police, 27 March 1924, No.38, R/20/A/1285.

This situation produced a marked increase in the number of deportations, especially of Somali women.[65]

Little else can be ascertained about VD control during the war but the end of the conflict saw a resurgence of concerns about infection among British and Indian servicemen, and there were new discussions about how best to deal with the problem. One proposal was to create official 'lines' for prostitutes in Sheik Othman, which was singled out on account of the large number of prostitutes believed to reside there.[66] While it was agreed that this was a good idea in theory, most officials, including the resident, thought that it would make little difference to the spread of infection, as the majority of women would continue to work privately; many residing with husbands or other family members.[67] As far as the assistant medical director of the Aden Field Force was concerned, efforts should concentrate on the removal of 'doubtful characters'.[68] But there were doubts about intensifying this policy and whether or not it worked. The officer commanding Sheik Othman thought that deporting women because they frequented houses notorious as brothels would simply drive them onto the streets. He pointed out that the military authorities were already struggling to arrest women for loitering with the intent to sell sex. Many of them had been scheduled for deportation.[69] Others thought that deportation would do little to address the root cause of the problem, which was a huge imbalance of the sexes. There were apparently four

65 Note by Political Resident, 28 March 1921, No.29: Epidemic Disease – Report of the Prevalence of Venereal Disease at Sheik Othman, R/20/A/1285.

66 Superintendent of Police, Sheik Othman, to First Asst. Resident, 18 October 1919, No.29, R/20/A/1285.

67 Note from Political Resident, 23 October 1919, No.29, R/20/A/1285.

68 Asst. Director of Medical Services, Aden Field Force to First Asst. Resident, 22 September 1919, No.29, R/20/A/1285.

69 OC Sheik Othman to Headquarters, Aden Field Force, 1 October 1919, No.29, R/20/A/1285.

times as many men as women in Aden. It was also difficult to identify women suitable for deportation. Ascertaining their marital status was particularly difficult as Sharia law permitted temporary marriages and easy divorce. The marital status of women changed constantly, with relationships being particularly fluid in the Somali community.[70]

There was, it seems, a sense of fatalism about what could be achieved in Aden and, for the next few years, the campaign against VD began to flag. There was even confusion about what measures had been attempted in the past, with some officials – mostly military – claiming that there was a precedent for deporting diseased women from the cantonment area to Sheik Othman and police officials claiming that no such expulsion had taken place. The idea of establishing prostitutes 'lines' in that division was revived only to be dropped again.[71] Energy was dissipated on projects that came to nothing, one being a proposal to establish a separate brothel for British soldiers and sailors; that is, one distinct from Indian troops. Such a facility was requested by the commanding officer of the Royal Fusiliers, presumably because Indian soldiers were thought to be more heavily infected with VD. But the proposal was rejected because it created ill feeling among Indian troops, many of whom were already angered by the military police preventing them from visiting public prostitutes in The Crater.[72]

---

70 Note from Asst. Resident in charge of Police, 23 October 1919; Deputy Supt. of Police to AR in charge of Police, No.29, R/20/A/1285.

71 G.A. Richardson, Asst. Resident in charge of Police to First Asst. Resident, 17 March 1921; K.M. Dadina, Deputy Supt. of Police, Aden, to Asst. Resident in charge of Police, [no date] March 1921, No.73: Re the complaint made by the officer commanding Yemen Infantry that prostitutes suffering from venereal disease are deported from Aden to Sheik Othman, R/20/A/1285.

72 Report from Inspector of Police, The Crater, 14 January 1921; Lt.-Col. M. Hancock, Officer Commanding 2nd Battalion Royal Fusiliers, to Headquarters, Aden Field Force, 21 January 1921; Note of 10 February 1921, forwarded by Deputy Asst. Adjutant General, Aden Field Force to First Asst. Resident;

Soliciting, surveillance and registration

As there had been no movement on the issue of brothels in Sheik Othman, the focus of anti-VD measures returned to surveillance and deportation, particularly of women found soliciting. The focus was again on 'private' prostitutes who were loitering near military facilities or in areas frequented by off-duty soldiers. In 1923 and 1924, there was a spate of deportations of prostitutes and pimps following arrests by civilian police.[73] In addition to regular patrols, some officers were involved in plain-clothes surveillance. This appears to have been a new departure and led police to enter private residences and offices that were being used for illicit prostitution. On the night of 26 April 1924, two plain-clothes policemen search some huts near the wireless station in Sheik Othman, where they discovered three 'gaudily dressed' women and two sweepers standing near them, said to be pimps. The sweepers threatened to assault the police and refused to hand the women over. The police went to the nearby artillery battery, where the sergeant-major agreed to lend six gunners to assist the police and brought the women and the two men to Maala police station. Following their arrest, five persons were put up for deportation: three Somali women (aged 36, 38 and 40) and two men (aged 23 and 40). The latter was the husband of one of the women. The deputy superintendent of police concluded his report on this incident with the following sentences, 'From secret inquiries made it appears that this group of huts, is the rendez-vous of bad women. It is situated in an out-of-the-way place and is easy of access. I suggest that

---

Note by Political Resident, 10 February 1921, No.31: Re the proposal to reserve a brothel for the British soldiers and sailors, R/20/A/1285.

73 E.g. Asst. Resident in charge of Police to First Asst. Resident, 26 April 1923; Notes by First Asst. Resident, 27 March 1924 and 26 February 1924; Acting Deputy Supt. of Police, Aden, to First Asst. Resident, 27 March 1924, 24 April 1924 and 26 May 1924, No.277: Prostitutes – Deportation of all women found soliciting, R/20/A/1285.

families of sweepers should not be permitted to live [there] at Khormaksar.'[74]

It is unclear whether this advice was followed, but Khormaksar remained a primary focus of police surveillance. Even so, surveillance and deportation failed to make much difference. VD rates remained high and there was renewed concern over the disorder created by prostitution, which had now become a political issue. In the late 1920s, groups critical of British rule attempted to make political capital out of the spread of disease and the immoral behaviour that the British seemed to condone by tolerating prostitution. Some opponents of British rule began to mobilise around the banner of moral purity and the defence of Islam, although in some cases employing the rhetoric of international health and hygienic modernisation. This agitation seems to have had political objectives, but the campaign also provided a vehicle for individuals harbouring personal grievances. Most of their demands were rejected but they ushered in a new era of surveillance and control.

The first petition of this kind came from Awad Abdulla of Sheik Othman, a *qadi* or magistrate of a sharia court. Abdulla and dozens of other signatories pleaded with the political resident to increase the number of women deported for soliciting on moral and public order offences associated with prostitution. He claimed that 'there was hardly a street which does not contain a few prostitutes living side by side with respectable family men, setting thereby a very bad precedent and most unfortunate example to the rising generation of girls and boys. Apart from this ... these prostitutes and their dependents are simply a public nuisance. They beat drums, create alarums every now and then and make life a burden.' The *qadi* went on to protest about the

74 Acting Deputy Supt. of Police, Aden, to First Asst. Resident, 28 April 1924, No.277, R/20/A/1285.

spread of venereal disease among the young and the failure of the British to inspect, treat and segregate women involved in prostitution.[75]

This petition failed to impress the magistrate of Sheik Othman, who claimed that he knew the number of prostitutes residing in his division but was 'not previously aware that so many professing puritans also had their habitation there'. He went on to explain that such women tended to live on the edge of the town, which was surely far better than having them walk about the centre, adding that 'the question of quantity is regulated by demand – as in all commercial projects'. This demand, he claimed, was 'created by the very people who append their names to this petition, and their co-religionists. It is well known that the easy laws of marriage and divorce allowed by the Sharia is the primary cause of prostitution in the East.' He stated that it was his policy to recognise prostitution as a 'necessary evil' and to 'endeavour to keep it under control'. He also believed that:

> this petition has been organised by some individual with an axe to grind... The Qazi [*qadi*], who with considerable voracity collects fees from the temporary marriages and rapid divorce which I regard as the chief cause of the extensive female prostitution, heads the list of petitioners. The majority of the landlords whose signatures are appended own the houses in which these unfortunate women live. I have never yet had a suit for ejectment on moral grounds filed in my court from any of them.[76]

---

75 Petition from Awad Abdulla and other residents of Sheik Othman, 11 October 1928, No: 589A: Sheikh Othman: Application from Awad Abdulla, Qadi of Sheik Othman and other signatories complaining against alleged prostitution at Sheik Othman, R/20/A/1285.

76 Magistrate, Sheik Othman, to Resident, 12 November 1928, No.589A, R/20/A/1285.

There is no way of knowing whether or not these allegations were true, but the first assistant resident, Lt.-Col. B.R. Reilly, was asked to investigate the matter, which entailed questioning a number of the petitioners. They claimed that there were about two-hundred women working as prostitutes in Sheik Othman, distributed in around eighty houses. For the last few months, they had apparently drawn more attention to themselves by 'roaming about on the streets in motors ... shouting and making noises which disturb ... the public peace.' Several residents also complained that prostitution had gone hand in hand with an increase in the consumption of alcohol, several grog shops being closely associated with prostitution. For these reasons, there appeared to be a general feeling that these prostitutes should be confined to a particular locality.[77]

The findings of this inquiry suggest that the magistrate was somewhat complacent about the level of discontent in Sheik Othman. Indeed, other petitions soon began to reach the political resident. One came from Sheik Ahmed Taha al-Hitari, the imam of the largest mosque in Tawahi division. The imam informed the resident of 'the restlessness of the inhabitants of Maalla and Sheik Othman are put to, on account of the large number of prostitutes living in private houses in both localities', who appeared 'in the veil of inchastity, displaying their finery in a shameful manner and in such a nature as is contrary to the general rules of morality.' He added that these rules were not only those of Islam but were to be found throughout the British empire and in all civilised countries. In addition to the offence given to moral values and disturbance of the peace, al-Hitari wrote of the spread of venereal disease and degeneracy among the young, and was critical of attempts to control it by medical

77 Memo by First Asst. Resident, Aden, 17 November 1928, No.589A, R/20/A/1285.

inspection of prostitutes, as this condoned immoral behaviour. In support of his argument, he cited part of a speech given by a British peer (probably Lord Knutsford[78]) at the League of Nations in 1927, in which the peer claimed that experts were unanimous in thinking that medically regulated prostitution was unsupportable on medical and moral grounds. The imam echoed his calls for a crackdown on pimps and prostitution. Finally, he reminded the resident of the potential harm to the reputation of the British among Muslim subjects of the empire, if people came to ask: 'Do you like that the English should rule over your own country so that your daughters and wives may become degenerate as a result of the enjoyment of this abhorred freedom.'[79] Another petition from Maala protested about the ubiquity of prostitution in the division but focused more on the disturbance to family life (predominantly from Somali immigrants) and decency rather than abstract notions of purity and morality.[80]

Emanating from two divisions, these and subsequent petitions suggest that there was widespread discontent with the trouble caused by prostitutes in Aden. But the petitions differ in tone. Only the imam's suggests something like a determined anti-colonial or Islamist agenda. Nevertheless, there was enough in these petitions to concern the political resident, who may have made a connection between this agitation and the rise of Salafism in the settlement during the 1920s. Adherence to this strain of

78 The name which appears in the petition appears to read 'Kushdon' but there is no peer of this name and it probably refers to Sidney Holland, 2nd Viscount Knutsford (1855–1931), chairman of the London Hospital House Committee from 1896 to 1931. Knutsford sometimes spoke on the issue of venereal disease.

79 Petition from Sheik Ahmed Taha al-Hitari, to First Asst. Resident, 19 November 1928, No.598A, R/20/A/1285.

80 Petition to First Asst. Resident from Abdulla Haji Khan and others, 14 December 1928, No.598A, R/20/A/1285.

Islam was initially most apparent among Yemenis (which may explain the frequent references to Somali women) but they were increasingly concerned to create a regional alliance of Muslims under the banner of moral purity (Reese 2012; 2014). This had become evident in Cairo and Alexandria during the First World War and such sentiments were increasing throughout the region (Vatikiotis 1991). At any rate, the resident ordered that a list of public prostitutes living in the division be compiled, showing their names, place of origin, length of stay in Sheik Othman and whether they had been registered or not.[81] These lists resembled those complied in the prewar years, although the new ones were less detailed and aimed to record all prostitutes regardless of whether they were classed as private or public. As far as the British were concerned, there was no prospect of any general crack-down on prostitution to appease the petitioners but they hoped that improving surveillance would help them to better manage disruptive behaviour, using deportation if necessary. The resident may have calculated that such measures would be enough to satisfy some of the less politically motivated petitioners.

The majority of women identified by the new search in Sheik Othman were classified as previously unregistered, which confirmed the impressions of observers over the previous decades.[82] Remarks on character were made sporadically by comparison with previous lists because the main focus was now on registration. However, those that were made reveal a similar picture – of women who had drifted into prostitution on account of divorce, death of their spouse or uncertain income from other sources. Several women appeared to be living with

81 First Asst. Resident to Capt. Falconer, Sheik Othman Police, 20 November 1928, No.598A, R/20/A/1285.

82 E.g. Statements showing the names of prostitutes living in Sheik Othman, sections A-D, December 1928, No.589A, R/20/A/1285.

at least one parent and practising prostitution to meet the needs of the entire household.[83] Other comments show chaotic family circumstances – one woman in Tawahi having apparently been divorced; her former husband had shot her brother who was protecting her.[84] The main places of prostitution were confirmed as Sheik Othman, with sixty-four resident prostitutes, and Maala with forty-eight.[85] It was reported that no prostitute of any description was living in The Crater but women from the other divisions went there regularly.[86] Only nine women resident in Tawahi were recorded as working in prostitution.[87]

Although the police and other authorities in Aden had a clearer idea of the nature and extent of prostitution than they had had for some time, it made little immediate difference to the control of prostitution or the perception of the problem among the public. The resident continued to receive petitions complaining of the 'great and regular nuisance' caused by prostitutes in Sheik Othman, for example.[88] The police in Aden had recently acquired additional powers to close premises designated as brothels as the result of the extension of the Bombay Police Act to the settlement, but they were, on the whole, reluctant to use them.[89] The view that prostitution was a necessary evil was paramount and only the most egregious cases of soliciting were now acted on. This view was also compatible with another turn in the policing of venereal disease

83 E.g. numbers 3–5, Tawahi register, December 1928, No.589A, R/20/A/1285.

84 Number 1, Tawahi Register, December 1928, No.589A, R/20/A/1285.

85 Registers for Maala and Sheik Othman, December 1928, R/20/A/1285.

86 Memo, Supt. of Police, Aden, 17 December 1930, R/20/A/1285.

87 Register for Tawahi, December 1928, No.589A, R/20/A/1285.

88 Petition from Mohammed Saeed El Aonay and three others, 9 March 1929, No.589A, R/20/A/1285.

89 Note by First Asst. Resident, 28 March 1929, No.589A, R/20/A/1285L.

during the final years of Aden's rule by the Bombay Presidency – a shift from prevention to treatment.

Whether in the form of medical regulation or intensified surveillance and policing, prevention made little impact on prostitution or rates of disease. The police continued to clamp down on public soliciting and occasionally closed brothels but venereal disease remained rampant.[90] Women were sometimes compelled to seek treatment following contact-tracing but such cases were rarely brought before the police. A new direction was required and the introduction of the Indian CD Act of 1868 (long repealed in India) was considered for a time. However, the idea was eventually dismissed as 'politically unfeasible' because of circumstances in Aden and the probability of an adverse reaction to such a measure in Britain.[91] The settlement authorities opted for a less coercive approach in keeping with a suggestion made by the chief civilian medical officer, Maj. Bilderbeck of the Indian Medical Service, who warned that 'Repressive measures are unlikely to effect their purpose in respect of prostitution and venereal disease.'[92] These sentiments were broadly in line with the recommendations of the social hygiene movement in Britain (Tomkins 1993), although pragmatic political considerations were probably more important in the case of Aden.

In the course of 1929, momentum gathered behind Bilderbeck's proposal to extend facilities to treat venereal infection, with the political resident, G.S. Symes, restating the opinion that 'remedial measures will be more likely to be effective than repression'. In addition, the resident favoured the continuance of the partial segregation of prostitutes, the restriction of attempts to make brothels alluring (e.g. removing external lights

---

90 Note by Resident, 24 May 1929, No.176: Venereal Disease, R/20/A/1285

91 Note by Resident, 13 June 1929, No.176, R/20/A/1285.

92 Bilderbeck to First Asst. Resident, 11 June 1929, No.176, R/20/A/1285

and decorations), the prevention of public soliciting, and the restriction of liquor licenses in areas notorious for prostitution.[93] The latter measures aimed to reduce the nuisance to those who lived in the area. The main problem was how to expand the facilities available for treatment. By 1930, it was agreed that the most effective way of doing so was to make use of the hospital run by the Keith-Falconer Mission under the auspices of the Church Missionary Society.[94] The mission initially insisted that all those it treated should attend Christian services which was a problem because most prostitutes were Muslim. However, it later dropped this condition and a contract was drawn up for a six-month trial to equip the hospital to treat the poor free of charge, commencing in January 1931.[95] During this period, the results were satisfactory and the scheme was extended until at least March 1933.[96] Treatment free from stigma or punishment had replaced surveillance and coercion.

Conclusion

The measures implemented in the final years of Aden's rule by Bombay amount to an admission of the impossibility of curbing prostitution among a large, diverse and transient population. Prior to the 1930s, anti-VD measures aimed to control prostitution through policing and surveillance, varying in character and intensity in accordance with political and military needs. Initially, 'sanitary surveillance' was directed towards women registered as prostitutes and this reflected the military and naval

93 Note by Resident, 9 July 1929, No.176: R/20/A/1285.

94 Lt.-Col. E.S. Phipson, IMS, Chief Civil Administrative Medical Officer, Aden, to First Asst. Resident, 26 July 1930, R/20/A/1285.

95 Lt.-Col. E.S. Phipson to First Asst. Resident, 22 September 1930; Note by Chairman, Aden Settlement, 21 February 1931, No.176, R/20/A/1285.

96 Note of 5 July 1932; approved by Resident 7 July 1932, R/20/A/1285.

preoccupations of the settlement's authorities. But in the years before the First World War, the purview of surveillance widened and lists of private or 'amateur' prostitutes were compiled from 1908. These measures were driven by the police rather than the army and reflected growing concerns over public order rather than venereal infection. The latter concerns emerged again, following the demise of intensive surveillance in 1913, but were again subsumed by considerations of public order, this time, following the rise of political Islam.

As in other colonies, the primary aim of surveillance was to define and 'fix' colonial subjects (Berda 2013). But this was easier said than done, in view of the diversity and mobility of the population. The authoritarian impulses of some officials were also frustrated by magistrates, political officers and even by the police themselves. Intervention to prevent deportation or other harsh measures was relatively common. Appeal procedures provided a safeguard which some women used to good effect. The utility of surveillance was also reduced by bureaucratic friction and indifference. Maintaining registers was a painstaking business and the accuracy of much of the intelligence that informed them was questionable. As time went on, the objectives of surveillance changed, too. Although venereal disease and political disorder remained important concerns, surveillance was increasingly intended to appease sections of the Arab population, critical of the authorities' toleration of prostitution. The result was a compromise that satisfied few people and had very little impact on rates of VD infection. The move in the 1930s from policing and surveillance to treatment was an acknowledgement of the intractability of these problems rather than a reflection of progressive trends.

References

Berda, Yael (2013), 'Managing Dangerous Populations: Colonial Legacies of Security and Surveillance', *Sociological Forum*, 28(3): 627–30.

Corbin, Alain (1990), *Women for Hire: Prostitution and Sexuality in France after 1850*, trans. A. Sheridan, Cambridge, MA: Harvard University Press.

Gavin, R.J. (1975), *Aden Under British Rule: 1839–1967*, London: C. Hurst & Company.

Harrison, Mark (1994), *Public Health in British India: Anglo-Indian Preventive Medicine 1859–1914*, Cambridge: Cambridge University Press.

Harrison, Mark (1995), 'The British Army and the Problem of Venereal Disease in France and Egypt during the First World War', *Medical History*, 39: 135–158.

Harrison, Mark (2018), 'Health, Sovereignty and Imperialism: The Royal Navy and Infectious Disease in Japan's Treaty Ports', *Social Science Diliman*, 14(2): 490–75.

King, Gillian (1964), *Imperial Outpost: Aden: Its Place in British Foreign Policy*, Chatham House Essay Series.

Kour, Z.H. (1981), *The History of Aden*, London: Frank Cass.

Levine, Philippa (2003), *Prostitution, Race and Politics: Policing Venereal Disease in the British Empire*, New York: Routledge.

Reese, Scott S. (2012), 'Salafi Transformations: Aden and the Changing Voices of Religious Reform in the Interwar Indian Ocean', *International Journal of Middle East Studies*, 44: 71–92.

Reese, Scott S. (2014), '"A leading Muslim of Aden": Personal Trajectories, Imperial Networks, and the Construction of Community in Colonial Aden', in James L. Gelvin and Nile Green (eds), *Global Muslims in the Age of Steam and Print*, Berkeley: University of California Press, pp. 59–77.

Reese, Scott S. (2018), *Imperial Muslims: Islam, Community and Authority in the Indian Ocean*, Edinburgh: Edinburgh University Press.

Smith, F.B. (1971), 'Ethics and Disease in the Late-Nineteenth Century: The Contagious Diseases Acts', *Historical Studies*, 25: 118–35.

Smith, F.B. (1990), 'The Contagious Diseases Acts Reconsidered', *Social History of Medicine*, 3: 197–215.

Tomkins, S.M. (1993), 'Palmitate or Permanganate: The Venereal Prophylaxis Debate in Britain, 1916–1926', *Medical History*, 37: 382–98.

Vatikiotis, P.J. (1991), *The History of Modern Egypt from Muhammad Ali to Mubarak*, London: Weidenfeld and Nicholson.

Wald, Erica (2014), *Vice in the Barracks: Medicine, the Military and the Making of Colonial India, 1780–1868*, London: Palgrave Macmillan.

Walkowitz, Judith R. (1980), *Prostitution in Victorian Society: Women, Class and the State*, Cambridge: Cambridge University Press.

Chapter 2

Surveillance and Subversion: Reporting Vital Statistics in Colonial Burma

Atsuko Naono[1]

Introduction

Improvements in medicine in nineteenth-century Europe made the prevalence of diseases in tropical environments, such as malaria and cholera, a crucial element of the European conceptualisation of indigenous society and people (Arnold 2013: 345–352; Harrison 1998: 11–18). New devices, such as the combination of mapping and medical statistics, also played important roles in visualising the disease environment. Pamela Gilbert, for example, examines how plague mapping in colonial India helped to perpetuate the perception of India as a homogenously tropical place with a stagnant culture that denied melioration, thus being 'guilty of disease production' (Gilbert 2003). Pointing to Benedict Anderson's 'total surveyability' of a colonial state, Takeshi Onimaru argues, in the introduction of this volume, that it was the areas of colonial medicine, public health, and policing that most required 'total surveyability' for maintaining colonial order because the threats were not usually visible, being 'hidden in the local society and people'. In order to make indigenous society and people 'scientifically' legible, a range of methods, including surveys, were introduced in colonies such

1 This research was supported by the Wellcome Trust (grant reference number: 203132/Z/16/Z).

as India and the economic and social life of the local population were scrutinised to provide a 'qualitative understanding of risk' to the colonial economy (Bayly 1996; Kalpagam 2000: 48–9; Polu 2012). Although their impacts have not been fully examined, among these methods, medical surveys were crucial for the colonial government.[2]

One of the most important approaches to medical surveillance in the colonies was the system of gathering various kinds of medical data from colonial subjects through the registration of vital statistics, such as deaths and births. The introduction of this system to Burma (part of India until 1937) was consistent with the 'colonial enclave' model of health protection that prioritised the well-being of the European military and civilian populations in the colony by gathering local health information (Arnold 1993: 61–115; Ramasubban 1988). From a medical perspective, vital statistics could provide a measure of success in conquering disease and improvements in well-being in the colony. Towards this end, they were intended to help reveal the distribution of diseases, enabling the colonial medical administration to evaluate the health and strength of the colony and assess the probability of epidemics.

Vital statistics was also a political 'tool' of empire (Headrick 1981). As Arjun Appadurai explains, the British had to 'know' places like India and Burma through 'countable abstractions' in order to 'imagine' that they ruled them (Appadurai 2013: 244–249). Colonial statistics provided apparent (although often inaccurate) details about the colony's makeup. Nevertheless, having statistics of some kind was a self-deception that granted

2 Sunil Amrith's discussion of the post-WWII development of public health points to the absence of more direct forms of government information gathering on health, such as 'medical police' and medical infrastructure, and, as a result, the 'virtual impossibility of medical surveillance' in South and Southeast Asia (Amrith 2006: 167).

the British the confidence that they had power over the colony. However, this confidence could be shaken when the use of statistics was subverted; applying vital statistics to local health inadvertently empowered indigenous agency to challenge the state. As vital statistics became more accurate over time, local doctors and politicians gained a means to measure how much or how little the colonial state was doing to protect the health and wellbeing of the indigenous population.[3] The data revealed for all to see the weaknesses of the colonial medical establishment and its health policies. Europeans were clearly better protected than the indigenous population and medical resources and infrastructure were clearly being directed mainly at the European cantonment and urban populations. This fed the equation promoted by indigenous nationalists of the sicknesses of indigenous life with the neglect of colonial rule. This transformed a tool for building empire into a weapon for challenging the legitimacy of imperial rule.

In this chapter, I look at several episodes that shaped and redirected the emerging colonial medical surveillance in Burma. I attempt to identify why the system of vital statistics was set up, how it was implemented, and why it failed. I seek to demonstrate that even though the colonial medical establishment continually revised the system, medical surveillance in Burma was never a complete success for the colonial state. The main reason for chronic failure was the continuing inability to produce a reliable system of collecting and reporting health data. However, even the imperfect system revealed important and telling patterns of birth, disease, and death, providing indigenous politicians with an important tool for hastening the retreat of colonial rule.

---

3 Kalpagam noted this dual nature of colonial statistics, which 'generated the data used for evaluating its own performance' (Kalpagam 2000: 44). Kanbur (2016) pointed out the similar impact of famine statistics.

Registration of births and deaths

Vital statistics, or the use of numbers in medicine, had been emerging as an important technology in England since the seventeenth century. William Farr at the General Registrar Office, created under the 1836 Registration Act, was the central figure for the development of a new registration system of births, marriages and deaths and for supervising this system once established (Magnello and Hardy 2002; Higgs 2002). Among other things, an important historical function of vital statistics was to evaluate the strength of the state. Dorothy Porter, for example, discusses the historical link between the health and wealth of modern nations which led to the introduction of various ways of counting the population and quantifying its economic well-being and health condition. According to Porter:

> Counting and evaluating the strength of the state was supported by the political philosophy of mercantilism which viewed the monarch's subjects as his paternalistic property and equated the entire well-being of society as coterminous with the well-being of the state, as embodied by the sovereign. (Porter 1999: 49)

She notes that imperialism stimulated the development of censuses for that purpose. The system of registration of births and deaths as well as the census in colonies such as Burma was a device to more accurately visualise the size and makeup of the population, and the residents' health and disease condition through numbers. Accordingly, Burma's colonial medical establishment made a sincere effort to produce a reliable system of collecting and reporting health data. The numbers and variety of annual medical reports which included some form of vital statistics increased dramatically. The main series of medical reports would eventually include the following:

- *Annual Report of the Health Officer for the City of Rangoon* (1925–1934)
- *Report on the Sanitary Administration of Burma* (1902–1921)
- *Annual Report on Mental Hospitals in Burma* (1878–1940)
- *Report on the Rangoon Lunatic Asylums* (1877–1906)
- *Annual/Triennial Report on Hospitals and Dispensaries in Burma* (1867/68–1939)
- *Notes and Statistics on Hospitals and Dispensaries in Burma* (1899–1940)
- *Annual Report of the Port Health Officer, Rangoon* (1913–1922)
- *Report on Vaccination in British Burma* (1867–1933)
- *Report on Lock Hospitals, British Burma* (1873–1888)
- *Report on Public Health and Vital Statistics, British Burma* (1867 & 1868)
- *Report on the State of Public Health Administration of Burma* (1867–1922, continued by *Report on the Public Health Administration of Burma* 1923–1939)
- *Report of the Harcourt Butler Institute of Public Health* (1926–1940)
- *Annual Report on the Working of the Burma Government Medical School Rangoon* (1923–1939)

Historians of British India have observed that public health measures were initially put in place to protect the European military and civilian population in the colonies who were confined to a limited enclave, and the needs of the Indian population were largely neglected (Arnold 1993: 61–115; Ramasubban 1988). As Mark Harrison explains, the urgent introduction of the registration of deaths in India originated in the realization of its importance in protecting British troops from diseases such as cholera (Harrison 1994: 78). The military imperative of public sanitation and disease control first became apparent among the British soldiers who had returned to metropolitan Britain after the Crimean War, which led to the creation of a Royal Commission in 1857. Similar concerns were raised in India after the Mutiny of 1857 when large numbers of British troops suffered epidemic diseases, leading to the foundation of the Royal Commission on the Sanitary State of the Army in India in 1859 (Ritchell 2006: 58). These developments would initiate the first phase of public health efforts in British India.

The increasing appetite for data soon extended medical data collecting in India and Burma to the indigenous population, becoming increasingly intrusive in rural and local indigenous life over the course of the nineteenth century. Interest in indigenous health grew out of concern for European well-being, the intimacy between Europeans and their household servants, and the potential for indigenous people to be carriers of disease. British medical officers began to realize that the good health of the British soldiers and civilians required controlling epidemic diseases, which could not be achieved without improving the health of the indigenous population with whom Europeans were in daily contact.

Nevertheless, the original provincial sanitary commissioners served in an advisory capacity and had no executive powers, so their involvement was limited to reporting vital statistics rather than medically intervening in rural areas. Annual medical reporting to Calcutta from Burma began during this period, with specialization leading to an increasing number of annual reports from the 1860s. In 1868, the Royal Commission recommended that each provincial sanitary commissioner be responsible for the registration of births and deaths. The Presidency of Bengal's Sanitary Commission was initially responsible for Burma as well until Albert Fytche, Chief Commissioner of British Burma, was tasked with this work in 1869 (Richell 2006: 58–59). Until 1869 data was only collected in the principal towns of British Burma and was initially collected by non-medical authorities. Native agents collected the data under the supervision of the district officers or magistrates.[4] The responsibility of the civil surgeons at this time was limited to remarking on the figures in the submitted returns; they were not tasked with evaluating their veracity.

Later, when local records were kept in rural areas, they remained purely of local relevance and were not sent anywhere beyond the local administrative centre. For example, the 'Permanent Sanitary Record' and 'Village Sanitary Inspection Book' were kept at district and township headquarters and not included in the data to be sent to Rangoon, Calcutta, or London. The disinterest in indigenous health was clear. As one sanitary commissioner reported in 1908, for example, the '"Village Sanitary Inspection Book" is very little used'.[5]

The aforementioned enclavist characteristic of the initial introduction of the registration of births and deaths in Burma continued throughout the colonial period. Nevertheless, extending the system to the entire civilian population elucidated the

4 *Report on the Administration of the Province of British Burmah* for 1865–66: 48; henceforth *RAPBB*.

5 *Report on the Sanitary Administration of Burma*, 1909: 19; hereafter, *RSAB*.

disease distribution in Burma, even though the early registration of births and deaths does not seem to have been coercive. The colonial administration solicited data rather than forced its provision. As the *Report of the Administration of the Province of British Burma for 1865–66* stated:

> The machinery is doubtless rude and the Returns often incorrect, but the system has one feature of good in it, which is, that it is free from the imputation of being an engine of oppression or annoyance to the people.[6]

This benign approach to the indigenous population in the collection of vital statistics in Burma may have been a natural extension of administrative practices from British India. Harrison points to the residual 'lingering shadow of the mutiny' in late nineteenth century India that made the colonial administration hesitant to enforce public health interventions that might conflict with indigenous cultural practices (Harrison 1994: 60). According to Arnold, it was only after the 1890s that intensive colonial public health interventions were conducted under the rubric of the new field 'tropical medicine' (Arnold 1993: 13). The prolonged delay in bringing Western medicine to the indigenous population of India and the non-coercive nature of the registration of births and deaths was security related.

Towards speedier and more reliable returns

In the precarious political milieu of the mid nineteenth century, vital statistics provided a means for the British government in India to know its colonial subjects. The colonial state would continue to rely upon this intelligence for the duration of colonial

6 *RAPBB* 1865–66: 48.

rule. However, the importance of timely and accurate statistics to detect and report the outbreak of epidemics gradually became increasingly evident through a series of failures by the colonial medical administration to detect and contain epidemics in the early 1900s, sparking sustained efforts to improve the reliability of vital statistics in Burma. The shortcomings of vital statistics in Burma were attributed to various factors, such as (1) chronic delays in submitting returns of reports, (2) the unreliability of the data collected by native officers, mostly village headmen,[7] (3) the lack of comparative data, and (4) the lack of information sharing. Data processing errors had the potential to create serious problems, and such problems recurred throughout Burma into the 1930s.

The system of vital statistics in Burma was initiated in 1870. Village or ward headmen prepared the village registers of births and deaths, which were then collected by the police. Around the end of the month, the local police stations forwarded them to the township officer, who used them to prepare the township return form, which was in turn sent to the deputy commissioner to prepare the district return, which was then forwarded to the sanitary commissioner. Despite this seemingly simple system for collecting vital statistics, however, recurring epidemics revealed serious shortcomings and forced the colonial administration to seek significant improvements in the system of reporting deaths. The first major province-wide revision of the system would not occur until the beginning of the twentieth century.

As in other parts of the world, colonial Burma periodically suffered from frequent epidemics. The demographic historian Judith Richell explained that 'the health authority's measures

7 'The registration is, however, inaccurate and incomplete owing partly to the illiteracy of the headmen and partly to the fact that the headmen have to bear the expense and trouble submitting their returns and thus often omit or forget to do so' (Cherry 1930: 23).

were essentially reactions to outbreaks rather than preventive actions.' As late as 1908, the sanitary commissioner showed 'a lack of clear policy to control outbreaks' when he declared that the best way to deal with epidemics was by voluntary evacuation until the epidemic passed (Richell 2006: 178). A series of plague epidemics hit Burma during this period. One plague pandemic began in Yunnan and moved eastward to Hong Kong in 1894, then westward to Bombay in 1898 before reaching Burma in 1899 where it was slow in having an impact. The mortality rate was relatively low until 1905 when it reached epidemic proportions, causing 8637 deaths in 1906 and 9249 deaths in 1907.[8]

Various public health measures were introduced to arrest the spread of the plague even though heavy-handed public health interventions had triggered a huge outcry in India, resulting in the assassination of W.C. Rand, Chairman of the Plague Committee in 1897. A similarly forceful intervention in Burma included burning plague victim's clothes, disinfecting plague patients' houses, and killing rats. However, in Burma, plague patients were not forcibly isolated from their family members. The colonial medical administration was very careful to incarcerate only persons considered untrustworthy and likely to abscond from the infected locale. Instead of segregation, a system of 'exemption certificates' was adopted, which required those persons concerned to report to the health authority once a day for six consecutive days.[9]

Importantly, indigenous people learned the lesson that drawing attention to their homes and villages as the site of deaths from an epidemic disease was to invite the destruction of their worldly possessions and livelihoods without recompense. Some appear to have been willing to bet on their chances of

8 *RSAB* 1906: 9; *RSAB* 1907: 10.

9 *RSAB* 1906: 9.

survival with the disease rather than to report the outbreak to state officials. Plague deaths in many towns and villages began to be concealed both physically and statistically. In one case, for example, the headman of the village of Sittang did not report a significant spike in the number of deaths. The civil surgeon inadvertently became aware of the sudden increase of deaths in the village and investigated. He identified a plague outbreak and learned from villagers that 'rats had been dying in the village before the recent epidemic broke out.' The civil surgeon took immediate action to control the epidemic, but only after considerable mortality had already occurred.[10] This incident highlighted the fact that not only were the vital statistics inadequate to prevent the outbreak of an epidemic, but their accuracy deteriorated as the crisis progressed, as the indigenous people sought to make themselves invisible to the colonial state by strategically fixing their returns.

Lenore Manderson found similar issues with the accuracy of data in the Federated Malay States, where accuracy was compromised by 'official incompetence, poor compliance from populations, reluctance of estates and mines to comply and report sickness and deaths and understaffing' (Manderson 1996: 39). She also suggests that information collected at the hospital was unreliable, because it was compiled by 'an unqualified dresser' whose reported causes of death were approximate only.

The colonial medical establishment increasingly blamed the village headmen for the unreliable data. In 1902, the sanitary commissioner wrote to the Secretary to the Government of Burma, arguing that the current system of the registration of vital statistics was faulty and required some changes to improve

10 *Burma Proceedings. Home (Medical) Department, Burma,* August 1909 IOR/P/8069, 'More expeditious publication of the monthly Vital Statistical Return and the forms to be used.'

their accuracy. The sanitary commissioner was concerned about the inaccurate classification of disease or cause of death reported by village headmen. These headmen did not 'possess any educational qualifications on which they may be allowed to pose as being capable of classifying diseases, nor indeed do any of the other compilers of the vital statistical returns possess this qualification'.[11] The general distrust of the mortality and mobility data provided by village headmen was no doubt influenced by the Sanitary Department's bitter experience dealing with the unreliable data of smallpox vaccination reported by native superintendents. Negative comments made about the native staff's reporting are plentiful in the official documents; for example, 'These figures do not inspire confidence', and 'Inspection revealed that many of the returns sent by the vaccinators were falsified', etc.[12]

However, as the sanitary commissioner had pointed out, the headmen were unqualified for the task, and other problems with the system of vital statistics itself contributed to its failure to accurately categorise diseases in Burma. Until 1902, the weekly mortality report from Rangoon categorized diseases according to the Royal College of Physicians' *New Nomenclature of Diseases* (1868). Even though the terms were revised a few times and they were becoming more familiar to the village headmen, in 1902, the Government of India ordered the Government of Burma to stop using the 1868 edition and instead rely on the Royal College of Physicians' updated nomenclature of 1896.[13]

11 *Burma Proceeding. Medical* IOR/P/6507.

12 *Burma Proceedings Home (Sanitary) Department, Burma,* August 1900 IOR/P/5799. 'Resolution on notes on the Statistics of Vaccination in Burma for the year 1899–1900.'

13 *Burma Proceedings Home (Sanitary) Department, Burma*, July 1902 IOR/P/6274. 'Orders regarding the preparation of the weekly statement of deaths in the town of Rangoon.'

The later classification included many changes. For example, 'dropsy' was removed from the 'general diseases' category while 'general injuries' and 'poisoning' were added to it. Further changes included 'non-tubercular phthisis' which entered the diseases of the respiratory systems, and 'spleen disease' was moved from diseases of the digestive system to diseases of the lymphatic system.[14] These changing categories may have been quite confusing for the village headmen, who already had more than enough details to consider when determining causes of disease. For example, the single category of 'All other diseases' included twenty-two groups of causes of disease.[15] R.H. Castor would attempt to rectify this confusion with the publication of *Nomenclature of Diseases in Burmese* (1922).

Further, in determining the causes of disease, it is important to consider the extent to which Burmese village headmen's pre-existing notions of disease categories clashed or conflicted with the new Western categories demanded by colonial vital statistics. These issues are beyond the scope of this chapter, but an analysis of different categorisations of disease between Western medicine and Burmese traditional medicine is needed to fully understand how Burmese village headmen classified and reported disease for the purposes of vital statistics. A comprehensive effort to understand the indigenous system of medicine did not begin until 1928 when the 'Committee of Enquiry into the Indigenous System of Medicine' was established by the

14 Ibid.

15 'Summary of deaths from different causes grouped together under the head "All other diseases" in the weekly statement of deaths' included: 'Tubercle of the lungs, Other tubercular affections, leprosy, Premature birth, Debility and Anæmia. Old age, Other general disease, Diseases of the nervous system, circulatory system, respiratory, digestive, lymphatic, urinary, generative, organ locomotion, connective tissue, skin, Other local diseases, Drowning, Other general injuries, and Poisoning' (*Burma Proceedings* IOR/P/6274).

Ministry of Education. This suggests that the colonial medical establishment most likely did not consider variances in the data that resulted from different village headmen, who lacked not only medical training but Western education altogether, and had difficulty making sense of categories.

Standardising data collection

The Government of India considered that greater uniformity across provinces could help to resolve the delay and that more careful disease verification could help to fix the unreliability of data or at least improve upon them. In 1904, the sanitary commissioner thus proposed that the classification of diseases could be more rigorously checked by the civil surgeons:

1. The village headman should refrain from giving a classification of causes of death. Rather, they should make sure to include 'the more prominent symptoms of the disease'.

2. After township officers checked the village vital statistics, the return should be sent to the Civil Surgeon instead of the Deputy Commissioner to be reviewed carefully with his own clerk. The Civil Surgeon should then forward the returns to both the Sanitary Commissioner and the Deputy Commissioner.[16]

The Lieutenant-Governor of Burma supported the proposal to make the civil surgeon responsible for the returns, as was the practice in Bengal, and suggested that the deputy commissioner's clerks work with the civil surgeon. The commissioners

16 *Burma Proceedings* IOR/P/6507.

of Burma's eight divisions were divided in their reactions. Most of the commissioners opposed loaning their respective deputy commissioner's clerks to the civil surgeon, but some were pleased that the civil surgeon would assume this burden and spend more time checking the data. However, some commissioners were concerned with how well the civil surgeon could control the headmen and the township officers. As the deputy commissioner of Myingyan predicted, 'I imagine that the civil surgeon, if they take on the work, will soon cry out that in spite of their endeavours the headmen will not be taught, will not understand, and will not take interest'.[17] Other commissioners were concerned that strengthening the civil surgeon's power to investigate cause of death while imposing stricter reporting orders upon the village headman could strain their relationships with the latter. As the commissioner of the Meiktila Division wrote, 'The headman is at the base of the official pyramid. We cannot afford to make the post unpopular. I confess to a fear that "prompt enquiry into the causes of all anomalous and doubtful phenomena" may be stronger treatment than the village system can bear'.[18] The commissioner of Minbu District was against the transfer of responsibility. He pointed out that the accuracy of the return would not improve 'unless something is done to make the original entry by the headman a more reliable source of information'.[19] In response, some deputy commissioners raised the need for 'a simple classification in Burmese of the different diseases'.[20]

Despite these objections, authority for the compilation of vital statistics transferred from the deputy commissioner to the

---

17 Ibid.
18 Ibid.
19 Ibid.
20 Ibid.

civil surgeon in 1904.[21] Around the same time, the Government of India indicated its desire to encourage municipal authorities to cooperate in devising uniform ways of reporting health statistics because Calcutta, Rangoon, Bombay, and Madras were all following different methods of tabulating their statistics. A suggestion to convene a conference of health officers, however, was rejected by the finance sub-committee of Rangoon on the grounds that they could not afford to send their health officer to a conference as there were more important things for him to do.[22]

As timely and reliable returns remained elusive, the need for more accurate vital statistics to combat the spread of plague around the empire became ever more pressing and prompted further consideration. Around 1909, a severe outbreak of malaria in Upper India and Bombay had raised a red flag to the Government of India, which began to express a need to make the system of registering births and deaths faster and more effective at reporting outbreaks of epidemics. In a letter to the Secretary to the Government of Burma, P.W. Monie, an undersecretary to the Government of India, explained that the local governments had not given prompt notification to the Government of India about the magnitude of the malaria epidemic nor of the measures taken to prevent it. The local government of Bombay, for example, only reported the data after the Government of India specifically requested it by telegraph. In the end, the Government of India received a significantly delayed and redundant report on the

21 *RSAB* 1904: 1

22 *Burma Proceedings. Home (General) Department, Burma,* February 1904 IOR/P/6735. 'Adoption of a uniform system of exhibiting the Health statistics of the Presidency Towns and Rangoon.'

malaria outbreak forwarded by the sanitary commissioners.[23] The Government of India subsequently requested they be provided 'full and prompt information regarding epidemics of this nature' and queried 'whether the monthly returns of mortality and birth statistics could not be forwarded to the Government of India much earlier than at present, and in any case not later than four weeks after the end of the month to which they relate'.[24]

In response, the Sanitary Commissioner of Burma, Major C.E. Williams, expressed doubts about the feasibility of reporting unusual mortality in a timely manner in Burma and cited the chronic delays in the submission of local vital statistics, especially from remote districts. For example, the return from Shwebo for the quarter ending 31 March was received on the last day of August, which was three months and eleven days late, which delayed production of the quarterly return by more than five months.[25] Table 2.1 indicates the significant delays in submission of vital statistics to the Sanitary Commissioner's Office from Pegu District in 1908.

Furthermore, about a quarter to a third of all districts were constantly delinquent in their submission of returns. Table 2.2 shows the number of districts (29 in total) which submitted returns within one week of the due date.

According to the Sanitary Commissioner of Burma, it typically took more than two months for information of an epidemic to reach the district health officer (civil surgeons) through the vital statistics of the township. This was too late for

23 *Burma Proceedings, Home (Medical) Department, Burma,* February 1909. IOR/P/8068. 'Reports of unusually severe outbreaks of epidemic diseases to be made to the Government of India. More expeditious publications of the monthly vital statistical returns.'

24 Ibid.

25 *Burma Proceedings.* IOR/P/8069.

the deputy commissioner or civil surgeon to take effective action against the outbreak of epidemics.[26] Furthermore, Williams noted an important oversight in the rules regarding reporting the outbreak of an epidemic. Williams explained that the *Burma Village Manual*, which provided detailed instructions for village headmen, stipulates:

> it is incumbent upon every headman to at once report any occurrence of cholera or small-pox within his village tract, to the Township Officer, or to the Subdivisional Officer or Deputy Commissioner, if these officers are nearer than the Township Officer.[27]

But he found that plague had not been included in this requirement.[28]

The series of deadly epidemics including plague between 1905 and 1908 with smallpox in 1906 played a significant role in changing the functions of vital statistics by about 1910. But problems with the collection of vital statistics were again

26 Sanitary Commissioner of Burma, Major Williams, gives an example of the flow of data and time as follows:

> A Police Officer visits a village in his Police circle on, say, the 19th December, and brings away with him all vital statistics foils available in the Headman's registers. These foils will in due course ... be sent by the officer in charge of the police-station to the Township Officer. The Township Officer will prepare a statement of births and deaths for the villages in question for the month of December, but since the information he has about occurrences at this village only date up to 18th or 19th December, his return for that month will be incomplete. This must happen in the case of many villages. He, however, will forward his returns for December to the Civil Surgeon on 1st February and those returns include many occurrences which have taken place in November. The Civil Surgeon will send them to the Sanitary Commissioner by 20th February. (*Burma Proceedings, Home (Medical) Department, Burma,* August 1909 IOR/P/8069).

27 Ibid.

28 Ibid.

Table 2.1: Delays in reporting vital statistics

Return for	Due in Sanitary Commissioner's Office	Received in Sanitary Commissioner's Office
January 1908	20th March	25th May
February 1908	20th April	8th September
March 1908	20th May	10th August
April 1908	20th June	3rd November
May 1908	20th July	3rd November
June 1908	20th August	26th November
July 1908	20th September	10th December
August 1908	20th October	14th December
September 1908	20th November	15th December
October 1908	20th December	Not received as of 16th February 1909
November 1908	20th January	Not received as of 16th February 1909
December 1908	20th February	Not received as of 16th February 1909

Source: IOR/P/8069 Proceedings July to December 1909

Table 2.2: Number of districts submitting reports within one week of the due date

Month	Jan	Feb	Mar	Apr	May	Jun	Jul	Aug	Sep	Oct	Nov	Dec
	7/29	8/29	10/29	11/29	9/29	12/29	11/29	8/29	12/29	10/29	8/29	9/29

Source: IOR/P/8069 Proceedings July to December 1909

revealed in a scandalous incident in Minbu District in 1913. The Commissioner of the Magwe Division, Lieutenant-Colonel D.J.C. Macnabb furiously accused the Civil Surgeon, Mr. Wells, of ignoring his responsibility to report in a timely way a serious outbreak of malaria in Pwintbyu Township caused by the opening of the Mon Canal or to take adequate measures to contain the outbreak. Macnabb wrote:

> If the Civil Surgeon had detected the epidemic when it began, as he could and should have done, and had seen that the village headmen were well supplied with quinine and taken the steps now taken to give the sufferers medical aid and advice in their

> homes, we should at least have been able to save some 50 per cent. of those who have died. The Civil Surgeon has, therefore, on his conscience what to me as a lay man appears to be, 1,000 preventible deaths.[29]

When Macnabb learned of the malaria outbreak, he checked the mortality returns for the Pwintbyu police station and noticed that the death toll in June 1912 was almost twice as high as that for June 1911. Even with the slow reporting of data, Macnabb believed that the civil surgeon should have noticed this issue in August when compiling his report. Furthermore, in September, when Mr. Dunn, an officer of the Indian Civil Service wired the civil surgeon to report a serious outbreak of malaria in Pwintbyu and asked for help, the civil surgeon was slow to respond. Then, a month later, the civil surgeon visited Pwintbyu, but his subsequent report to the sanitary commissioner 'made no mention whatsoever of the malaria epidemic'.[30] Macnabb found this surprising as the malaria death tolls in September 1912 were already four times as high as in September 1910. He thus wired the sanitary commissioner twice to demand an investigation of this outbreak, and Major Williams dispatched his assistant surgeon and sub-assistant surgeon to visit Pwintbyu separately. However, one of them did not even take any quinine to distribute to villagers. Frustrated, Macnabb personally visited Pwintbyu in late December and found the outbreak had become more serious. The death toll in November 1912 had reached 460 in Pwintbyu Township while there were only 55 deaths in 1911 and 33 in 1910. The fact that the civil surgeon took Christmas leave during this outbreak further angered Macnabb.

---

29 *Burma Proceedings, Home (Medical) Department. Burma,* June 1913 IOR/P/9124.

30 Ibid.

Macnabb's frustration was no doubt exacerbated by the fact that he had foreseen the possibility of a malaria outbreak in Pwintbyu and had given a public warning about it in a speech at the opening ceremony of the Mon Canal in July 1911. In that speech, he advised village headmen to ensure adequate supplies of quinine and encouraged villagers to take them as a preventive measure against malaria, reminding all of the malaria outbreak that followed the opening of the Punjab Canal in India. As he predicted, there was a big jump in mortalities in the region after the Mon Canal opened. However, to his dismay, 'the epidemic found the sub-treasuries insufficiently supplied with quinine, and great delay was experienced in getting fresh supplies from the Rangoon depot'.[31] Macnabb also inquired about the responsibility of the sanitary commissioner who should have known about the great risk of a malaria epidemic in this region after the opening of the canal and asked whether the sanitary commissioner had ordered local medical officers to look out for any report which indicated the outbreak of malaria cases there. It is easy to imagine that Macnabb felt that a great opportunity had been missed to save lives and replaced with a similarly great tragedy due to faulty systems and lack of care of certain medical officers.

The scandal resulted in changes to the way that health statistics were recorded in Burma. The seriousness of the episode and charges of mismanagement triggered a flurry of correspondence between a wide range of officials involved in colonial medical surveillance at various levels. These included the Commissioner of Magwe Division, the Sanitary Commissioner, the Officiating Secretary to the Government of Burma, the Inspector-General of Civil Hospitals, the Civil Surgeon of the Minbu District (Mr. Wells), the Sub-Divisional Officer (Maung Tok Gale), and the

31 Ibid.

Township Officer (Maung Po Gyi). Their correspondence illuminates a number of the most important shortcomings of the reporting of vital statistics.

In response to Macnabb's query, the sanitary commissioner excused himself for not ordering local officers to look out for any sign of outbreak of malaria due to him being abroad when he was informed about the opening of the canal and that an acting sanitary commissioner at that time was not informed about this news. Further, despite agreeing with Macnabb's points in general, he stated that it was actually the deputy commissioner who had the authority to order hygienic measures as well as to receive early information about outbreaks of diseases from local officers. However, the Secretary to the Government of Burma requested that Mr. Wells explain his failure to detect the huge increase in mortality as well as his neglect to take prompt action such as drawing the attention of the deputy commissioner to the abnormal incidence in mortality. Wells was also asked to explain the delays in his reporting of vital statistics. Wells claimed the delays were unavoidable. First, he explained that the vital statistical clerk was not a full-time post and that compiling the vital statistics was not given priority. He complained that it took considerable time to check the figures sent by each township before he could submit correct statistics. The civil surgeon was supposed to submit his vital statistics by the 20th of each month. However, frequent delays in the returns from different townships had a rolling effect, which caused further delays in the compilation of his own report.[32]

32 According to a letter from the Sanitary Commissioner, there were frequent and serious delays in the Vital Statistics Returns in 1912 for Minbu District (Mr. Wells in charge). For example, the returns for July were received on October 11th, the ones for September were received on November 18th, and October returns were received on December 30th (*Burma Proceedings IOR/P/9124*).

As we have seen, many of these were systemic or structural issues, and there is reason to sympathise with Wells' position. Even today, timely and accurate reporting of an epidemic remains a major issue for the WHO and other organizations seeking to contain the spread of disease. Even with globalised communication and information technology, preventing pandemics remains a major challenge.[33]

But the 1913 incident was exacerbated by a structural failure to share information. Macnabb complained that the vital statistics data was not shared with him. He only came to know about this outbreak from a conversation with the previously mentioned Mr. Dunn. A serious outbreak was occurring in his division, but the commissioner was not aware of it because the vital statistics were reported to the Sanitary Commissioner's Office. Thus, the vital information was not shared among relevant personnel like Macnabb. The latter therefore requested that the Secretary to the Government of Burma arrange that each of the vital statistical returns (monthly and quarterly) submitted by the civil surgeon to the sanitary commissioner be sent to the commissioner of the division and that the office copy be shared with the deputy commissioner as well.[34] Macnabb explained that the 'system over-centralises responsibility and control and the measure of decentralisation I now propose is absolutely essential to Commissioners of Divisions'.[35]

The issue of who was in charge of the work and compilation of the district returns seems also to have been an important one. As mentioned, the authority over vital statistical data collection had been transferred from the deputy commissioner

---

33 "Brilliant's Wish: Disease Alerts" in *WIRED* Feb. 23, 2006 (https://www.wired.com/2006/02/brilliants-wish-disease-alerts/)

34 *Burma Proceedings* IOR/P/9124.

35 Ibid.

to the civil surgeon in 1904, but the problems in 1913 revealed remaining uncertainty over who was in charge. In response to Macnabb's criticism, the sanitary commissioner defended the civil surgeon, instead blaming the deputy commissioner for neglecting to take the necessary steps to control malaria. According to the sanitary commissioner, his civil surgeon was not 'the Sanitary authority of the District', but rather was 'the Executive Health Officer and the Sanitary Adviser to the Deputy Commissioner'. Further, he explained that the deputy commissioner was the authority empowered to order hygienic measures to be taken by subdivisional officers and headmen. Thus, while recognising the civil surgeon's responsibilities, on the one hand, the lines of authority in public health were blurred and confusing on the other. The civil surgeons further claimed that the deputy commissioner enjoyed early access to the statistical information from local subordinate officers in the district while the civil surgeon was hampered not only by a lack of executive power to order public health intervention but also from the systemic delays in reporting from the townships.[36] While the commissioner of the division complained that the sanitary commissioner had too much power regarding the collection of statistical information, the sanitary commissioner complained about his men's lack of authority compared to that held by the deputy commissioner.

The 1913 episode also highlighted the systemic failure to use the statistical data reported in the forms for early detection of epidemics. The returns of statistics did not provide a way to compare the mortality for each month and year. Wells had complained that the statistical return Form B did not include columns showing the monthly and quarterly mortality rates of either the entire district or the local police-station circles. Such

36 *RSAB* 1904: 1.

columns would have clearly indicated the jump in deaths and would have helped him to detect the seriousness of the malaria outbreak in the Mon Canal area. The sanitary commissioner similarly observed the deficiencies arising from the statistical clerks' duty in compiling vital statistics. He wrote:

> Unless the statistical clerk compared the returns for any month very carefully with those for the same area for preceding months of the same year or for the corresponding month of earlier years he would be apt to overlook even a considerable increase in mortality in any of the police circles.[37]

Macnabb also recognised the problems of the forms used to collect vital statistics, which provided no adequate data to compare the death rate. He proposed an amendment by which Form A would give additional data for each township as follows:

> (a) population by last census; (b) normal death-rate per mille per mensem; (c) the number of deaths for the corresponding period of the previous year; (d) the death-rate per mille per mensem represented by the deaths reported for the month.[38]

Another problem with colonial medical surveillance revealed that by 1913 there was still no agreement on a uniform classification of diseases in the statistics. The *Report of the Sanitary Administration of Burma* includes many references to the unreliability of the figures as a result. According to the reports, the village headmen who prepared the returns did not have the ability to correctly classify the diseases reported to them by villagers.

37 *Burma Proceedings* IOR/P/9124.

38 Ibid.

> The actual heading under which deaths in rural districts are returned appears to be of little practical value for statistical purposes. The diagnosis of the cause of death is dependent in rural areas on the selection by the relatives of the deceased, or the village headman, of a named disease from their very limited medical vocabulary, which they think will fit in with the symptoms exhibited during the course of the illness and most illnesses not referable to 'fever' can only, owing to the peculiar nomenclature of disease adopted among the lower classes of Burmans and Indians, be included by the superior registering agency under the very indefinite heading of 'all other causes.'[39]

As we saw in the previous section, from the introduction of the system of registering births and deaths in British Burma, the problem of inaccurate data, especially from rural districts, was mentioned in almost every report. The village headmen who collected the raw data from villagers were consistently blamed for this in the colonial medical reports. The first stage of the reporting system in colonial Burma operated at the village (rural areas) or ward level (towns). Each village or ward headman collected information on the recent deaths and births in their area. This data was submitted to the police headquarters. The earliest government reports on the vital statistics system, during the 1870s, demonstrated an understanding that appears to have been lost in later years, pointing out the impossibility of headmen producing accurate data because they were already burdened by revenue collection work in certain periods of the year and did not have time to work on birth and death registers.[40]

---

39 *RSAB* 1904: 4.

40 *Report on the Administration of British Burmah* 1872–73: 159.

The accuracy of the data submitted by village headmen was evaluated after the report was sent to police headquarters. One of the main tasks for civil surgeons and vaccinators was to investigate the accuracy of returns of births and deaths registers. Civil surgeons, their vaccinators, and district officers all visited registered villages to conduct inspections.[41] As one civil surgeon described his 1919 tour in Upper Burma to inspect the vital statistics returns: 'The Civil Surgeon rides up to the Thugyi's house, a table and chair are brought out, and the birth, death, vaccination and other registers [are] produced for inspection' (Entrican 1919: 2). The civil surgeon then went through the registers carefully to judge if they were accurately completed. Civil surgeons and vaccinators reported the results of these investigations to the sanitary commissioner's office.[42] Omissions were found every year and those who were found guilty of making faulty reports or those that were missing data were punished in various ways such as through fines and demotion, etc.

Making colonial rule count: The subversion of medical statistics

As mentioned, the colonial government ironically contributed to its own undoing. Its efforts to improve the reliability and speed of gathering medical statistics proved to be double-edged. While the colonial government was making improvements in medical surveillance through the system of vital statistics, questions were also emerging regarding the extent to which the colonial administration had achieved its goals and how this impacted the indigenous population. The 1920s and 1930s saw the emergence

41 *RSAB* 1905: 1.

42 *RSAB* 1906: 20.

of Burmese politicians who asked what the colonial government had done for the betterment of the Burmese (Charney 2009). As the colonial administration penetrated the life of the indigenous population through medical surveillance, it was provided with a powerful and persuasive means to measure how well the colonial state was doing at improving the indigenous population's health. While doing so, it revealed for all to see the weaknesses of the colonial medical establishment and its health policies. What had been largely invisible to the indigenous population before, their medical neglect, was now increasingly replaced by awareness, made possible through the medical statistical data.

The problems in the system of vital statistics (chronic delay, unreliable data, lack of supervision) which had been cited as important concerns by the colonial medical officers were in fact problems of colonial medical administration itself. But the archival sources such as the proceedings and the colonial government reports I have examined were written from the colonial medical establishment's perspectives and it is true that they expressed their concerns for their own data gathering system regarding its inadequacies. It seems that there was a chronic and formulaic vilification and scapegoating of indigenous village headmen for the unreliable data because they were uneducated and their rudimentary medical knowledge was inadequate for accurately diagnosing the causes of deaths. However, as we have seen, the complicated and frequently changing categorization of diseases and their nomenclature with which the village headmen were presented caused great confusion. Also, as mentioned, especially in the early years of collecting medical data, village headmen had their hands full with other responsibilities such as dealing with revenue reports. On top of that, especially in some of the more remote areas, village headmen were responsible for vast areas which made it impossible to report births or deaths in a timely fashion.[43]

It became clear that the colonial medical administration failed to protect the health of the indigenous population at least in part due to the defective systems they relied upon. The problems regarding relaying and submitting the vital statistics reports, especially with the issue of its flow of information, were also sometimes caused by the power relationships within the colonial administration. In the case of British India, Harrison has demonstrated that the Indian government's attempt to introduce a system to centralise information collection into the hands of the Sanitary Commissioner, J.M. Cunningham, by bypassing civil surgeons and provincial sanitary commissioners was a reflection of the Indian government's desire to 'prevent the imposition of custodial measures such as cordon sanitaires' and to 'deprive provincial governments and medical officers of the initiative in dealing with epidemic disease' (Harrison 1994: 78–79). In the case of Burma, as we have seen, the absence of a system for sharing information among the divisional commissioner, civil surgeon, and sanitary commissioner about sudden increases in deaths from malaria caused a delayed response against the outbreak of malaria and led to a major epidemic in Minbu. This demonstrated the lack of an effective system of warning against the appearance of epidemics. There were also technical problems with the available forms.[44] If the

43 There is clear evidence that the colonial government was aware of the limitations in its collection of medical data. For example, it sanctioned the commissioner of the Irrawaddy division to enlist ten villages in the Myaungmya district to the category of 'Irregularly Patrolled areas' due to their remoteness (*Burma Proceedings, Home (Sanitary) Department, Burma,* November 1901 IOR/P/6035. 'Addition of certain villages to the irregularly patrolled areas in the Myaungmya district for the collection of vital statistics').

44 *Burma Legislative Council,* 1 September 1931, p. 99; henceforth *BLC.*

forms included the data from previous months and years, it would have been easier for the civil surgeon to notice sudden hikes in the number of deaths from a certain disease. The indigenous population understood these failures as indicating that the protection of their health was not a significant priority of the colonial government.

The perception of neglect was compounded by frequent indications that the colonial administration's main priority remained the health of European residents. Sometimes this evidence was qualitative. Mr. J.K. Munshi (council member for Rangoon West), for example, argued in 1923 against the claim made by the Finance Member that there were no racial distinctions in the private wards of the hospital. According to Munshi, only European gentlemen were allowed to use the second floor; all Indian, Burman and other non-European men were restricted to the right wing of the first floor, while ladies used the left wing. His complaint was regarding the discriminatory usage of public funds. As he explained, 'I cannot understand why this distinction is observed in the hospital in a paying ward where all the patients pay equally and where the hospital is maintained from the funds of the general tax-payer'. However, the poor patients who went to the hospital and waited there for three days without being attended by a doctor were worse off.[45]

But evidence that indicted the colonial state's neglect of indigenous health also came from the colonial state's own statistical reports. In 1932, at a meeting of the Burma Legislative Council, U Ba Shin (member from Myingyan North), requested that the council confirm the vital statistical data which revealed an excess in the death to birth rate in Myingyan. The Minister for Education affirmed this was the case and although the excess was partly due to defective registration, he admitted that

45 *BLC*, 24 March 1923: 412.

part of the rapid increase was due also to a failure in health administration in the town. Statistics had again been used by indigenous politicians to point to the failures of colonial medicine as evidence of what otherwise would have been a largely invisible development.[46]

By 1930 it was common for Burmese members of the Legislative Council to ask the government to present official medical statistics that revealed how indigenous health was faring under the colonial medical establishment,[47] even for such remote areas as Cheduba. For example, in 1929, U Pu (member for Toungoo South) requested that the government present a table of the number of attacks and deaths from tuberculosis in all schools and colleges in Burma for each year from 1921.[48] Similarly, at the outbreak of beriberi in Cheduba in 1930, U Kyaw Mya (member for Arakan South) asked for statistics. including the number of deaths as well as the measures that the government had taken to combat it.[49] Soon, the Burmese began to understand that the success or failure of public health intervention could be measured by statistics. U Po Yi (member for Mandalay town) asked the government what anti-malarial measures it had undertaken and 'what actual success has resulted from these measures supported by published statistics?'[50]

Despite their usefulness to its opponents, however, from the government's perspective, vital statistics continued to be essential state intelligence. Even into the 1930s, the Burmese Sanitary Commissioner continued to use vital statistics to report a connection between economic conditions and the mortality

46 *BLC*, 1 September 1931: 88–89.

47 *BLC*, 13 February 1930: 41.

48 *BLC*, 18 February 1929: 143.

49 *BLC*, 6 August 1930: 86.

50 *BLC*, 1 September 1931: 99.

rate (Richell 2006: 213). However, the fact that vital statistics had become a tool that could be used to hold the colonial state to account for the well-being of the indigenous population was also clear. The colonial government had in this way made itself accountable to indigenous political leaders.

Conclusion

The system of registering births and deaths in colonial Burma provided the colonial government with various kinds of important information about the medical and sanitary conditions of Burma on a yearly basis. The colonial medical surveillance systems cultivated the image of colonial control on paper, but the utility of the data in practice proved fleeting once these returns, especially those from remote villages, were investigated. It was a porous system. The colonial medical establishment's distrust of the information prepared by the indigenous village headmen, chronic delays in submitting mortality statistics, constant failures in reporting the outbreaks of epidemics, and the lack of sharing of vital information among various offices of the colonial administration were all obstacles to the colonial medical establishment using medical surveillance as an effective device to legitimate their rule. These failures of medical surveillance had dire consequences for efforts to actually control disease and save local lives. More importantly, the problems of the vital statistics system played a role in revealing the weaknesses of the colonial administration itself as statistical numbers demonstrated to the indigenous population the colonial government's unwillingness to fully commit to their health. In other words, statistics became an effective measurement for indigenous political leaders to understand the nature of the colonial state and to pressure it to act for the benefit of the indigenous people. In short, statistics ultimately made colonial rule count.

References

Amrith, Sunil (2006), *Decolonizing International Health: India and Southeast Asia, 1930–65*, Cambridge Imperial and Post-Colonial Studies, Basingstoke: Palgrave Macmillan.

Anderson, Benedict (2006), *Imagined Communities: Reflections on the Origin and Spread of Nationalism*, London: Verso.

Appadurai, Arjun (2013), 'Numbers in the Colonial Imagination', in Saul Dubow (ed.), *The Rise and Fall of Modern Empires, Volume II, Colonial Knowledges*, London and New York: Routledge, pp. 243–268.

Arnold, David (1993), *Colonizing the Body: State Medicine and Epidemic Disease in Nineteenth-Century India*, Berkeley and Los Angeles: University of California Press.

Arnold, David (2013), 'Introduction: Disease, medicine and empire', in Saul Dubow (ed.), *The Rise and Fall of Modern Empires, Volume II, Colonial Knowledges*, London and New York: Routledge, pp. 343–368.

Bayly, Christopher A. (1996), *Empire and Information: Intelligence Gathering and Social Communication in India, 1780–1870*, Cambridge: Cambridge University Press.

Castor, Richard H. (1922), *Nomenclature of Diseases in Burmese*, Rangoon: Office of Superintendent, Government Printing.

Charney, Michael W. (2009), *A History of Modern Burma,* Cambridge: Cambridge University Press.

Cherry, Major H.C.C.C. (1930), 'Public Health Conditions and Administration in Burma', *Journal of the Royal Sanitary Institute*, LI. (1)1: 23.

Curtin, Philip (1989), *Death by Migration: Europe's Encounter with the Tropical World in the Nineteenth Century*, Cambridge: University of Cambridge Press.

Entrican, James (1919), 'A Civil Surgeon "on Tour" in Upper Burma', *Indian Medical Gazette* 54(1): 1–5.

Gilbert, Pamela K. (2003), 'Mapping Colonial Disease: Victorian Medical Cartography in British India', in George Sebastian Rousseau (ed.), *Framing and Imagining Disease in Cultural History*, Basingstoke: Palgrave Macmillan, pp. 111–128.

Harrison, Mark (1994), *Public Health in British India: Anglo-Indian Preventive Medicine 1859–1914*, Cambridge: Cambridge University Press.

Harrison, Mark (1998), '"Hot beds of disease:" Malaria and civilization in nineteenth-century British India', *Parassitologia*, 40(1–2): 11–18.

Headrick, Daniel R. (1981), *The Tools of Empire: Technology and European Imperialism in the Nineteenth Century*, New York: Oxford University Press.

Higgs, Edward (2002), 'The Annual Report of the Registrar General, 1839–1920: A Textual History', in Eileen Magnello and Anne Hardy (eds), *The Road to Medical Statistics*. Amsterdam and New York: Clio Medica 67, Editions Rodopi B.V., pp. 55–76.

Kalpagam, U. (2000) 'The colonial state and statistical knowledge', *History of the Human Sciences*, 13(2): 37–55.

Kanbur, Ravi (2016), 'Statistics for Colonial Rule, for the Independence Struggle, and for Inclusive Development', presentation, IMF Fourth Statistical Forum, Washington, DC, 17–18 November, https://www.imf.org/external/np/seminars/eng/2016/statsforum/pdf/Kanbur.pdf.

Magnello, Eileen and Hardy, Anne (2002), 'Preface', in Eileen Magnello and Anne Hardy (eds), *The Road to Medical Statistics*. Amsterdam and New York: Clio Medica 67, Editions Rodopi B.V., pp. v–vii.

Manderson, Lenore (1996), *Sickness and the State: Health and Illness in Colonial Malaya, 1870–1940*, Cambridge: Cambridge University Press.

Polu, Sandhya L. (2012), *Infectious Disease in India, 1892–1940: Policy-Making and the Perception of Risk*, Basingstoke: Palgrave Macmillan.

Porter, Dorothy (1999), *Health, Civilization and The State: A History of Public Health from Ancient to Modern Times*, London and New York: Routledge.

Ramasubban. Radhika (1988), 'Imperial health in British India, 1857–1900', in Roy MacLead and Milton Lewis (eds), *Disease, Medicine, and Empire: Perspectives on Western Medicine and the Experience of European Expansion*, London: Routledge, pp. 38–60.

Richell, Judith L. (2006), *Disease and Demography in Colonial Burma*, Singapore: NUS Press and Copenhagen: NIAS Press.

Royal College of Physicians (1868), *New Nomenclature of Diseases*, London: Royal College of Physicians.

Royal College of Physicians (1896), *The Nomenclature of Diseases*, London: Royal College of Physicians.

Chapter 3

A Province Behaving Like a State: The Expulsion of Offenders Act (1926) and the Territoriality of Colonial Burma

Noriyuki Osada[1]

Introduction

A common strategy for a modern state seeking to govern its realm effectively is to develop preventive measures against its perceived threats by creating powerful surveillance apparatuses that persistently observe and gather detailed information about a wide range of objects. An elaborate legal-bureaucratic apparatus of this nature, however, requires vast resources, both financial and in personnel. A colonial state, generally with a limited budget and a workforce of questionable allegiance, is far from omnipotent and needs to find energy-saving methods for governance. Those methods tend to be characterised by arbitrary and summary execution of power based on relatively coarse knowledge rather than detailed information (Singha 2015). This chapter describes how the colonial authority in Burma developed an arbitrary expulsion policy which it

1 This chapter is based on my research on border control in colonial Burma, particularly its main port city of Rangoon (Osada 2011; 2014; 2016a; 2016b). An early version of this chapter was read at the international conference on Burma/Myanmar Studies held at Chiang Mai University on 26 July 2015. A Japanese version was published as Chapter 3 of my monograph (Osada 2016b). At various stages in revising the early English version, the members of this book project and Nick Cheesman provided insightful comments for which I am grateful.

increasingly used to remove undesirable persons and maintain order at minimal cost.

Another focus of this chapter is the spatial connotation of the expulsion policy in Burma. Expulsion is relevant to the territoriality of the modern state. Although it is taken for granted today that the power to deport undesirable persons, along with the other rights for border control, forms a part of the external sovereignty of the state, the arts of border control are a product of modern history where governing states increasingly needed to respond to global movements of people and things. Some scholars have convincingly argued that modern border control measures originated in the United States in the late nineteenth century and were adopted with varying degrees of localisation worldwide by the 1930s (McKeown 2008; Bashford 2014). Burma's expulsion policy developed in this historical context. However, the Burma case differs in terms of territorial sovereignty from the widely studied white settler societies such as the United States and Australia. While border control measures in the latter countries were developed to restrict vast immigration of Chinese who were obviously foreigners to those countries, Burma's peculiar colonial settings made things more complicated. During the early decades of the twentieth century, the territory of Burma was not only under British colonial rule but was governed as a local administrative unit within British India. In this context, migration from the Indian subcontinent to Burma was regarded as a domestic move of British subjects within British India, and the local administration's power to deal with it was limited. Under those circumstances, nevertheless, the development of the government of Burma's expulsion policy had the effect of enhancing the territoriality of Burma, even before its formal separation from India in 1937.

The expulsion policy in Burma targeted persons whom the authority regarded undesirable and as being 'foreign' to Burma.

The policy's climax was the promulgation of the Expulsion of Offenders Act in 1926, authorising the government of Burma to expel 'non-Burman offenders' from its territory. Its primary target was Indian criminals in Rangoon, the port capital city of Burma, where more than half of the population were immigrants from the Indian subcontinent and their descendants. Historians have paid little attention to this act. A rare study by Usha Mahajani, a comparative historian of Indian communities in Southeast Asia, attributes the expulsion policy to the rise of Burmese nationalism and its antagonism against Indians based on her analyses of the debates between Burmese and Indian politicians in the legislative council of Burma at the time (Mahajani 1960: 42–44). However, she did not adequately consider the intentions of the colonial government. Burmese nationalists certainly provided support for the law, but were not its direct cause. It was the provincial government of Burma that needed the measures.

In this chapter, I argue that the government of Burma enacted the Expulsion of Offenders Act for the practical necessity of urban governance, and it did so by drawing on two precedents within the corpus of British colonial legislation: preventive policing in British India and the deportation policy of the Straits Settlements. This chapter introduces the historical settings of colonial Rangoon and the immigration issue there, then traces the two predecessors to the Expulsion of Offenders Act, and finally, examines the act itself through the controversies over it and a case of proceedings under the law.

Migration and urban governance

The British defeated the last Burmese kingdom through three successive wars during the nineteenth century and gradually incorporated its territory into British India. The newly acquired territory formed the province of Burma as a local administrative unit within India until 1937 when it was formally separated from India and became an individual crown colony. Beginning in the late nineteenth century, the British attempted to develop the vast and sparsely-populated plains of the Irrawaddy Delta into the leading rice supplier of the British Empire. Under this imperial imperative, the colonial authorities encouraged labour migration from the Indian subcontinent to the Irrawaddy Delta in the beginning. They later adopted a laissez-faire policy on migration because it became increasingly clear that many Indians voluntarily came to Burma without governmental interference. While most cultivators in the delta were Burmese-speaking people who had come down from the middle Irrawaddy basin, which had been the demographic core of the traditional kingdoms in Burma, many Indian migrants were absorbed in the growing urban labour market of Rangoon, which was the provincial capital as well as the main port for exporting rice from the delta (Chakravarti 1971).

The population of Rangoon grew rapidly from 98,745 in 1872 to 234,881 in 1901 and then to 400,415 in 1931 (Osada 2016a). In the early twentieth century, Rangoon became one of the largest cities in British India, next to Bombay, Calcutta, and Madras. Like other port cities around the Indian Ocean and Southeast Asia, Rangoon had a cosmopolitan characteristic, with residents of many cultures. Still, the most visible in the city were Indians. Though the term 'Indian' was rather rough considering their diversity in terms of birthplace, language and religion, here I use the term as it was used by colonial officers at the time. According to decadal censuses in the early twentieth century, Indians constituted more than half the population of Rangoon. At the same time, Burmese-speaking people (hereafter Burmese), the majority in the province, comprised about one-third of the city's population. Other 'indigenous races' in Burma were numerically negligible in Rangoon. Middle-class Indians included traders, moneylenders, and subordinate officials, while many Indian labourers came to work as rice millers, stevedores, sampan rowers, rickshaw pullers, etc., and most returned home after a few years of working. Some people repeatedly travelled back and forth. The average numbers of migrants crossing the Bay of Bengal to and from Rangoon were about 300,000 immigrants and 240,000 emigrants per year between 1908 and 1929 (Andrew 1933: 221). One immigration controller at the time boasted that Rangoon 'now occupies pride of place as the first immigration and emigration port of the world' (ibid.: 5, See also Amrith 2015: 148). Thus, the urban society of colonial Rangoon always comprised a large floating population that government authorities could not easily monitor or control. This increased the risks of contagious diseases and crime in the city. Because Rangoon was the province's capital city, the local British officials of the government of Burma were, of course, more concerned over these risks than those in Calcutta and London. In a nutshell, the immigration control in Rangoon formed a policy area where the economic interests of the British/Indian empire and the interests of the local administration of Burma might conflict, if so with the former taking precedence over the latter.

The previous literature has not paid enough attention to this characteristic of the immigration policy in colonial Burma. First, socioeconomic historians stress the colonial power's economic motivation to mobilise cheap labour from India's famine-afflicted areas to Burma's promising agricultural regions (Furnivall 1957: 71–73; Cheng 1968: 117–124; Adas 1974). This understanding assumes that the British colonial government in India deliberately allowed unrestricted migration within British India while at the same time beginning to restrict emigration to other countries, ostensibly to protect Indian labourers. Scholars who studied Indian communities in Burma have been especially critical of the colonial administration forcing Indian labourers in Rangoon into miserable living conditions (Chakravarti 1971: 43–55). However, while correctly identifying the imperial economic imperatives, these scholars tend to treat the colonial power as monolithic and centralised. They overlook that it was a sprawling and complex bureaucracy of offices and divisions and sub-divisions ranging from Rangoon to Calcutta to London. They rarely recognise the local government of Burma as an agent acting on its own initiative to address local challenges. In fact, the government of Burma improvised measures to deal with social unrest in Rangoon, which deteriorated due to unrestricted migration, taking care not to hamper the labour supply. In other words, the local government could not restrict the number of migrants but it sought to control the quality of migrants, although the qualities it favoured were those that reduced risks from a governmental perspective, and had little regard for the welfare of labourers.

Second, political historians have treated migration control as a political issue. They understood it as part of the larger question of the separation of Burma from India and that any movement towards migration control or separation was promoted by Burmese nationalists in the colonial legislature.[2] The British gradually decentralised India's state apparatus to reduce the central government's burden and respond to the rise of Indian, and to some extent Burmese, nationalism, especially

2 There have been numerous studies on the extent to which Burmese nationalism affected colonial policies. For example, Usha Mahajani points out that Burmese members of the legislative council introduced many 'anti-Indian' bills during the rising tide of nationalism in the 1920s (Mahajani 1960). In contrast, Robert Taylor argues that Burmese politicians were economically dependent on Indian capitalists, which posed a dilemma for Burmese nationalism, as the politicians' demands for migration control had to be tempered lest they harm their benefactors' interests (Taylor 1987: 162–174). But whatever their differences, both studies focus on the behaviours of Burmese politicians in the colonial legislature rather than the colonisers' intentions or interests.

during the global tide of self-determination following World War I. The status of the provincial administrator of Burma was elevated from Chief Commissioner to Lieutenant Governor in 1897 and to full Governor in 1923 when the dyarchy system was introduced to Burma with a delay of four years from India proper. In this process, a legislative council was established in 1897 as an advisory body to the government and gradually expanded its scale and function as the council's elected representatives increased. While this limited democratisation increased the Burmese nationalists' influence on the policy-making processes, substantial power remained in the hands of the local British officials, who were granted greater discretionary power with the increasing decentralisation of administrative control of the Indian empire. Previous studies have largely failed to consider why the British government of Burma not only authorised but also initiated border control measures in Rangoon. The direct motives of the local government were to address practical problems in urban Rangoon, such as epidemics and 'foreign' criminals. The government of Burma developed border control measures to address these issues by drawing on experiences elsewhere, both within and beyond British India.

Preventive policing in colonial India

The Expulsion of Offenders Act in Burma was, in many respects, a further development of crime prevention measures implemented in other parts of the British Raj in India. According to Radhika Singha, a historian of criminal law, there was 'hectic legislative activity' in India in the 1860s and 1870s, which resulted in 'a dual but intersecting pathway for dealing with habituality in crime.' The 'Criminal Tribes Act (Act XXVII of 1871) ... authorized provincial governments to set out rules for the collective registration and surveillance of "hereditary criminal castes and tribes,"' while 'the "security for good behaviour" sections of the Indian Code of Criminal Procedure (CrPC 1861) ... allowed vagrancy and bad-livelihood to be assessed "by evidence of general repute or otherwise"' (Singha 2015: 243–244).[3] These two laws became the bases for further preventive measures, granting colonial authorities the arbitrary power to place under surveillance not only convicted criminals but also those who were merely suspected of habitual criminality.

The introduction and tightening of preventive measures coincided with ever-increasing concerns about the deleterious effects of urbanisation in the colonies. Since the end of the nineteenth century, the major cities in India had been linchpins of the colonial economy and governance, both demanding and fuelling a huge influx of working-class men from the regions. Urban riots, the ever-expanding informal economy and the general culture on the streets, all fed colonial anxieties about maintaining 'public order' (Kidambi 2007: 117–127). The government of Burma established the Rangoon Town Police in 1899 modelled on the Bombay police and began seeking mechanisms to criminalise undesirable characters in the city, such as '*badmaash*' (Kidambi 2007: 127–155; Singha 2015: 242).

At the same time, colonial officials considered that the mass migration of undesirable characters to the cities had been caused by the decaying traditional order in rural areas (Singha 2015: 242–243, 260–263). Hence, in addition to establishing a police force in towns, the colonial administration constructed a 'village system' to enable constant monitoring of the rural population through appointed village headmen (Lalita 2015: 68–92). Notably, British administrators considered Burma to be one of India's most crime-ridden provinces at the time.

---

3 My understanding of the development of crime prevention measures in colonial India throughout this section rely heavily on her argument.

Broad discussions about this alleged problem both within and outside officialdom prompted various changes in the criminal administration in the province of Burma during the 1910s and 1920s (Christian 1942: 157–164; Furnivall 1957: 137–141).

Burma's over-crowded prisons were frequently cited as evidence of its notorious crime-rate. According to Ian Brown, in the mid-1910s, Burma's average daily inmate population was around 20,000. As a proportion of the province's total population, at just under 140 per 100,000, it was almost three times higher than the United Provinces and five times higher than Bengal (Brown 2007a: 248–249; Brown 2007b: 294). Moreover, about a quarter of all inmates in Burma were concentrated in two prisons in Rangoon, the Rangoon Central Prison and the Insein Prison, each holding over two thousand prisoners (Brown 2007a: 230). A considerable number of prisoners were convicted of trivial offences such as theft, housebreaking, and vagrancy, and their sentences were relatively short (Brown 2007a: 249). In some cases, because of the colonial government's concern for the health conditions of prisoners, it was perhaps easier for criminals from the lower classes to survive inside prisons than outside (Brown 2007a: 235–236). These circumstances could stimulate a tendency toward recidivism that has been considered a problem in Rangoon since the end of the nineteenth century.[4]

In Burma, preventive policing was considered necessary for easing this heavily burdened prison administration, leading to the Burma Habitual Offenders Restriction Act in 1919 (Lalita 2015: 126–139). The object of this law was 'to gain a greater hold over the habitual offender by keeping a closer control over his movements, either by confining him to a certain village or area or by requiring him to report himself at stated times and

4 *Report on the Rangoon Town Police*, henceforth: RRTP 1899: 21.

places, or by doing both.'[5] In other words, it strengthened the arbitrary power that had previously been vested in the colonial authority. Practically, a district magistrate could issue an 'order of restriction' to any person he considered should be closely monitored by a village headman. The intention was to restrict an undesirable mobile person to a stable village society, even if the stability was only an ideal rather than real.

In the evolution of criminal law in India, the Burma Habitual Offenders Restriction Act's immediate predecessor was the Restriction of Habitual Offenders (Punjab) Act, 1918. During World War I, the government of India strengthened its powers to restrict the movement of people. Following this trend, the local government of Punjab moved toward provincial enactment. The central government accepted this movement despite considering it 'a departure from the principle that major changes in codified law should be introduced only in the Central Legislature' (Singha 2015: 265). The government of India considered that this case was exceptional and should not be followed. However, the Burma Habitual Offenders Restriction Act was enacted the following year. Subsequently, other provincial enactments for crime prevention appeared, such as the Bengal Goondas Act of 1923 and the United Provinces Goondas Act of 1932. Whereas the Habitual Offenders Acts sought to restore rural order by interning undesirables within the villages, the Goondas Acts reflected the colonial imaginary that criminalised urban *goondas* (gangsters, ruffians, or crooks) who could lure migrant labourers into criminal businesses and sought to expel those *goondas* from the city (Nandi 2010; 2014; Singha 2015: 266–267).

5 Statement of Objects and Reasons for the Burma Habitual Offenders Restriction Bill, 1919 (*Burma Gazette* 1919: Pt. III, p. 3). See also *Burma Code*, 6th edition, 1934: 607–611.

In colonial Rangoon, the fluidity and anonymity of the vast floating population made it difficult for the authorities to police the city. The number of recognised crimes rapidly increased, especially after the middle of the 1910s.[6] The Rangoon Town Police attributed the social unrest to inflationary prices and the expansion of the city rapidly outpacing the expansion of the police force.[7] Criminal immigrants, both from surrounding districts and from abroad, often organised *ad hoc*, sometimes hybrid, groups in the city to commit crimes collectively, such as dacoity (armed robbery), robbery, or theft.[8] In his book *Crime in India,* published in 1924, Bombay's ex-Commissioner of Police, S.M. Edwardes, wrote that 'Of all the cities [in India], Rangoon perhaps suffers most from dacoity' (Edwardes 1924: 42). In addition, the ward headman system, which was created in Rangoon as an urban variation of the village system in Burma, was largely ineffective, not only because of the impossibility of monitoring the floating population in the city but also because the ward headmen were granted only vague and weak power, in contrast to the village headmen.[9]

---

6 From 1911 to 1921, for example, serious offences against the person (murder, hurt, kidnapping, etc.) increased by 66% from 148 to 245 cases, serious offences against person and property, or against property only (dacoity, robbery, lurking, etc.) increased by 179% from 139 to 388 cases, and minor offences against property (theft, criminal breach of trust, etc.) increased by 49% from 1259 to 1879 cases. Considering the population increase in the same period was only 17%, these increases are remarkable (RRTP 1921: 1).

7 RRTP 1916: 6; 1917: 8; 1919: 3; 1920: 1; 1922: 19.

8 The annual Rangoon Town Police report in 1922 noted, 'When one reflects how easy it is for a criminal from the districts to slip into Rangoon, rent a room in a tenement house and gather round him a few shady characters from the Town, an especially easy matter if he possesses a revolver; the wonder is, that not more cases are committed' (RRTP 1922: 17). The hybridity of criminal groups was mentioned in the report as early as 1916 (RRTP 1916: 7–9).

9 RRTP 1909: 9; 1921: 11; 1922: 26; 1923: 10.

The Burma Habitual Offenders Restriction Act did not greatly benefit Rangoon. To deal with criminals 'who have come in from districts surrounding Rangoon and are following a life of crime in the town,' the act was amended in 1923 so that the authorities in Rangoon would 'have power to return such men to their native village.'[10] However, the Rangoon Town Police continued to complain that the Burma Habitual Offenders Restriction Act was not a legal basis for expelling Indian criminals to their native places and that restricting them within the city of Rangoon was only 'a farcical punishment'.[11] In these circumstances, the Rangoon Town Police requested the government of Burma pass further legislation to 'get rid of the numerous natives of India who prey on Rangoon' and cited two existing laws: the previously mentioned Bengal Goondas Act of 1923 and the Foreigners Act of 1864.[12] The latter law, which was Indian central-level legislation, had been operated in the province of Burma for more than ten years until then, as we will see in the next section.

Deporting outsiders: From Chinese to Indians

When the Burma Habitual Offenders Restriction Bill was discussed in the province's legislative council in 1919, the problem of Indian criminals had already been identified not only by the administration but also by non-governmental members of the council. J.E. DeBern, a representative of domiciled Europeans and Eurasians and a member of the select committee to consider

10 Statement of Objects and Reasons for the Burma Habitual Offenders Restriction Amendment Bill, 1923, in File No. 3300 (1923) 'Burma Habitual Offenders Restriction Law, 1919,' Public and Judicial Department Annual Files, Asia, Pacific and Africa Collections, the British Library, London (IOR/L/PJ/6/1851).

11 RRTP 1924: 20.

12 RRTP 1923: 19–20.

the bill, reported that the committee had not raised the question of the Indian habitual criminal because the bill was a very urgent matter. Still, he expressed anxiety about this issue, saying that 'if he [the Indian habitual criminal] comes across here to prey on our population, I think he should be treated as our Chinese habitual criminal is and be prevented from residing anywhere in Burma'.[13] He is invoking expulsion by the Foreigners Act of 1864 in mentioning the treatment of Chinese criminals here.

Disturbances in Rangoon's Chinatown at the turn of the twentieth century pushed the government of Burma and the Rangoon Town Police to take stringent measures against Chinese ruffians (Osada 2014). Referring to the policy in the Straits Settlements, especially Singapore, where Chinese immigrants comprised most of the population, the government of Burma based its policy of expelling Chinese undesirables on the Foreigners Act of 1864. A 'foreigner' was defined in the law as a person 'not being either a natural-born subject of Her Majesty ... or a Native of British India.' Its section 3 prescribed that:

> The Governor-General of India in Council may, by writing, order any Foreigner to remove himself from British India, or to remove himself therefrom by a particular route to be specified in the order; and any local Government may, by writing, make the like order with reference to any Foreigner within the jurisdiction of such Government.[14]

This law laid a specific claim to the territoriality of British India as a state and distinguished British subjects from outsiders (Banerjee 2003: 78–81).

---

13 *Abstract of the Proceedings of the Council of the Lieutenant-Governor of Burma* 1919: 565.

14 *A Collection of the Acts passed by the Governor General of India in Council* 1864: Act III of 1864.

Most Chinese in Rangoon and surrounding areas were foreigners from southern China, such as Fukien and Canton, while some Chinese were British subjects by dint of birth in the British colonies, such as the Straits Settlements, or by naturalisation. In 1909, the government of Burma deported some Chinese accused of rioting from the territory of British India for the first time. During the 1910s, the government of Burma began to view expulsion as a powerful tool for controlling the local Chinese communities, especially in urban Rangoon, where Chinese comprised between five and seven percent of the population (Osada 2014).

In 1919, DeBern suggested extending this power to expel foreigners to Indian criminals, but immigrants from the Indian sub-continent, who comprised the majority of colonial Rangoon, were outside the purview of the Foreigners Act because they were natural-born British subjects. In this context, in 1923, the Rangoon Town Police expressed a need for 'some machinery whereby the Police can get rid of the numerous natives of India who prey on Rangoon'.[15]

A few pieces of local legislation in the early 1920s paved the way for expelling undesirable British subjects from Burma. The Burma Suppression of Brothels Act in 1921 authorised the deportation of European, including British, prostitutes.[16] The British authority had long been anxious that the presence of European prostitutes diminished British prestige in the colony, assuming that the local people did not distinguish British people

15 RRTP 1923: 19.

16 Section 17. The text of the law was included in File No. 2987 (1916) 'Prostitution in India: Suppression of Brothels in Rangoon: Consideration of the Burma Suppressions of Brothels Bill, 1921,' Public and Judicial Department Annual Files, Asia, Pacific and Africa Collections, the British Library, London (IOR/L/PJ/6/1448).

from other Europeans.[17] Although, this section was not put into effect until 1923, the number of deportees was negligible,[18] and it was quite different from later laws targeting Indian criminals, it pioneered the deportation of British subjects from Burma.

The next target was beggars. The problem of immigrant beggars from India had been repeatedly raised in Burma since the turn of the twentieth century. In 1914, the provincial legislative council requested the government of Burma take measures to prevent the influx of immigrant beggars and return them to their native places.[19] Fearing such measures would negatively affect the labour supply from India to Burma, the government instead criminalised begging within Rangoon City.[20] However, fines and imprisonment were not sufficient deterrents. In 1922, seeking a better solution to this problem, the government of Burma amended the Rangoon Police Act again and gave the Commissioner of Police in Rangoon the power to deport from Rangoon a person who had been convicted of begging twice.[21] Because systems had to be put in place to maintain records of convictions and to identify previously convicted beggars, there were only four deportations in the first year.[22] However, seventy-

17 Letter No. 13124—14A, from W. H. Tarleton, Commissioner of Police, Rangoon, to the Chief Secretary to the Government of Burma, dated the 19th November 1913, in File No. 1M-42 (1913) 'Measures for the suppression of pimps who profit by the prostitution of foreign women in India,' Government of Burma Police Proceedings A, Asia, Pacific and Africa Collections, the British Library, London (IOR/P/9126). This is reminiscent of discussions on colonial desire by Ann Stoler (2002) and others.

18 For example, the numbers were 4, 6, 4 respectively in 1923, 1924, 1925 (RRTP for each year).

19 *Burma Gazette* 1914 Pt. III: 56–61.

20 According to section 41A of the Rangoon Police Act, created by amendment in 1907, begging was punishable with a fine of up to fifty rupees, or with imprisonment of up to one month, or both (*Burma Code* 1934: 377).

21 *Burma Code* 1934: 378.

22 RRTP 1922: 23.

Table 3.1: Number of deportations from Burma by the Foreigners Act, 1922–1938

	1922	1923	1924	1925	1926	1927	1928	1929	1930	1931	1932	1933	1934	1935	1936	1937	1938
Chinese in Rangoon	10	7	19	147	118	37	66	102	57	72	194	212	113	60	122	112	109
Chinese in districts	0		2		41	45	19	27	28	24	22	27	6	8	10	8	4
Others	0	nd	8	7	3	0	3	2	4	0	0	0	0	3	14	2	0
Total	10	7+?	29	154	162	82	88	131	89	96	216	239	119	71	146	122	113

Source: RRTP 1926–1938; PLCGB, 1925–1926, vol. V, p. 224

one people were deported in the second year, and dozens were usually deported in each successive year until 1938, with some years, such as 1932 and 1933, seeing hundreds of expulsions.[23] Though this provision mentioned neither race nor ethnicity as a factor for expulsion, the Rangoon Town Police reported that almost all deported beggars were Indians, particularly from Chittagong.[24] The removal orders for these Indian beggars were executed by putting them on board ships proceeding to their home country.

The beginning of the mass deportation of beggars corresponded with the shift in the operation of the Foreigners Act. The scope of the Foreigners Act was widened, and the number of deportees increased drastically from the early 1920s. In the previous decade, expulsions by the Foreigners Act averaged only four per annum, and most of them were notorious gangsters. However, in 1922, ten persons were deported and by 1925 they numbered around one hundred or more (Table 3.1). The police reported in 1925 that expulsion under this law 'had a very wholesome effect in reducing theft'.[25] The expanded use of the Foreigners Act, together with the mass deportation of beggars

23 RRTP each year.

24 RRTP 1923: 18; 1924: 18.

25 RRTP 1925: 14.

by the Rangoon Police Act, suggests that the scope of targets in the expulsion policy was enlarged substantively by including petty criminals (Osada 2014: 89–90).

The Expulsion of Offenders Act

The expulsion policy transformed into more direct and summary measures to govern the urban poor in the 1920s. The culmination of this process was the promulgation of the Expulsion of Offenders Act in 1926. The formal name of the act was 'An Act to authorise the Expulsion from Burma of non-Burmans who have been convicted of certain criminal offences or ordered to furnish security for good behaviour'.[26] After U May Oung, Home Minister of the province of Burma, first introduced the bill in the legislative council on 10 March 1925, it was fiercely criticised both within and outside the council. The primary complaint was that the bill was anti-Indian. Another bill, the Burma Tax on Sea Passengers Bill, was submitted by the Financial Minister on the same day, seeking to impose a tax of five rupees on every passenger who arrived in Burma by sea. As its primary target was the Indian labourer, Indian representatives in the legislative council accused the government of revealing its anti-Indian attitude by submitting these two bills on the same day. In the council, the commercial and Indian representatives stood against these bills, whereas the governmental and Burmese representatives supported them.[27] Outside the legislative council, the *Rangoon Daily News*, an English newspaper owned and

26 *Burma Code* 1934: 1078.

27 See the discussion in the legislative council about the Burma Tax on Sea Passengers Bill (*Proceedings of the Legislative Council of the Governor of Burma* (hereafter PLCGB) 1925 Vol. III: 42–57, 390–446, 517–519) and the Expulsion of Offenders Bill (PLCGB 1925 Vol. III: 57–74; Vol. IV: 175–199) respectively, and Mahajani's analysis of these discussions (Mahajani 1960: 39–44).

managed by an Indian leader in Burma, regularly published dissenting opinions.[28]

Despite the objections, the government of Burma got both bills through the council with minor revisions. The governor-general of India, however, rejected the Burma Tax on Sea Passengers Bill while approving the Expulsion of Offenders Bill.[29] The legislative assembly of India resolved to recommend to the governor-general that the government of India immediately move that the Secretary of State disallow the expulsion act. On that basis the India Office in London seriously considered taking the extraordinary measure of disallowance.[30] In the end, the governor-general of India rejected the legislative assembly's resolution and the bill was enacted, but, as we will see, the India Office dictated that the government of Burma immediately amend the act to address some objections.

The controversy surrounding the Expulsion of Offenders Bill had three points at issue. First was the law's validity from the British Empire's perspective. Indian representatives in the legislative council of Burma and the legislative assembly in India claimed that when the government of India was requesting other

---

28 These articles were collected and published as a book (Indo-Burma Unity 1929). The *Rangoon Daily News* had a comparatively large circulation of 3000 and its tone was considered 'moderate' by the colonial authorities (*Statement of Newspapers and Periodicals Published in the Province of Burma* 1926: 10–11). Its proprietor Mohamed Auzam was a leader of the Muslim community in Rangoon at the time as well as a member of the legislative council elected by an Indian constituency in Rangoon (Indo-Burma Publishing Agency 1927: 12).

29 The governor-general of India explained his reason for withholding assent: 'the Act embodies a principle of taxation which I am unable to approve' (Indo-Burma Unity 1929: 17).

30 File No. 1645 (1925) 'Introduction in Legislative Council of (1) Burma Sea Passengers Bill to impose tax on persons entering Burma by Sea & (2) Expulsion of Offenders Bill for deportation of convicted offenders. As to refusal of sanction to Bills,' Public and Judicial Department Annual Files, Asia, Pacific and Africa Collections, the British Library, London (IOR/L/PJ/6/1906).

colonies in East and South Africa to improve the conditions in which Indian migrants were treated, it was quite improper to make anti-Indian legislation inside the Indian empire.[31] The India Office also considered this to be a problem. Acknowledging that Burma would be separated from India in due course, a high-ranking official in the India Office wrote:

> so long as the two countries form part of one administrative system it seems difficult to defend acquiescence in legislation of this character, as difficult as it would be to defend Parliamentary legislation or Orders in Council giving power to the Home Secretary to deport to Scotland any Scotsman convicted in England of any one of a large range of criminal offences.[32]

Nevertheless, despite the India Office's view that the law was 'both politically and constitutionally undesirable,' the government of Burma's decision was finally upheld.[33]

The second point of contention was the vague definition of 'non-Burman,' the target of this law. The first definition of the term in the original bill was a 'person born elsewhere than in Burma, or born in Burma of parents who were not habitually resident in Burma, and who are themselves neither domiciled nor habitually resident in Burma'.[34] Although it was defined by the place of birth and the permanence of residence, many members of the legislative council pointed out that the meanings of 'domiciled' and 'habitually resident' were not clearly prescribed. A particularly sharp response came from Charles

31 PLCGB 1925 vol. IV: 178, 180–181.

32 Note by Vernon Dawson, Principal at the India Office, dated the 27th of January 1926, in File No. 1645 (IOR/L/PJ/6/1906).

33 Note by Vernon Dawson, Principal at the India Office, dated the 23rd of March 1926, in File No. 1645 (IOR/L/PJ/6/1906).

34 PCLGB 1925 Vol. III: 60.

Haswell Campagnac, a representative of the Anglo-Indian community, who said with some irony:

> For my part the most objectionable thing which I find about this Bill is the definition of non-Burman. It seems to me that that definition is far too wide. If that definition is allowed to stand, it will mean that a person like myself will come under the category of non-Burman. My father has resided in this country for nearly half a century; my mother was born in Burma but happened to be in Calcutta when I was born, and shortly after I was born, I was brought to Burma by my mother to remain here until I went to England to pursue my education. Not having been born here, and not having resided continuously here for 18 years I shall be classed as a non-Burman. If I am convicted of a criminal offence, I am liable to be sent away. Sent away where to? (Laughter)[35]

Campagnac appeared to be confident that the category of 'non-Burman' could not apply to him, and the government of Burma appears to have agreed. The home minister responded that 'the question of domicile depends on what is termed in law the *animus manendi* and must in each case be considered with regard to the facts of that particular case and it is impossible to lay down a comprehensive definition'.[36] The legal term *animus manendi* refers to an intention to remain. The definition of 'non-Burman' in the enacted law was 'any person neither of whose parents is or was a member of race indigenous to Burma and who in addition is not himself domiciled in Burma'.[37] In this definition, though, the term 'domiciled' was still not clearly defined, and the place of birth criterion was replaced by race. However,

35 PLCGB 1925 Vol. III: 70.

36 Ibid.: 72.

37 *Burma Code* 1934: 1078.

according to the home minister, even a person like Campagnac, neither of whose parents was regarded as belonging to any 'race indigenous to Burma,' could be exempted from the scope of deportation, based on *animus manendi* and decided on a case-by-case basis. A similar attitude can be seen in the government of Burma's operation of the Foreigners Act in the earlier period, in which Chinese undesirables who had long been engaged in commercial activities within the province of Burma were rarely expelled (Osada 2014: 86–87).

The third point in the controversy concerned the kinds of offences deserving of expulsion. The bill's original draft was very broad, including defamation as a reason for expulsion. Indian members of the legislative council suggested that the real purpose of this legislation would be to restrain the political activities of Indians.[38] The government of Burma agreed to reduce the scope of expulsions to some extent. The enacted law listed two sets of offences.[39] The first list included severe crimes such as murder, robbery, and grievous bodily harm. Once convicted of those crimes, an offender could be expelled. The second list included lighter crimes, such as theft, for which an offender would be expelled only after being convicted of two offences. The latter list also appeared to show that the application of crime preventive measures such as 'security for good behaviour' or 'order of restriction' had the same effect as the conviction of those lighter offences. Even if never convicted, one could be expelled after receiving an application of the preventive measures twice (At least the government that enacted the law considered it as such. We will come back to this point later). Thus, although reduced, the scope of the law was still considerable.

---

38 PLCGB 1925 Vol. III: 68.

39 *Burma Code* 1934: 1081.

Regarding political offences, defamation was removed from the lists, but offences against the state, including sedition (section 124A of the Criminal Code in India), remained. During the debate in the legislative council, the Home Minister, May Oung, plainly stressed the need for measures to expel political offenders, citing the Mandalay conspiracy case involving the Ghadar party in 1915.[40] Moreover, in the 1920s, the colonial authorities were increasingly aware that many Bengali terrorists fled into Burma to avoid enhanced surveillance in Bengal (Mukherji 2001; Ghosh 2006), which would have deepened the government of Burma's need for some machinery to expel political offenders. Thus, the Expulsion of Offenders Act first enacted in 1926 had wide scope against political offenders. However, immediately after its enactment, as briefly mentioned above, the India Office issued an order requiring the Burma government to amend the act to remove political offenders from its purview,[41] which they did, and all offences against the state were removed from the attached lists.[42]

Despite the amendment, the government of Burma had largely succeeded in creating mechanisms for excluding Indian non-political criminal offenders. Whereas the category of 'non-Burman' was deliberately vague, leaving scope to exempt long-term settlers from deportation, the range of criminal offences that could result in deportation was considerable. The combination of the broad legal scope and the administrative discretion was consistent with the Raj's tradition of crime preventive measures.

---

40 PLCGB 1925 Vol. III: 73.

41 Letter No. 34-Public, from The Earl of Birkenhead, Secretary of State for India, to The Lord Irwin, Governor-General of India in Council, dated the 22nd April 1926, in File No. 1645 (IOR/L/PJ/6/1906).

42 *Burma Code* 1934: 1083.

Table 3.2: Number of deportations from Burma by the Expulsion of Offenders Act, 1926–1938

	1926	1927	1928	1929	1930	1931	1932	1933	1934	1935	1936	1937	1938
Indians in Rangoon	nd	19	31	70	72	46	90	94	115	93	75	47	60
Indians in districts	nd	2	6	8	9	16	11	11	13	6	14	48	16
Total	13	21	37	78	81	62	101	105	128	99	89	95	76

Source: RRTP 1926–1938

Operation on the ground

The operation of the Expulsion of Offenders Act started in 1926, and by 1929, it was in full swing. In the decade from 1929 to 1938, there was an average of around 90 deportees under the act each year (Table 3.2). The Foreigners Act for foreign (mainly Chinese) criminals, the Rangoon Police Act for beggars, and the Expulsion of Offenders Act for 'non-Burman offenders' constituted three pillars of the expulsion policy in Burma, which expelled several hundred undesirables from the territory of Burma every year in the 1930s.

While the numbers of deportees were recorded in annual police reports, it is less clear how these laws were enforced on the ground. However, the Indian Law Reports documents one case of proceedings under the Expulsion of Offenders Act that offers some insights. This case *King-Emperor v. Nga Po Sein Gyi alias Islam*[43] appeared in the law reports because the District Magistrate of Bassein referred to the Rangoon High Court, and the latter ruled on it. The respondent, Po Sein Gyi, was 'a Bengali Mohammedan by birth and has apparently lived in Burma for some 13 to 15 years.' When the proceedings started in 1928, he

43 *The Indian Law Reports. Rangoon Series* (hereafter ILR.R) 1929: 266–269. The following quotations are taken from here unless otherwise noted.

was residing in the Bassein district in the Irrawaddy Delta with a wife 'who, on the mother's side, is partly of Burmese blood' and several children by her. Po Sein Gyi had been convicted of theft and imprisoned for six months in 1926, and an 'order of restriction' was passed against him under the Burma Habitual Offenders Restriction Act in 1928. Shortly thereafter, the proceedings to expel him under the Expulsion of Offenders Act commenced.

The District Magistrate of Bassein probably referred the case to the High Court because of an inconsistency in the text of the Expulsion of Offenders Act 1926. One section of the law defined the term 'offenders' as including persons restricted under the Habitual Offenders Restriction Act. However, another section describing how an offender may be expelled, prescribed that the district magistrate may start proceedings 'when an offender becomes liable *by reason of his conviction of an offence* to be expelled from Burma.' Because applications of preventive measures such as 'security for good behaviour' and 'orders of restriction' were not convictions of offences, the High Court ruled that there was no mechanism to expel persons receiving an 'order of restriction' solely on the grounds of such restriction and not by reason of a conviction of an offence. Po Sein Gyi's proceedings were therefore referred back to the district magistrate because a conviction for theft alone was not grounds for expulsion.

The government of Burma, in response to the High Court decision, swiftly amended the act to 'fix' this 'technical defect' in the text to fulfil the intention of the act 'to enable the Local Government to expel all non-Burmans under the Habitual Offenders Restriction Act and the Criminal Procedure Code'.[44]

44 Remarks by the Home Ministry in the legislative council on 12 December 1929, in File No. 1645 (IOR/L/PJ/6/1906).

This seems to reconfirm the importance for the government of crime prevention measures. In Po Sein Gyi's case, the proceedings to expel him started shortly after issuing an 'order of restriction'. This suggests that the restriction order might have been issued as a pretext to expel someone whose conviction for theft was not sufficient grounds. Despite the discrimination between severe and lighter crimes in the law's text, those preventive measures made it possible for a single conviction of theft to be grounds for expulsion if the concerned district magistrate felt so inclined.

Moreover, the High Court pointed out another problem in Po Sein Gyi's case. The respondent had long lived in Burma. Thus, the High Court judge remarked that 'by birth, he is a non-Burman, but it may be that he has acquired a domicile in Burma; and, if that is so, he would not be a non-Burman' within the definition of the Expulsion of Offenders Act.[45] Nevertheless, before the district magistrate, Po Sein Gyi had reportedly admitted to being non-Burman, and the district magistrate seemed to have acted on this. In this case, the proceedings were returned to the district magistrate because of a conflict in the original law. However, it suggests that in other cases district magistrates made arbitrary judgments on the question of who was non-Burman. Although the fate of Po Sein Gyi and his family after this ruling is unknown, it is supposed that the circumstances for people like them became much more difficult in the 1930s, which saw the mass deportation of petit criminals who were rendered as 'foreign' to Burma.

45 ILR.R 1929: 266.

Conclusion

Burma's expulsion policy mainly aimed at maintaining order in Rangoon. However, the Foreigners Act and the Expulsion of Offenders Act were enforced in the hinterlands as well (Tables 3.1 and 3.2). Expulsion, in general, is premised on a certain territory and a corresponding population. While the Foreigners Act, based on the territory of British India, gave the government of India the power to expel undesirable non-British subjects, the Expulsion of Offenders Act was based on the territory of the province of Burma. Though the province of Burma was a local administrative entity within British India, the legislation gave the government of Burma the power to expel 'non-Burman offenders' from Burma. The cumulative expulsions then served to distinguish and enhance the territoriality of Burma as an individual state, at least in this specific field of border control administration.

Many studies on the state-making process in Burma have examined the development of its modern administrative apparatus (Furnivall 1939; Taylor 1987). Typically, it has been described as but one, albeit peculiar, variation within the broader process of state-making in British India. But these studies rarely asked how the territorial framework of the province of Burma became a separate state from India. While some have studied the delineation of the provincial territory of Burma on the map (Thant Myint-U 2001: 20; Woodman 1962: 205–335; Thongchai 1994: 72–80), the practical border-making of Burma has not been thoroughly studied, although there is growing interest in this issue (cf., Tagliacozzo 2004; Osada 2011; 2014; 2016a; 2016b; Guyot-Réchard 2021). The process by which the government of Burma developed the expulsion policy reveals the local politics of border-making and sheds light on the relationship between population and territory in the emerging colonial state of Burma.

By creating the category of 'non-Burman', the Expulsion of Offenders Act brought an Indian who was a British subject as well as a native of British India under the purview of its expulsion policy. In effect, this legislation treated Indians in the same way as foreigners like the Chinese. This category of 'non-Burman' as defined in the law was both racial and territorial, with the latter weighted more than the former. In the Expulsion of Offenders Act in 1926, someone who was not regarded as a member of any indigenous race could nevertheless be 'Burman' by demonstrating *animus manendi*, the intention of remaining. This was a quite different conception of 'Burman' from the one evoked by Burmese nationalism, which evolved with the notion of race at its core (Phyo Win Latt 2019).

However, while the British definition of 'Burman' in this law was much broader than the Burmese nationalists' or the current Myanmar citizenship law in 1982 (Taylor 1993; Cheesman 2017), it must be noted that this seemingly liberal categorisation of people was a product of colonialism that served the interests of empire. While the government of Burma had to ensure the continuous supply of labour and capital from 'outside' the province, they also had to maintain social order among the diverse and fluid population, and with a limited budget. Expulsion came to be seen as a powerful, economical, and convenient measure, with the categories of those to be deported defined vaguely enough to allow the arbitrary interpretation of individual cases.

References

Adas, Michael (1974), *The Burma Delta: Economic Development and Social Change on an Asian Rice Frontier, 1852–1941*, Madison: University of Wisconsin Press.

Amrith, Sunil S. (2015), *Crossing the Bay of Bengal: The Furies of Nature and the Fortunes of Migrants*, Harvard: Harvard University Press.

Andrew, E. J. L. (1933), *Indian Labour in Rangoon*, n.p.: Oxford University Press.

Banerjee, Paula (2003), 'Aliens in a Colonial World,' in Ranabir Samaddar (ed.), *Refugees and the State: Practices of Asylum and Care in India, 1947–2000*, New Delhi: Sage Publications, pp. 69–105.

Bashford, Alison (2014), 'Immigration Restriction: Rethinking Period and Place from Settler Colonies to Postcolonial Nations,' *Journal of Global History*, 9(1): 26–48.

Brown, Ian (2007a), 'South East Asia: Reform and the Colonial Prison,' in F. Dikötter and I. Brown (eds.), *Cultures of Confinement: A History of the Prison in Africa, Asia and Latin America*, London: Hurst & Co., pp. 221–268.

Brown, Ian (2007b), 'A Commissioner Calls: Alexander Paterson and Colonial Burma's Prisons,' *Journal of Southeast Asian Studies*, 38(2): 293–308.

Chakravarti, Nalini Ranjan (1971), *The Indian Minority in Burma: The Rise and Decline of an Immigrant Community*, London, New York: Oxford University Press for the Institute of Race Relations.

Cheesman, Nick (2017), 'How in Myanmar "National Races" Came to Surpass Citizenship and Exclude Rohingya', *Journal of Contemporary Asia* 47(3): 461–483.

Cheng, Siok-Hwa (1968), *The Rice Industry of Burma, 1852–1940*, Kuala Lumpur: University of Malaya Press.

Christian, John LeRoy (1942), *Modern Burma: A Survey of Its Political and Economic Development*, Berkeley: University of California Press.

Edwardes, S. M. (1924), *Crime in India: A Brief Review of the More Important Offences Included in the Annual Criminal Returns with Chapters on Prostitution & Miscellaneous Matters*, London: Oxford University Press.

Furnivall, J. S. (1939), 'The Fashioning of Leviathan: The Beginnings of British Rule in Burma,' *Journal of Burma Research Society*, 29(1): 3–137.

Furnivall, J. S. (1957), *Colonial Policy and Practice: A Comparative Study of Burma and Netherlands India*, New York: New York University Press.

Ghosh, Durba (2006), 'Terrorism in Bengal: Political Violence in the Interwar Years,' Durba Ghosh and Dane Kennedy (eds.), *Decentring Empire: Britain, India and the Transcolonial World*, New Delhi: Orient Longman, pp. 270–292.

Guyot-Réchard, Bérénice (2021), 'Tangled Lands: Burma and India's Unfinished Separation, 1937–1948,' *Journal of Asian Studies* 80(2): 293–315.

Indo-Burma Publishing Agency (1927), *Who's Who in Burma: A Biographical Record of Prominent Residents of Burma with Photographs and Illustrations*, Calcutta, Rangoon: Indo-Burma Publishing Agency.

Indo-Burma Unity (1929), *Burma Government's Crusade against Indians*, Bombay: Sunshine Pub. House.

Kidambi, Prashant (2007), *The Making of an Indian Metropolis: Colonial Governance and Public Culture in Bombay, 1890–1920*, Aldershot and Burlington: Ashgate.

Lalita Hingkanonta Hanwong (2015), *Policing in Colonial Burma*, Chiang Mai: Center for ASEAN Studies.

McKeown, Adam (2008), *Melancholy Order: Asian Migration and the Globalization of Borders*, New York: Columbia University Press.

Mahajani, Usha (1960), *The Role of Indian Minorities in Burma and Malaya*, Westport: Greenwood Press.

Mukherji, Susmita (2001), 'The Bengali Revolutionaries in Burma, 1923–33,' in *Proceedings of the Indian History Congress: Millennium (61st) Session, Kolkata, 2000–2001*, Kolkata: Indian History Congress, pp. 1104–1117.

Nandi, Sugata (2010), 'Constructing the Criminal: Politics of Social Imaginary of the Goonda,' *Social Scientist*, 38(3–4): 37–54.

Nandi, Sugata (2014), 'Inventing Extraordinary Criminality: A Study of Criminalization by the Calcutta Goondas Act,' in Shaunnagh Dorsett and John McLaren (eds.), *Legal Histories of the British Empire: Laws, Engagements and Legacies*, Abingdon: Routledge, pp. 92–106.

Osada, Noriyuki (2011), 'An Embryonic Border: Racial Discourses and Compulsory Vaccination for Indian Immigrants at Ports in Colonial Burma, 1870–1937,' *Moussons: Recherche en sciences humaines sur l'Asie du Sud-Est*, 17, pp. 145–164.

Osada, Noriyuki (2014), 'Discovery of "Outsiders:" The Expulsion of Undesirable Chinese and Urban Governance of Colonial Rangoon, Burma, c. 1900–1920,' *Journal of Sophia Asian Studies*, 32: 79–96.

Osada, Noriyuki (2016a), 'Housing the Rangoon Poor: Indians, Burmese, and Town Planning in Colonial Burma,' IDE Discussion Paper, No. 561.

Osada, Noriyuki (2016b), *Taidō suru kokkyō: Eiryō Biruma no imin-mondai to toshi-tōchi* (The border in embryo: Immigration and urban governance in colonial Rangoon), Tokyo: Yamakawa Shuppan-sha.

Phyo Win Latt (2019), 'Protecting Amyo: The Rise of Xenophobic Nationalism in Colonial Burma, 1906–1941,' Ph.D. dissertation, National University of Singapore.

Singha, Radhika (2015), 'Punished by Surveillance: Policing "Dangerousness" in Colonial India, 1872–1918,' *Modern Asian Studies*, 49(2): 241–269.

Stoler, Ann Laura (2002), *Carnal Knowledge and Imperial Power: Race and the Intimate in Colonial Rule*, Berkeley: University of California Press.

Tagliacozzo, Eric (2004), 'Ambiguous Commodities, Unstable Frontiers: The Case of Burma, Siam, and Imperial Britain, 1800–1900,' *Comparative Studies in Society and History*, 46(2): 354–377.

Taylor, Robert H. (1987), *The State in Burma*, Honolulu: University of Hawaii Press.

Taylor, Robert H. (1993), 'The Legal Status of Indians in Contemporary Burma,' in K. S. Sandhu and A. Mani (eds.), *Indian Communities in Southeast Asia*, Singapore: Times Academic Press; Institute of Southeast Asian Studies, pp. 666–682.

Thant Myint-U (2001), *The Making of Modern Burma*, Cambridge: Cambridge University Press.

Thongchai Winichakul (1994), *Siam Mapped: A History of the Geo-body of a Nation*, Honolulu: University of Hawaii Press.

Woodman, Dorothy (1962), *The Making of Burma*, London: The Cresset Press.

Chapter 4

Surveillance and Repression of Communists in the Indochina Colonial State

Tomokazu Okada

Introduction

According to Charles Founiau and Patrice Morlat, the French gradually adopted the repressive devices (*appareils répressifs*) of the Indochina colonial state from 1885 to 1930 in response to the Vietnamese nationalist movement (Forniau and Morlat 2015: 109–10). The Cần Vương movement (1885–1889; against French colonial rule), Phan Bội Châu's Đông Du Movement (1905–1909), and the Vietnam Modernization Association (Duy tân Hội) sent Vietnamese students for training and education in Japan. The Annamite Patriots Association raised their demands for self-determination internationally at the Paris Peace Conference after World War I. The 1930–1931 Yên Bái mutiny, launched by the VNQDĐ (Việt Nam Quốc Dân Đảng: Vietnamese Nationalist Party), and the uprising of the Nghệ-Tĩnh soviets led by communist organizations, including the Indochinese Communist Party (ICP), marked a turning point for the Indochina colonial state and its repressive devices.

World War I was a watershed for colonial issues. The petition 'Annam People's Request' that Nguyễn Ái Quốc (Hồ Chí Minh) submitted at the Paris Peace Conference shocked the world. Post-war France expressed its gratitude to the Indochinese people for their cooperation and began working towards a type of 'colonial autonomy', both to reward them and to develop Indochina. Subsequently, an existing system of local political representatives developed and increased the number of native members and voters in the Chamber of the People's Representatives (*Chambre des représentants du peuple*), Chamber of Commerce, and Chamber of Agriculture (Okada 2010: 7). The colonial administration also experimented with developing a public education system with primary and advanced courses similar to those in Metropolitan France to train native officials in Indochina (Trinh 1995; Bezançon 2002).

The national liberation movements also changed after World War I. After the Đông Du Movement, Indochina nationalists escaped to China and Southeast Asia. Many secretly built international networks to create opportunities to revolt in the 1920s. In response, the Indochina colonial state reorganized and strengthened its police organization. The colonial state worked closely with the police, the administration of Metropolitan France, and embassies. They had some success in the surveillance and control of overseas revolutionary groups (Goscha 1999: 65, 72–73), but their repressive devices remained ineffective in Indochina.

Since the creation of the union (Tonkin, Annam, Cochinchina, and Cambodia in 1887; Guangzhouwan in 1898; and Laos in 1899), the Indochina colonial state assimilated its local peoples, disregarding their ethnic diversity. Instead, it explored colonial autonomy with a policy called '*politique d'association*', which encouraged cooperation among the locals while retaining local political structures and customs (Morlat 2006: 27–28).[1] In this dual regime, French colonial powers could not directly oversee police operations everywhere and were reliant on the diverse

1 The theory of '*politique d'association*' was formulated in the 1860s, and its application to Indochina began to be discussed by the French Radical Socialist Party around 1908 and was subsequently debated in parliament.

kingdoms and municipalities to police the territories outside its direct control, making it difficult to detect early signs of dangerous movements and uprisings. The French colonial power was therefore unprepared for the Yên Bái mutiny and the uprising of the Nghệ-Tĩnh soviets in Vietnam in 1930–1931, to which it responded with extreme force, resulting in remorse for their overreaction. Thousands of protesters were killed or imprisoned almost indiscriminately (Brocheux and Hémery 2001: 309).[2] Activists who narrowly escaped repression were then forced to go underground.

However, this unlimited use of force threatened to fundamentally overturn colonial rule, which was based on cooperation with the local people. The 1930–1931 experience became a warning of failure for both the oppressors and oppressed. To maintain order, the Indochina police forcefully sought information from prisoners and suspects in prison. Subsequently, they created files detailing the appearances and identities of persons considered dangerous. Moreover, securing collaborators who could provide reliable information was a primary objective. Thus, the Indochina colonial state strengthened its policing and provided new repressive devices to identify and monitor dangerous people, both domestically and internationally.

This chapter focuses on police monitoring and control of dangerous people in Indochina during the 1930s. During that time, Indochina police surveillance targeted communists,[3]

2 According to reports, 3,000 farmers were killed, and 9,000 to 10,000 people were imprisoned in Nghệ An and Hà Tĩnh provinces. Additionally, according to one testimony, 2,978 people were arrested and 1,228 were convicted between February 1930 and May 1931. RST (Résidence supérieure au Tonkin), NF (Nouveau Fonds), 6546, ANOM (Archives nationales d'outre-mer), France.

3 The Indochina police also targeted nationalists, but they are largely beyond the scope of this chapter. In a nutshell: A representative organization, the VNQDĐ, was founded in 1927 by Nguyễn Thái Học, but began to split internally around 1929. Members who remained in Indochina launched

who did not stop their activities even after the uprising of the Nghệ-Tĩnh soviets was crushed. The ICP and its actors became more cautious and cunning, avoiding foolhardy and dangerous demonstrations and trying to earn the sympathy of the public by using 'legal' methods as much as possible. Communists in Indochina in the 1930s were split into two groups: agents of Comintern and 'indigenous communists', distinguished simply by the fact that some of them had attended Comintern and the rest had not. Agents of Comintern, called 'return from Russia,' had many members who went to study in Moscow in the 1920s and who, after the uprising of the Nghệ-Tĩnh soviets, escaped into southeastern China, where they were active in underground revolutionary networks. However, after the Popular Front government appointed the first socialist prime minister in France in 1936, Comintern agents were allowed to be openly active in ICP headquarters in Saigon. The 'indigenous communists' did not qualify as members of the ICP, but acted in sympathy with communism (Kurihara 2005: 211–243). Most of the 'indigenous communists' were Vietnamese intellectuals who had completed higher education at the University of Indochina. They were not colonial bureaucrats but in diverse professions, such as private school teachers, journalists, lawyers, doctors, and engineers, who helped reconstruct and operate ICP activities (Trinh 2004). The Indochina police had a lot of trouble dealing with these 'indigenous communists' who operated behind the scenes of the ICP's legitimate activities around 1936.

---

the Yên Bái mutiny in 1930, but it was put down by the French and its leaders were all executed. Meanwhile, another faction, which continued to operate outside Indochina (Guangdong and Yunnan in China), continued in the footsteps of their leader Phan Bội Châu, who had been arrested in Shanghai in 1925, and planned a revolutionary political movement with the aim of achieving independence for Indochina (Hammer 1955: 82-84; Duiker 1976: 164-165). However, the Indochina police closely monitored the nationalists and prevented them from returning to Indochina. GGI (Gouvernement général de l'Indochine), 65444, ANOM, France.

In this chapter, I clarify how the Indochinese police attempted to control communists, focusing on two cases: the activity of the ICP Local Committee, which in 1935 was based in the northern Vietnam border region with China (in the Protectorate of Tonkin), and the communist involvement in organizing the general strikes in Hanoi in 1936–1937. These two cases reveal the characteristics of Indochina's colonial state and its repressive devices. A key issue was the local activists seeking autonomy / self-determination, and the colonial state seeking ways to grant greater autonomy to the locals in the colonial state, a dynamic peculiar to Indochina, its police administration system, and its legal standards for crimes. These cases also illustrate some of the issues raised in the introduction to this book: civilization, 'francization', control through information, and the 'twilight zone'.

Police organization in Indochina

First, I provide an overview of the formation of police organizations in Indochina. During the 1890s, the French colonial authorities mobilised military forces to quell the Cần Vương insurgency, a movement seeking to restore sovereignty to the Nguyễn dynasty of Vietnam. It then shifted to a civilian system and established a police organization to maintain domestic security in the early twentieth century.

Initially, police services relied on municipal police organized in large cities. There were concerns over the emergence of the Đông Du Movement by Vietnamese nationalists, and a more extensive police organization was needed. In addition to the Attorney General, the local executive secretary (*Résident supérieur*) created a system for supervising the police with greater authority.

According to the Governor General's decree (*arrêté*) on 26 November 1908, establishing the Tonkin Police Organization, the purpose of the police was to 'maintain public order, protect personal property and freedom, monitor morality, ensure security and deter crimes, and punish offenders'. These missions were conducted under the direction of the Central Police Chief of Hanoi. Central police chiefs and other police officers were appointed by the Governor General of Indochina or the local secretary, of which there were 68 in 1907 and 70 in 1908.[4] They were deployed to police stations throughout the country[5] and each had several officers, as required.

In the administrative divisions, such as rural areas and city blocks, there was a police box (*Poste de police*) under the control of the Indochina police, where the militia and vigilantes of the pre-colonial protectorate countries were organized under the name *Garde indigène*.[6] This means that the existing militia and vigilantes, such as those of the Nguyễn dynasty or the Kingdom of Cambodia were reemployed as policeman by the French colonial authorities. Similar systems existed in other French colonies. In Madagascar, for example, the French empire had been able to entrust local security forces with policing and maintaining security for the 'prosperity of the colonial state', rather than merely to sustain the colonial order (Courtin 2012: 63).

Police services were also outsourced to locals in the *phố trưởng* system in Vietnam. The *phố trưởng* (舗長: *chef de rue*)

---

4 GGI, 3817, 3824, ANOM, France.

5 In 1911, there was a central police station (*Commissariat central de police*) each in Hanoi, Saigon, and Phnom Penh. There were three police stations (*Commissariat de police*) in Hanoi, one in Hải Phòng, one in Huế, one in Tourane (Đà Nẵng), two in Phnom Penh, one in Battambang, one in Vientiane, and one in Guangzhouwan (GGI, 17196, ANOM, France).

6 GGI, 17196, ANOM, France. In 1911, there were 159 regional police boxes in Cochinchina, 169 in Tonkin, 72 in Annam, 33 in Cambodia, 15 in Laos, and 7 in Guangzhouwan.

is a representative of a street in a city block, elected by the residents, responsible for issuing various public certificates, and assisting in duties such as tax collection, night watch, sanitation management, and resident dispute arbitration (Gouvernement général de l'Indochine 1905: 24–25). This was a form of colonial self-management. The *phố trưởng* initially relied on local people's initiative and volunteer services, but the city administration began to pay an allowance in 1926. Furthermore, workers became 'public agents' of the colonial administration[7]. The local administrative system of the municipalities or villages, such as the *phố trưởng*, were expected to function as a repressive device of the Indochina colonial state.

Central Service of Information and General Security

Albert Sarraut, a member of the Radical Party, held the second Indochina Governorship from 1917 to 1919, and was a leader in setting French colonial policy after World War I.[8] During the interwar period, he served as colonial minister, interior minister, and prime minister of France. Sarraut aimed to construct a self-governing colonial state based on the idea of *association*. On the one hand, he declared that the governor general must have greater powers of initiative and activities to develop the colony and request defence from the home country. On the other hand,

7 FMH (Fonds de la Mairie de la ville de Hanoi), E.98-2230, VNAC-I (Vietnam National Archive Center-I)-Hanoi, Vietnam.

8 With the support of the economic organization *Union coloniale*, Sarraut represented a group called the colonial party in the National Assembly, which protected the interests of the colony. He was a defender of the French empire, who was trying to maximise autonomy (and thus self-determination) of the colonial state but denying the liberation or independence of local peoples. His aides during Governor General Sarraut's second term, formed a faction supporting Sarraut (Sarratist), from which Louis Marty, Pierre Pasquier, and René Robin became the governors general of Indochina in the 1920s and '30s (Cf. Morlat 2006).

he stressed the need to strengthen the systems for collaborating with local people for self-government (Sarraut 1923: 65, 105). Naturally, this idea risked the colonies becoming independent. Nevertheless, under the Third French Republic's approach to colonialism, Sarraut and his successors attempted to realize a 'perfect and supreme state form' that might escape France's influence but cooperate with France (William 1973: 122).

First, the autonomy of the Indochina colonial state was manifested in the centralization of the Governor General. The Governor General's Ordinance on 28 and 29 June 1917, established the Central Service of Information and General Security (*Service central de Renseignements et de Sûreté* Générale); it became a central police agency under the direct control of the Governor General. Sarraut appointed Janbreau, his daughter's husband, the director of the new agency, to oversee the reorganization of the intelligence and security services. The police services, and command structures as well as their local administration functions all came under the remit of the new director of the Central Service of Information and General Security.[9] Accordingly, the number of police management personnel (*cadres*) increased, with most of the new personnel assigned to the regions (Cochinchina, Tonkin, Annam, Cambodia and Laos). Priority was given to the coordination of central and local organizations, and their rationalization and sharing of roles.

In 1922, the Central Service of Information and General Security merged with the Political Affairs Directorate. Police operations and political affairs services shared many overlapping concerns about the tensions between colonial rule and local society. The Central Service of Information and General Security, which became a division of the Directorate of Political Affairs and General Security (*Direction des affaires politiques et de la sûreté*

9 RST, NF, 2030, ANOM, France. See also Faivre 2023: 50–59.

Générale), was able to investigate and monitor more diverse cases with jurisdiction over political affairs and other concerns that were not under their previous remit. The ability to collect and centralize information promised efficiencies in handling the caseload, but it appears that realising such efficiencies would take some time: the capacity to detect signs of uprisings and pre-emptively suppress dangerous political movements was not developed in time to prevent the Yên Bái mutiny and the Nghệ-Tĩnh soviets in 1930–1931.

The scope of operations of the Indochina police was clearly outlined by the governor general on 1 December 1934.

> The Directorate of Police and General Security in the General Government has the following responsibilities: To centralize information concerning the internal and external security of Indochina and to gather reports from administrative and judicial authorities on facts concerning public order; To direct political information services abroad and at home and to ensure control of foreigners; To control the functioning of the various police services and to coordinate their efforts to accomplish the tasks incumbent upon them; To study all questions relating to the organization of the various police forces of Indochina.[10]

Personnel (mostly French) belonging to the Central Service of Information and General Security were selected and assigned to managerial positions across all regions of Indochina (Table 4.1). The total number of personnel was 157 in 1926, 237 in 1931, and 452 in 1937. The organization and function of the police in Indochina was divided into: special police, judicial police, city police, border police, and police research institutes.

10 RST, NF, 6, ANOM, France.

Table 4.1: Staff members of the Central Service of Information and General Security in 1937

	HQ-Hanoi	Cochinchina	Tonkin	Annam	Cambodia	Laos	**Total**
Contrôleur	1	3 (1)*	1	1	1	0	7
Commissaire	3	14 (2)*	14 (5)*	4 (2)*	6 (3)*	0	41
Inspecteur	2	45 (3)*	45 (3)*	16 (2)*	12 (2)*	3 (2)*	123
*Brigadier***	2	46	26	0***	16	0	90
sous — Brigadier	0	39	33	0***	15	0	87
stagiaire (trainee)	1	13	10	0***	5	0	29
Secrétaire	5	21 (1)*	15 (1)*	3 (1)*	6	0	50
*Labo. SIP.*****	0	15	5	2	3	0	25
Total in 1937	14	196	149	26	64	3	**452**

* ( ) is the number of special police staff.

** *Brigadier* organizes and directs squads at each assignment.

*** In Annam, a military reserve unit, *Garde indigène* (generally known as '*Corps Bleu*'), performed patrol duties[11].

**** Personnel of *Laboratoires et Services d'Identité des Police* (Police research institute).

Source: Gouvernement général de l'Indochine 1938: 414–443.

Special police were called political (administrative) police. They were chosen by the manager (*contrôleur*), superintendent (*commissaire*), and detective (*inspecteur*), with the aim of monitoring and suppressing anti-social behaviour in the political system. Their task was to collect information on foreigners and security risks (especially political) both within and outside the country. For this purpose, they worked with police officers and administrative department officials. Special police personnel were under the direct control of local police department

11 Agefom (Agence française d'outre-mer), carton 269, dossier 440.

managers. According to the 1937 Administrative Yearbook, seven people were assigned to Cochinchina, nine to Tonkin, five to Annam, five to Cambodia, and two to Laos (Gouvernement général de l'Indochine 1938: 414–423). They often hired local informers to gather information.

The judicial police investigated and repressed felony and misdemeanour offenses and deployed detectives, police officers (*brigadiers*), deputy police officers (*sous-brigadiers*), and police managers (who had functions similar to those of prosecuting attorneys, deciding whether or not to prosecute, and presenting the state's case to the judiciary) mainly to police stations located in the larger cities.

The city police was under the jurisdiction of the Central Service of Information and General Security, but had its own personnel from the city's budget. The chief was a police manager who held the title of *commissaire central* or *commissaire d'arrondissement* who reported directly to the mayor. Although the city police aimed mainly to maintain urban law and order (sometimes state security in cooperation with the special judicial police), they also inherited a duty traditionally performed by police since the French Revolution: city sanitation management (Berlière 1996: 10). For example, unsanitary areas of Paris tended to have higher crime rates. Police intervention in citizens' private life was meant to cut off crime. In fact, in 1924, Hanoi police officers patrolled houses in the city one by one to investigate sanitation conditions.[12]

Border police were responsible for the customs and security of the French, locals, and foreigners on both sides of the

12 FMH, E.98-2230, VNAC-I-Hanoi, Vietnam. However, the city police had no jurisdiction over criminals beyond the city's border. For example, in 1930, the Hanoi police announced there were 3,000 illegal prostitutes in the city, but in fact, according to Joyeux, director of the hygiene department of Hanoi city, there were twice as many within city limits. Notably, the Hanoi

colony's sea and land borders. They were under the control of the local police department chief and the local secretary and cooperated with the armed forces deployed at the border for defence purposes.

The Police Research Institute's main task was to collect personal data on inmates, suspects, dangerous persons, and immigrants for criminal investigations. In December 1931, Tonkin's Chief Executive Tholance and Regional Police Manager Arnoux warned that communist inmates, suspects, and released persons could create underground networks. The police created personal data (photos, anthropometric data, charges, a summary of judgments, and statements of criminal intent) for all suspects and sent copies to the police at the suspect's place of origin.[13] Police research institutes had compiled data from 237,000 individuals (including non-communists) by 1941. This was four times the number of files from 1927 to 1928 (Brocheux and Hémery 2001: 112).

After the 1917 and 1922 reforms, and the 1930–1931 repression, the Indochina colonial state established a police command and division system that rationally collected and concentrated information. The aim was to maintain public order in general, and, more particularly, to gather information that might provide advance notice of possible political movements and uprisings. Expectations were particularly high for the mission of the special police. The next section examines Indochina police surveillance and the control of communists in Tonkin in 1935–1937.

police could only arrest those prostitutes who could not escape from the city (Joyeux 1930: 12).

13 RST, NF, 6955, ANOM, France.

Identification and monitoring of dangerous persons

Tonkin local committee of the ICP

In March 1935, the Indochinese Communist Party held its first convention in Macao, China, four years after the uprising of the Nghệ-Tĩnh soviets. Around this time, the Indochinese Communist Party's domestic organization had recovered considerably. The party was based in the Tonkin Highlands (the provinces of Lạng Sơn, Cao Bằng, and Bắc Giang) on the border with China in the northeastern part of Indochina. It maintained a 'local committee' (*Xừ Ủ y*) there from which it tried to stimulate propaganda activity in Hanoi and Tonkin Delta, with many Thô people (now Tày-Nùng) working in the area as collaborators.[14] In fact, one of the Thô people was dispatched to Hanoi for propaganda work at the order of the local committee in May 1935. The Tonkin police obtained this information using reports from special police and police research institute profiling.

The Tonkin Police Annual Report, from June 1935 to June 1936, stated that 'the political situation in Tonkin was excellent during this period and the area's security was not threatened at any time.' Additionally, 'only on the Indochina northern border, have we confirmed activities of the illegal revolution group and the Indochina Communist Party, but no cases or attempts of demonstrations have been seen.' The border area with China was controlled by a military division, which strictly monitored entry and exit, including the crossing of many Chinese workers. After the ICP convention in Macao, Annamese (Vietnamese) communists who had gone abroad tried to re-enter Indochina by mingling with the Chinese workers, but the police discovered the plan in advance.[15] In May 1935, an extraordinary notification

14 RST, NF, 6546, ANOM, France.

15 RST, NF, 6546, ANOM, France. The Tonkin Police received information that approximately 100 Annamese communists were living in Marseille

was issued by the Governor-General of Indochina, instructing border control officers to, 'Please check the person who has been disguised as a drug seller; it is a party official'.[16] This notification indicates that the Tonkin police continued to regard the Indochinese Communist Party and its officials as potential threats even after repressing the Nghệ-Tĩnh soviets' uprising in 1931.

Interrogation and 'informers'

During the 1930–1931 period, the Indochina colonial state's repression gradually began to bear fruit. In the late 1930s, the most energetic, cunning men overseeing the monitoring of dangerous persons were Police Managers Arnoux and Laneque, who were in the Tonkin Special Police (Gouvernement général de l'Indochine 1938: 414–415).[17] The activities of the political police in Indochina can be found in their reports. As with any political police service, the primary activity was acquiring information. Two of their main sources of information were from the interrogations of inmates and suspects and from informers.[18]

(an exaggerated number), carrying counterfeit passports issued by the Chinese Communist Party. They were planning to travel to China in May–August 1935 and, guided by Chinese activists, would cross the border and enter Indochina.

16 RST, NF, 2032, ANOM, France.

17 Paul-Louis-Marius Arnoux and Charles-Alfred Laneque were elite police officers who entered the Indochina police in senior management positions in 1912 and 1927, respectively.

18 Informers were hired to assist the police, on similar terms to civil servants. They were paid a fixed monthly salary, with some bonuses when the information was particularly useful, and they had to do a precise job, with regular reports. There were both native Indochinese and French informers in France, who spent most of their time researching the archives of the Paris police headquarters, looking for new addresses of Vietnamese residents in the capital (Morlat 1990: 190).

Nguyỹn Văn Trạm,[19] who surrendered in May 1935 and entered a French consulate in Hong Kong, was immediately taken to Hanoi for questioning by the Indochina police. According to the report, he had received an order in January 1935 from 'KHIT' (Trần Huy Liệu), a member of the ICP headquarters in Macao, to establish links between the Tonkin Local Committee and the Tonkin Delta group. Based on this information, Laneque received further information from an informer named 'Leonard'. Leonard was (probably) an Annamese spy, who was fully integrated into the communist group in the Tonkin Highlands, and who reported the details and activities of its principal members to Laneque. Laneque focused on identifying dangerous individuals of unknown origin.

For example, although a person named CAO could not be precisely identified at first, he was tracked via Leonard, who had been in direct contact with CAO, and identified via interrogation (torture?) of an indigenous communist, Trần Văn Giàu, who had already been arrested. Information on CAO registered in the personal data file of the Police Research Institute was that he was about 28 years old, about 1 m 75 cm, with a bent back, sharp ears, and teeth. Similarly, with information sourced separately from Leonard and Nguyỹn Văn Trạm about a farmer named HOANG, nicknamed 'Cao Bằng's Stalin', the police identified him as Hoàng Đình Giong from the Thô people, who was a contact for a Chinese communist group.[20]

Leonard also reported that another dangerous individual known as the BEO used to work for the Ardin Publishing Company in Saigon. When Tonkin Police referred to the publication company through Cochinchina Police, it turned out that BEO had previously had dealings with the VNQDĐ (Vietnamese

19 'Return from Russia.' He had a relationship with Nguyễn Ái Quốc.

20 RST, NF, 6546, ANOM, France.

Nationalist Party) and had been arrested, but had escaped to China and later joined the ICP. Leonard seems to lose track of where BEO went after that. Around the same time, a person named Đặng Văn Ry, who had been linked to BEO, was arrested in Hanoi. If the police hadn't arrested Đặng Văn Ry, they could have continued to pursue the BEO. Laneque reported that 'his arrest was premature for grasping the flow of communists moving back and forth across the Indochina/China borders'.[21] Nevertheless, the Indochina police were able to understand the identities and activities of many communists in a fairly detailed manner.

Communist collaborators

However, their effectiveness was limited. According to Nguỹn Văn Trạm's testimony, in order to infiltrate Indochina, he needed an identification card, but a *lý trưởng*, an acquaintance of KHIT (Trần Huy Liệu), could create it. The *lý trưởng* (里長: *chef de village*) was the head of a village municipality and a public agent of the colonial administration authorised to issue identification cards. The identification card was based on family register information, and the *lý trưởng* created them in rural areas just as the previously mentioned *phố trưởng* did in the city. In other words, they were able to supply the communists with high-quality documents. They also collaborated in simpler ways, such as hiding suspects or failing to report their whereabouts.

The colonial authorities' distrust of *lý trưởng* and *phố trưởng* had a long history, expressed by Tonkin Executive Secretary Tholance in 1931:

21 RST, NF, 6546, ANOM, France.

> Too often, *lý trưởng* and the street chiefs [*phố trưởng*] who are responsible for carrying out the prescribed checks respond that the applicant is unknown in their village or sector, while he is in possession of his personal tax card. This practice constitutes clear evidence of negligence on the part of these authorities ... while making it difficult to establish regular documents. In order to remedy such a state of affairs, ... call the defaulting agents to order and give them all useful instructions so that these searches and identifications are truly effective.[22]

Tholance expressed further dissatisfaction a few years later after the Special Police received information about a *lý trưởng* working with the communists. In the Tonkin Executive Secretary's circular of 24 October 1935, Tholance reported:

> The information gathered by the Special Police and the interrogation of the propagandists of the Indochinese Communist Party recently arrested in the [Northern Tonkin] Highland and in the mining region of Hongay show that individuals from outside these regions can circulate there, stay in the villages, and frequently cross the Sino-Tonkinese border, without being reported by the responsible authorities. However, these individuals, some of whom have lived abroad for several years, most of whom are Annamese from the [Red River] Delta and have received at least basic French education, must necessarily attract the attention of the notables of the villages when they pass through, by their language, their costume and their behaviour, very different from those of the natives. This situation demonstrates the lack of police surveillance by the communal authorities and the district chiefs.[23]

22 RST, NF, 2248, ANOM, France.

23 RST, NF, 2091, ANOM, France.

This dissatisfaction lead Tholance to impose a 'duty to report to the authorities the visits of all outsiders, even friends' on all municipalities. From then on, outsiders were monitored by the new heads of municipalities, and had to provide information such as the purpose of their visit, destination, and identification cards to the police register (*registre de police*), which the secretary of the province regularly inspected. In short, existing officials such as *lý trưởng* and *phố trưởng* were no longer given police duties. It seems that the municipal power, secretary of the province, and other authorities assumed the role of monitoring outsiders.

Originally, public agents such as *lý trưởng* and *phố trưởng* were necessary to the police network, and their ability to provide and monitor information was assumed; however, this system did not always meet the expectations of colonial power. Sometimes, such agents betrayed the colonial powers. The repressive devices of the Indochina colonial state were based on a system of cooperation with the local people, which was a double-edged sword. This feature is apparent in the following cases.

Controlling semi-legal activities

Strike and Popular Front

From winter 1936 to spring 1937, workers held large strikes in Hanoi, the capital of French Indochina, corresponding with a nationwide general strike in France, where a left-wing three-party coalition had recently launched. Indochinese workers demanded wage increases from their employers and the same right to strike as workers in Metropolitan France. The French Popular Front conducted a survey of the food and housing situation and the working environment of the colonized populace from a humanitarian perspective. Although the Popular Front was reluctant to grant the right to strike, they were inclined towards granting freedom of association for the locals in Indochina. In addition, it issued modern labour regulations similar to the national law and released many political prisoners with a pardon. However, Indochinese workers were not given the same legal right to strike as French workers. The French Popular Front Government concluded: 'Every worker in the metropole can read and write, finish military service, maintain professionalism, and separate political and vocational requirements.' In contrast, according to Justin Godard's October 1937 report, colonial workers' 'level of education is inadequate, and they want the freedom to form labour unions just to cause strikes'.[24] French colonialists understood that the 'political and social movements caused by granting genuine freedom to the local population would spell the end of colonial rule' (Hémery 1975: 429–430). However, the leaders of the nationalist independence movement understood the reality even better. They believed that freedom from colonialism could be achieved only when they incorporated the tolerant, progressive, and modern French left-wing democracy and socialism into their own culture, while at the same time facing the reality that it is deeply imbued with the spirit of colonialism (Chafer and Sakur 1999: 4).

Le Travail group

The Indochina police identified a group of indigenous communists as the leaders of the general strike movement in Hanoi that began in the winter of 1936, based on the newspaper *Le Travail. Le Travail* group was a political organization disguised as a newspaper company under the guidance of the Tonkin

24 Guernut, 33, ANOM, France.

Local Committee and was regarded by the police as a 'legal division' of the ICP (Tô 1998: 532).[25] The Saigon-based ICP Central Executive Committee, together with the Stalinists and Trotskyists (Marangé 2012: 122), developed a party and democratic frontline in July 1936 to strengthen the masses' struggles. They sought to pursue all possibilities, combining legal and illegal activities. The party published a bulletin, *La Lutte*, in Saigon and the newspaper *Le Travail* in Hanoi. While describing the everyday lives of Indochina workers, farmers, and middle-class people in newspapers, it emphasized the need to unite to defend those people's interests, calling for improvements in working conditions and labour union freedom (*Le Travail*, 16 September 1936). *Le Travail* published an article about raising class consciousness and a concrete method for striking (*Le Travail*, 27 November 1936), playing a vital role in realizing the general strike movement (Okada 2015: 278).

The Tonkin and Hanoi police monitored the *Le Travail* group and closely observed general strikes. According to police records, there were 41 general strikes and demonstrations in Hanoi between October 1936 and July 1937.[26] More than 6,000 workers participated in the movement; however, only a few were arrested. Police repression was reserved for crimes such as violations, assaults, bribes, discouraging participants, and dismantling demonstrations. Thus, even though the Indochina colonial state did not recognize the right to strike, the general strikes had a 'semi-legal' status.

However, the *Le Travail* group activities were considered to be politically dangerous. The special police gathered details from their informer on *Le Travail* members connected with

25 The main members were Võ Nguyên Giáp, Trần Huy Liệu, Đặng Thái Mai, Trần Đìmh Long, and so on. RST, NF, 2960, ANOM, France.

26 RST, NF, 2960, ANOM, France.

the ICP, the 'Return from Russia', and indigenous communists and when, where, and with whom they met. Information about meetings of the thirteen key members of the *Le Travail* group on 29 November 1936, was sent in a secret report to all involved in the investigation on 3 December.[27] The police initiated legal proceedings to get a search warrant from a magistrate, raided the houses and offices of these thirteen people and their collaborators, and interrogated some of them.[28] The police confirmed that the *Le Travail* group included several former political prisoners who had been released by the Popular Front, and reported having seized VNQDĐ's founding plans and Marxist-Leninist documents as circumstantial evidence of guilt in their house searches. However, they did not have sufficient evidence to make any arrests. The Popular Front's position of legal procedures and human rights somehow restrained the security forces. The election of the French Popular Front Government played a role in keeping with their (communist) expectations.

Finally, the Indochina police banned the publication of *Le Travail* and arrested both the owner, Trịnh Văn Phú, and the editor-in-chief, Nguỹn Văn Tiên (16 April 1937). In Saigon, the main members of the *La Lutte* group were also arrested,[29] but the ban was suspended until September. It is thought that Tonkin and Cochinchina police were working together. In all cases, the charge for arrest was 'a crime of destructive and violent design over the freedom of the press and publication'. In short, the Indochina police were concerned that dangerous political and social movements had occurred and regarded the newspaper *Le*

27 RST, NF, 2960, ANOM, France.

28 ICP members, such as Trần Huy Liệu, were interrogated.

29 The punishment included three years in prison for Nguyễn An Ninh (patriot), two years for Nguyễn Văn Tạo (stalinist), and two years for Tạ Thu Thâu (trotskyist).

Travail itself as a 'dangerous incitement' that threatened public order and 'anti-France activity'.

The French Communist Party newspaper's response to the Indochina police and prosecutors' arrest of key members of Saigon's *La Lutte* group was: 'Unfair Arrest, House Search' and 'Torture Again'. In the home country, prominent intellectuals and politicians sent letters of protest to the colonial ministers.[30] In response to the arrest of the owner and editor-in-chief of *Le Travail* in Hanoi, members of the *Le Travail* movement sought intervention by the Socialist Party of France. For over a year, they gathered signatures from journalists' associations, workers, small-scale merchants, feminists, and students, and successfully petitioned for the parole of the two men.[31] Did public opinion compromise the colonial police power? On the one hand French colonialism had to preserve the systems for collaborating with local people for self-government, but on the other hand, during this period, Indochina colonial states cautiously exercised 'special powers' outside of the modern civilian judicial system based on the segregation of powers (Fourniau and Morlat 2015: 112), as exemplified in the following case.

Police's political intervention

The owner of the *Le Travail* newspaper company was a merchant named Trịnh Văn Phú, who ran a furniture store in Hanoi. His name appeared in police records and in an interrogation report by Tonkin's Special Police on 1 July 1930.[32] Laneque oversaw the interrogation. According to the report, Trịnh Văn Phú, born in

30 *L'Umanité*, August 20, 1937. INF (Indochine Nouveau Fonds), 330/2670, ANOM, France. For example, Francis Jourdain (painter), Romain Rolland (writer), and Andrée Viollis (journalist).

31 RST, NF, 4867, ANOM, France.

32 RST, NF, 6771, ANOM, France.

1906, inherited the business from his father, who operated as a lumber dealer at No.13 Rodony Street, Hanoi's Old Town. He was issued identification number T-32806 in 1924. He travelled to France at the age of 19 at the recommendation of a friend where he studied for several years at the *Lycée Mignet* in Aix-en-Provence in the south of France, the *Lycée Henri IV* school in Paris, and then Sorbonne University. According to the report, he often met a colleague in Paris and argued with him as he read the Communist Party newspaper *L'Humanité*. Nonetheless, he said that he was not a communist. He was arrested near the exit of the *Père Lachaise* Cemetery in Paris, where Indochinese students and workers gathered to protest the convictions of the 1930 Yên Bái mutiny participants. After being deported to Tonkin, he was not involved in any political activities, but was warned that even a minor political incitement attempt would result in his arrest and referral to court.

His name then reappeared in police records during the 1936 general strike movement. Deeply involved in the organization of the general strike as a significant member of the *Le Travail* group, he invited a worker representative to the *Le Travail* office to guide them through the strike method. Moreover, he met with both labour and management representatives and travelled to the city of Hanoi to negotiate arrangements.[33] However, in Indochina, these activities were illegal; Trịnh Văn Phú was openly engaging in the kind of 'political instigation' that Laneque had warned against.

Which raises the question: why was his behaviour tolerated by the authorities? Since World War I (or earlier), the Indochina colonial state sought colonial autonomy. Whether in an advisory

33 He was involved in the strike negotiations among the embroiderers, acupuncturists, barbers, and Renault employees in January 1937. RST, NF, 2960, ANOM, France.

body or a limited election, if there was a system in which the will of the people determined the local members, it was one of the ideal forms of autonomy for locals. It gave them hope. And the Popular Front government was unwilling to exclude anyone who could achieve autonomy for the colony, even if they were communists. Trịnh Văn Phú was one of the candidates for the Chambers of Tonkin People's Representatives at the election on 17 January 1937.[34] If elected, he could then publicly comment on the state of the political system in Hanoi City, the Tonkin region, and Indochina as a whole, as well as advise on how to correct social problems.[35] The dual purpose of the *Le Travail* group was to organize the general strike movement and to increase Trịnh Văn Phú's public support base. This was a semi-legal action conceived by the 'indigenous communists'.

The Indochina police found it difficult to arrest him because he was representing Hanoi.[36] The *Le Travail* group gathered approximately 400 volunteer election staff members (especially students and women), divided them into eight groups and allowed them to develop campaigns.[37] Trịnh Văn Phú was advertised not as a communist candidate but as 'a youth representative', 'a person familiar with European culture and having a fair attitude'. All sales tax-payers had the right to vote and many were in commerce and industry with small stores in the

34 There were two candidates: Trịnh Văn Phú and Trần Việt Bình. The election was in the merchant quota rather than the general candidate quota. The election became Ballottage (no candidate received the required number of votes in the first round), and the second round was held on 24 January. Of the 1073 valid votes, the former received 578 and the latter 499. The Chambers of Tonkin People's Representatives, founded in 1926, discussed, among other things, the revenue and expenditure of the local budget. approximately ninety local people were elected as members in twenty-one constituencies (provinces and cities) in Tonkin.

35 RST, NF, 409, ANOM, France.

36 Laneque did, however, closely monitor his activities via the informer 'DUCE'.

37 RST, NF, 4382, ANOM, France.

city.[38] According to a confidential police report, Trịnh Văn Phú's election staff were instructed to contact as many people as possible, round up the electors, and ask them to mark the ballot as 'Phú' in exchange for a 'fee'.

Having witnessed such a 'semi-legal' election campaign, Tonkin Executive Secretary Tholance was afraid the *Le Travail* group might win. He questioned the appropriateness of the candidate, saying the poster by Trịnh Văn Phú 'may have undermined the prestige of the French authorities in Indochina',[39] and reported to the Attorney General that the expression in the poster, 'The local people of the protectorate are obliged to be subjected to the regime of gag, the politics of terror, decadence, and public deception' is problematic. Moreover, he announced on 15 January, two days before the first round of voting, a ban on an election rally scheduled to be held at Trịnh Văn Phú's home.

This election demonstrated how the Indochina colonial state used repressive devices. Before the second election, Trịnh Văn Phú sent a telegram to the public prosecutor's office that read, 'There has been police interference in the election.' According to Phú, police agents ordered the *phố trưởng* of To Tick Street and Éventail Street to gather the ballots from several electors with the help of the Mayor of Hanoi.[40] In response, the police explained that they 'did not participate in any campaign, and the administration only intervened in order to ensure the strictest neutrality'. However, the truth of the matter is unclear; if there had been police or government intervention, it would not have been made public.

38 A total of 2,376 people were registered in the electoral roster, of which approximately 2,000 were business taxpayers (*petite patentés*) who ran small stores, such as tailors and launders.

39 RST, NF, 4382, ANOM, France.

40 RST, NF, 4382, ANOM, France.

Referring to the police intervention, Trịnh Văn Phú pointedly accused the *phố trưởng*, of collecting the ballots in response to the police order. Despite being a public agent of the colonial administration, he might have felt that the *phố trưởng* did not fully understand the basic rules of democracy. Trịnh Văn Phú was saying the administrative system that the Indochina colonial state had developed based on the ideas of autonomy, association, and collaboration was defective. This comment is, by extension, a harsh critique of French colonialism, which did not recognize Indochinese workers' right to strike because of their 'insufficient education level'. The Indochina colonial state of the 1930s was uncertain about its degrees of autonomy, and repression could only be exercised within certain limits. As a mature society, the Indochina colonial state was acutely aware that violent repression by special authorities would be openly criticized.

However, this criticism would not arise unless a crisis caused the collapse of the colonial state. The Indochina Police cleverly exercised their repressive functions. They silently watched Trịnh Văn Phú, overseeing the balloting process from beginning to end and confirming his winnings in the second poll on 24 January 1937. They then arrested him after taking the time to gather sufficient evidence. In doing so, they tried to maintain, in Saada's word, the 'dignity', 'prestige', and 'domination' of the colonial state of Indochina (Saada 2002).

On the eve of World War II, along with the collapse of the French Popular Front government, almost all communist groups and worker associations disbanded in Indochina. The main objective of the Indochina police since 1931 had seemingly been fulfilled.[41] Many 'indigenous communists' left the colonial

41 The Namky insurrection, led by the ICP, which occurred in Cochinchina in November-December 1940, was also quickly suppressed. According to

state of Indochina. Having relocated overseas, they had to wait until August 1945 to revisit their homeland after the arrival of Japanese troops and a coup d'état when the Indochina police and their repressive devices collapsed.

Conclusion

In the mid-1930s, the Indochina colonial state did not have a powerful police state. The French republican belief in liberty, equality, and fraternity meant that the ideal of achieving colonial autonomy was inescapable.

During the global Great Depression, Indochina suffered a recession and the labour class insisted on the same rights as workers in metropolitan France. The Popular Front government which took office in 1936, did not recognize the right to strike in Indochina, but it allowed workers' 'semi-legal' political and social movements. France found itself reconsidering the colonial state, but unwilling to allow any party (right or left) to destroy it. Under these circumstances, French colonial administration in the twentieth century was sensitive to subtle adjustments to its carrot-and-stick approach.

Tools of repression, however, are more difficult to fine-tune. The Indochina colonial state integrated the Central Service of Information and General Security and Political Affairs Directorate in 1922. This created an administrative agency to deal with both state security and public order simultaneously. The experiences

---

Chonchirdsin, after the Nam Ky insurrection had broken out the French authorities reviewed the situation and at least two reports were produced on the causes of uprising. Both reached the same conclusion – that the main cause of the insurrection was the lenient policy of the metropolitan and colonial governments during the Popular Front period in France. (Chonchirdsin 1997: 291)

of 1930–31 significantly influenced how the Indochina colonial state employed repressive techniques.

The Indochina police focused almost exclusively on the communist threat in the 1930s. International and indigenous communists worked together to evade police surveillance. The special police sought to identify dangerous persons through interrogations and informer reports, achieving significant results.

However, Indochina's systems of repression remained imperfect. As long as there were collaborators in villages and cities, the struggle between the police and communists was a cat-and-mouse game. As noted in the introduction to this book, some of those subjected to surveillance and control 'knew' that they were being 'monitored' by the colonial state and acted on the assumption that they were being watched. The police moved responsibility for monitoring 'outsiders' from the *lý trưởng* and *phố trưởng* to more loyal public agents, and the communists shifted their struggle to the legal and political arena following the launch of the Popular Front government. Despite obtaining a secret ICP document ordering the regional commission to 'organize a national strike movement', the police could not prevent the strike in Hanoi due to concerns about political sensitivities.

Trịnh Văn Phú's accusation of the police's political intervention in the Chambers of Tonkin People's Representatives election suggests the Indochina colonial state attempted to exclude communists from colonial political power. In 1936–37, the Indochina colonial state's repressive devices differed from previous questioning and surveillance strategies used in information gathering. The arrest, based on 'the crime of destructive and violent design over the freedom of the press and publication', was evidence of the police's violent additional functions. After all, as in 1931, eliminating the threat of communism was the best way to end the cat-and-mouse game decisively, and the police in Indochina had long searched for a way to resolve this issue.

References

Berlière, Jean-Marc (1996), *Le monde des polices en France, XIX*[e] *– XXe siècle*, Bruxelles: Complexe.

Bezançon, Pascale (2002), *Une colonisation éducatrice? L'expérience indochinoise (1860-1945)*, Paris: L'Harmattan.

Brocheux, Pierre and Hémery, Daniel (2001), *Indochine. La colonisation ambiguë, 1858–1954*, Paris: La Découverte.

Chafer, Tony and Sackur, Ammanda (eds.) (1999), *French Colonial Empire and the Popular Front. Hope and Disillusion*, New York: St. Martin's Press.

Chonchirdsin, Sud (1997), 'The Indochinese Communist Party and the Nam Ky uprising in Cochin China, November–December 1940', *South East Asia Research*, 5(3): 269–293.

Courtin, Nicolas (2012), 'La garde indigène à Madagascar. Une police pour la «splendeur» de l'État colonial (1896–1914),' in Jean-Pierre Bat and Nicolas Courtin (eds.), *Maintenir l'ordre colonial. Afrique et Madagascar, 19–20 siècles*, Rennes: Presses universitaires de Rennes.

Duiker, William J. (1976), *The Rise of Nationalism in Vietnam*, 1900–1941. Ithaca and London: Cornell University Press.

Faivre, Jean-Paul (2023), *Policiers et polices dans l'Indochine française 1864–1955*, Bordeaux: Memoring Editions.

Fourniau, Charles and Morlat, Patrice (2015), 'Mouvement national et appareils répressifs en Indochine (1885–1930),' in Chanson-Jabeur, Chantal, Forest, Alain, and Morlat, Patrice (eds.), *Colonisations et Répressions*, Paris: Indes savantes.

Goscha, Christopher E. (1999), *Thailand and the Southeast Asian Networks of the Vietnamese Revolution, 1885–1954*, London and New York: Routledge.

Gouvernement général de l'Indochine (1905), *Ville de Hanoi (Tonkin), Historique, développement financier, réglementation administrative, et fonctionnement des deivers servives municipaux de la Ville de Hanoi,* Hanoi: Imprimerie Taupin & Cie.

Gouvernement général de l'Indochine (1937), *Annuaire administratif de l'Indochine 1936*, Hanoi: Imprimerie d'Extrême-Orient.

Gouvernement général de l'Indochine (1938), *Annuaire administratif de l'Indochine 1937*, Hanoi: Imprimerie d'Extrême-Orient.

Hammer, Ellen J. (1955), *The Struggle for Indochina 1940–1955. Viet Nam and the French Experience*, Stanford, California: Stanford University Press.

Hémery, Daniel (1975), *Révolutionnaires vietnamiens et pouvoirs colonial en Indochine*, Paris: François Maspero.

Joyeux, B. (1930), *Le péril vénérien et la prostitution à Hanoi*, Hanoi: Imprimerie d'Extrême-Orient.

Kurihara, Hirohide (2005), *Comintern system to Indochina kyōsantō* (Indochinese Communist Party in the comintern system), Tokyo: Tokyo University Press.

Marangé, Céline (2012), *Le communisme vietnamien (1919–1991): Construction d'un État-nation entre Moscout et Pékin*, Paris: SciencesPo.

Morlat, Patrice (1990), *La repression colonialeau Vietnam (1908–1940)*, Paris: L'Harmattan.

Morlat, Patrice (2006), *Indochine-Années vingt, le rendez-vous manqué*, Paris: Indes savantes.

Okada, Tomokazu (2010), 'France shokuminchi teikoku ni okeru gentijin kanri seido – Indochina wo jirei ni (The French colonial empire's native civil service system: The case of Indochina)', *Shigaku-Zasshi* (Journal of historical science), 119 (6): 1–34.

Okada, Tomokazu (2015), '1936-37nen Hanoi ni okeru rōdōsha storaiki undō (The labour strike movement in Hanoi 1936–37)', *Tōnan Asia Kenkyū* (Southeast Asian Studies), 52(2): 267-94.

Saada, Emmanuelle (2002), 'The Empire of Law: Dignity, Prestige, and Domination in the "Colonial Situation"', in *French Politics, Culture & Society*, Summer, 20(2).

Sarraut, Albert (1923), *La mise en valeur des colonies françaises*, Paris: Payot.

Tô Huy Rứa and Học Viện Chính Trị Quốc Gia Hồ Chi Minh (eds.) (1998), *Thư tịc báo chi Việt Nam* (Vietnamese press documents), Hanoi: Nhà xuất bản giáo dục Việt Nam.

Trinh, Van Thao (1995), *L'école française en Indochine*, Paris: Karthala.

Trinh, Van Thao (2004), *Les compagnons de route de Hô Chi Minh, Histoire d'un engagement intellectuel au Viêt-Nam*, Paris: Karthala.

William, H. Frederick (1973), 'Alexandre Varenne and politics in Indochina 1925, in Vella, Walter F (ed.), *Aspects of Vietnamese history*, Honolulu: University of Hawaii.

Chapter 5

In Search of 'Invisible' Targets: Policing and Surveillance in Colonial Singapore in the late 19th and early 20th centuries

Takeshi Onimaru

Introduction

Southeast Asia experienced political, economic, social, and demographic changes from the mid-nineteenth to the early twentieth centuries. The primary driver of these changes was the expansion of Western colonial empires. Except for Siam, most of Southeast Asia was divided by Dutch, British, French, and Spanish (later American) powers, each of which began to build colonial states, implement law and order, and pursue economic profit from trade, plantations, and mining. In pursuit of rapid economic development in the colonies, colonial rulers encouraged mass labour migration, mainly from East and South Asia. Migrants brought their own cultures, customs, languages, religions, and sometimes diseases; so, as the population in Southeast Asia rapidly increased, ethnically, linguistically, culturally, and religiously diverse societies were formed. Singapore was one such colony of rapid population growth in which both the colonisers and migrants created distinctive political, economic, and social arenas.

When Singapore was established by Sir Stanford Raffles in 1819, it was a relatively unpopulated frontier. The total population of Singapore was around 1,000 in 1819 (Gillis 2005: 15), but the population grew rapidly, reaching more than 10,000

Table 5.1: The population in Singapore in the 19th century

Year	Total	Chinese	Ratio of Chinese
1824	10,683	3,317	31.0%
1834	26,329	10,767	40.8%
1849	52,891	27,988	52.9%
1860	81,734	50,043	61.2%
1871	97,111	54,572	56.1%
1881	139,208	86,766	62.3%
1891	141,300	100,446	71.0%

Source: Makepeace et al. (1991: 355–359)

Table 5.2: The trade of Singapore, 1824–1938 ($ million)

Year	Imports	Exports	Total
1824	6.6	5.0	11.6
1833	9.1	7.6	16.7
1843	13.1	11.5	24.6
1853	15.5	13.4	28.9
1863	29.8	25.7	55.5
1873	47.9	41.8	89.7
1883	79.2	68.2	147.4
1893	124.0	108.5	232.5
1903	299.3	257.7	557.0
1913	349.7	272.4	622.1
1923	573.0	402.7	975.7
1933	261.7	251.1	512.8
1938	369.6	320.2	689.9

Source: Wong (1991: 51)

five years later (see Table 5.1). By 1827, the ethnic majority in colonial Singapore was Chinese immigrants from mainland China. The number of Chinese immigrants increased in Southeast Asia and worldwide after 1860 when the Treaty of Beijing liberalised Chinese emigration from mainland China, which

Table 5.3: Direction of the trade of Singapore, 1825–1937 (percentage of total trade)

Year	The West	East Asia	Southeast Asia	Australasia	India	Others
1825	18	14	48	–	20	0
1835	19	14	46	–	20	1
1845	22	22	34	–	21	1
1855	25	18	40	–	14	2
1865	25	15	43	–	15	2
1875	26	10	52	–	11	1
1885	30	13	51	–	5	1
1895	25	15	52	–	6	1
1905	26	11	56	–	7	1
1915	29	9	56	–	4	3
1925	34	6	53	2	3	2
1935	37	14	39	5	3	3
1937	40	12	37	4	3	5

Source: Wong (1991: 50)

the Qing government had formerly prohibited. The colonial government of the Straits Settlements also had been promoting Chinese immigration as a labour force, and the number of Chinese immigrants had been increasing both in British Malaya, including Singapore, and all over Southeast Asia through Singapore (Shiraishi 2021: 54–55; Turnbull 1989: 36; Yong 1994: 2).

Singapore was established specifically to be the centre of British commerce in Southeast Asia and was declared a 'free port' where no customs duties were imposed on imports and exports. With this free trade policy and its prime geographical location at the southern tip of the Malay Peninsula and the south-eastern gate of Malacca Strait, Singapore became a major hub of intra-Southeast Asian trade from the 1820s (Kobayashi 2013) (see Table 5.2, 5.3).

To ensure Singapore's success as a regional trading centre, maintaining domestic order was one of the highest priorities of the colonial government. René Onraet, who served as director of the Criminal Intelligence Department and then Commissioner of Police in the Straits Settlements in the 1920s and 30s, described the main threats to British Malaya in his memoir as follows:

> From the very outset, subversive activities in Malaya were due to outside influences. There was no irritant within Malaya to give rise to such a reaction. There was no organisation within Malaya which was capable of producing such clever, political propaganda. All of it came from China. (Onraet 1947: 109)

For Onraet, all the troubles in Malaya came from China, reflecting the social, criminal, and demographic composition of the Straits Settlements, especially Singapore. More than half of Singapore's population was immigrant Chinese from the mid-nineteenth century onward, and thus, the majority of law-and-order issues in Singapore were crimes and disputes involving the Chinese. In the nineteenth century, the greatest threats to social order were massive riots and violent clashes between Chinese 'secret societies', while, in the early twentieth century, the primary threat was perceived to be underground communist activities.

The so-called 'secret societies' were social organisations from mainland China that immigrants recreated in Singapore. In fact, for the Chinese, there was nothing secret about these types of institutions, which played important roles in the Chinese communities of Singapore from the 1820s (Yen 1976: 12–13). But for British colonial rulers, who initially had no knowledge of Chinese languages, cultures or institutions, they looked like 'secret societies', and with no understanding of the causes of the frequent riots and disputes among these organisations, they were perceived to pose the most serious threats to colonial order in the nineteenth century.

Political movements in colonial Singapore emerged in the late nineteenth century and flourished, especially during and after World War I. Nationalist movements, both Chinese and Indian, communist movements, pan-Islamic movements, and anti-colonialism were all viewed as threats to the British colonial order in Singapore. Among these, the communist movement was considered to be the most dangerous in the 1920s and 30s after it organised a series of strikes and anti-colonial propaganda. The many regional and international links with communist organisations in neighbouring colonies and the Third International (the Comintern), and especially the communist uprising in the Dutch East Indies in 1926, all added to the authorities' concerns about communism in Singapore. Suppressing strikes and preventing a 'revolution' were necessary for maintaining law and order in colonial Singapore.

In dealing with these two threats, the Chinese secret societies in the nineteenth century and the communist movement in the early twentieth century, surveillance was crucial because both were 'invisible' to the British colonial rulers. However, their 'invisibility' differed. The Chinese secret societies were invisible because of the colonisers' ignorance of Chinese languages, cultures, and social customs, while the communists were invisible to the extent they succeeded in keeping their activities 'underground'. To some extent, their invisibility was enhanced by the fact that no one could identify who was a communist based on outward appearances. In both cases, the first step towards reducing these invisible targets was to identify them through surveillance measures; control and suppression measures followed based on information gathered through surveillance.

This chapter explores how the colonial government in Singapore policed Chinese secret societies in the nineteenth century and communist activities in the early twentieth century by developing its surveillance capabilities. Surveillance of the secret societies was conducted by the Chinese Protectorate and the colonial police forces, while surveillance of communist activities was primarily by the political police. The importance of secret societies and communist movements for British colonial rule in Singapore can be seen in their centrality to the study of Singapore's colonial history. The Chinese secret societies and their suppression has been studied by Pickering ([1867] 2000), Blythe (1969), Shiraishi (1975), Mak (1981), Yen (1986), Trocki (1990), and Lee (1991). The history and suppression of communist movements have been examined by Onraet (1947), Cheah (1992), Akashi (1994), Yong (1994, 1997a, 1997b), Hara (2009, 2017), Ban (2001), and Belogurova (2019). In all these studies, policing secret societies and communist movements have been treated separately. However, there was significant continuity between the measures taken against Chinese secret societies in the late nineteenth century and those against communist movements in the early twentieth century. Indeed, measures established to control and suppress Chinese secret societies in the late nineteenth century were applied to communist movements in the early twentieth century. This chapter reveals the continuity of measures taken by the colonial government in Singapore to monitor and control secret societies and communist movements, and the effectiveness and limits of these measures by comparing the methods deployed against the secret societies and the communist movements, based on a synthesis of previous studies and a fresh analysis of political police reports in British Malaya.

The development of the colonial police force in Singapore

The colonial police force in Singapore was established in 1820, less than a year after the establishment of Singapore itself. Francis Bernard was appointed to be the first Superintendent of police. Under his command, initially, was one constable, one jailer, one Malay writer, one Indian sailor (*tindal*), and eight peons (Turnbull 1989: 16).

From these modest beginnings, the colonial police in Singapore developed rapidly throughout the nineteenth century. It comprised 133 staff in 1843, 385 in 1865, and about 550 in the 1870s. The Inspector General of Police was established in 1871 when the police forces in Singapore, Malacca, and Penang were united. The Inspector General of Police was located in Singapore, and police superintendents were stationed in Malacca and Penang. Europeans dominated all the higher ranks, from police inspectors to inspector general, but Malays and Indians, mostly Tamils, occupied many of the lower ranks (Lee 1991: 53–54).

In 1871, when the police forces in the Straits Settlements were combined, the Police Force Ordinance[1] was enacted, officially defining the duties of the police forces as follows:

1. Preserving the public peace.
2. Preventing and detecting crimes and offence.
3. Apprehending, and causing to be apprehended, persons who shall have committed, or shall be charged with or suspected of having committed, or being about to commit, any crime or offence.
4. Regulating processions and assemblies in public places.

1 This ordinance, with slight amendments, was enforced until 1942.

5. Regulating the traffic upon public thoroughfares, and removing obstructions therefrom.

6. Preserving order and decorum in public places, and places of public resort, at public meetings, and in assemblies for public amusements; for which purpose Officers and Constables of Police, when on duty, shall have free admission to all places, meetings, and assemblies while open to any of the public.

7. Assisting in carrying out the Revenue, Excise, Sanitary, Conservancy, and Quarantine Laws.

8. Assisting in preserving order in the different ports and harbours in the Colony, and in enforcing the Port Regulations therein.

9. Executing summonses, subpoenas, warrants, commitments, and other process issued by the several Magistrates and Justices of the Peace on complaints or proceedings before them.

10. Exhibiting informations and conducting prosecutions for crimes and offences.

11. The protection of unclaimed and lost property, and the finding the owners thereof.

12. Taking charge of and impounding stray animals.

13. Inspecting weights and measures, for which purpose standard weights and measures shall be kept at each Chief Police Station.

14. Assisting in the protection of life and property at fires.

15. Protecting public property from loss or injury.

16. Attending the Criminal Courts and keeping order therein.

17. Escorting and guarding prisoners when being conveyed between the several Settlements, and to and from and at prisons and places of detention, and to and from, and at the places appointed for labour of prisoners.

(Morrah 1968: 40–41)

This Ordinance clearly stipulated that the police force would conduct not only judicial and administrative tasks but also surveillance of crimes and criminal suspects.

In 1881, a police training school was established, and a detective force was formed in 1884. Retired Sikh and European military officers were recruited as inspectors and constables after 1881, and in 1904, a cadet system was introduced to recruit young men in Britain to be colonial police officers and give them specialist training (Turnbull 1989: 88).

The colonial police force in Singapore developed throughout the nineteenth century and was charged with maintaining domestic order in the colony. According to Edwin Lee, policemen were unable to do so for a long time because their salaries were so poor and their duties were so difficult and dangerous that they quit quickly at the first chance (Lee 1991: 53). The most difficult and dangerous of their duties was policing riots, strikes, and bloody disputes among Chinese 'secret societies'.

The role of Chinese 'secret societies' in colonial Singapore

The history of 'secret societies' in Singapore dates back to the early nineteenth century, almost immediately after the establishment of Singapore. In 1824, these organisations already existed, and by the early 1840s, they had about 6,000 members (Gillis 2005: 24; Lee 1991: 25). William A. Pickering, who served as the first Protector of Chinese in Singapore in 1877, claimed that more than 60% of the Chinese population belonged to secret societies in 1867 (Pickering [1867] 2000: 311). Thus, secret societies were deeply rooted in Chinese communities in colonial Singapore, but what roles did they play, and how important were they for the Chinese?

Chinese immigrant workers were essential for the commercial development of Singapore. The proportion of Chinese to the total population in Singapore had been increasing throughout the nineteenth century, and the incessant influx of workers made Singapore a frontier city. Chinese migrants played important roles in colonial Singapore as dock workers, hawkers, rickshaw pullers, and plantation workers. Most were young and poor males who had never been to Singapore and came alone by contract. When they arrived in Singapore, they relied on Chinese organizations called *kongsi* (公司) or *hoey* (会) to find jobs, for mutual aid, and for protection (Shiraishi 1975: 82; Lee 1991: 26–27).

These *kongsi* and *hoey* played another important role in Chinese communities in colonial Singapore: protecting the economic interests of Chinese elites. Chinese societies in Singapore were divided into five topolect groups: Canton (広東), Hokkien (福建), Teochew (潮州), Hakka (客家), and Hainan (海南). Chinese business activities clustered around these topolect groups. For example, commerce was dominated by Hokkien and inland plantations were dominated by Teochew. Chinese business elites, called *Taukeh* (頭家), utilized *kongsi* and *hoey* for recruiting and controlling Chinese immigrant workers, and when their interests were threatened, *kongsi* and *hoey* were mobilised, fighting and killing each other to protect their topolects' economic interests (Blythe 1969: 2; Lee 1991: 27–28; Mak 1981: 41–43, 45, 49; Shiraishi 1975: 78–80).

Because of these disputes and riots, *kongsi* and *hoey* were regarded as 'violent' and 'criminal' organisations and referred to as 'secret societies' by the colonial government. However, the quite simple reason they were considered to be 'secret societies' was that there were almost no government officials who could understand Chinese languages until the 1870s. *Kongsi* and *hoey* were organisations bound by ritual and oath, and, for those who could not understand their rituals and practices because of a language barrier, these organisations appeared to be 'conspiratorial'.

Before they were outlawed in 1890, the colonial authorities made several attempts to regulate and control secret societies in Singapore. For example, in 1843, responding to public pressure, the colonial government drafted a bill to regulate the activities of secret societies, but it was not enacted. In 1854, the colonial government drafted a bill based on practices in Hong Kong to register the residents and secret societies, to empower the governor to deport unfavourable persons from the colony, and to recruit Chinese officers to maintain order in the districts. But again, it was not enacted. In each case, it was assumed that the problems caused by secret societies and immigrant Chinese could be solved by enlarging and improving the police force[2] (Blythe 1969: 2, 63–67, 80–82).

The police force was expected to suppress and control secret societies, but it was difficult for the police to accomplish these tasks. The most crucial barrier to policing the secret societies was that no police officers understood Chinese languages. The colonial government had not recruited Chinese for the police force due to concerns about secret society members infiltrating the police (Lee 1991: 35). But even though the government did not recruit Chinese, secret societies had influence over the police. For example, several police officers were fired because of

2 Jarman, Robert L. (ed.) (1998), *Annual Reports of the Straits Settlements, 1855–1941. (ARSS)* Vol. 1 (1855–1867), Archive Edition, p. 77.

their memberships of secret societies in the early 1860s.[3] Secret societies harboured suspects and criminals, and witnesses gave false testimonies out of fear of retaliation by the secret societies. During the period when there were no government officials who could understand Chinese languages, investigations relied on Chinese translators, who were frequently members of the secret societies (Blythe 1969: 2–3).

As membership in secret societies was not illegal, it was almost impossible for the police to control them. However, when their frequent disputes turned violent or spilt over into public riots, the colonial government had to ask for help from military forces or Chinese leaders to restore law and order. For example, in May 1854, a riot between Hokkien and Teochew Chinese broke out. On the first day of the dispute, Thomas Dunman, the Inspector General of Police, declared that the police could not control the situation and asked the military for help. The riot lasted more than 10 days, about 400 people were killed, and 300 houses were destroyed. Almost 500 people were arrested, and six men were sentenced to death (Lee 1991: 35–37). In another example, when a series of riots broke out in 1862–63, the government appointed the leaders of secret societies as Special Constables and asked for their cooperation in restoring order.[4]

Thus, riots, disputes, and crimes by secret societies were major disruptors of domestic order in Singapore, but the colonial government in Singapore did not introduce effective controlling measures against them until the late 1860s. This indicates that the colonial government in Singapore did not have a strong enough will to control the Chinese communities and let the communities govern themselves. The colonial government, for the most part, relied on Chinese business elites, *Taukeh*, to

---

3 Ibid., Vol. 1, p. 464.

4 Ibid., Vol. 1, p. 392.

maintain order in their own communities and societies. The *Taukeh*, in turn, were happy to oblige and employed the *kongsi* and *hoey* as highly effective tools for that purpose (Yen 1976: 16; Yong 2002: 86–89). Such 'outsourcing' of government functions and authority was common in colonial Southeast Asia.

Since Singapore was a 'free port', the colonial government could not raise revenue from trade and commerce, the most lucrative businesses in Singapore. Hence, to finance the colonial state, it needed to find stable and profitable revenue sources. It tried promoting the cultivation of commodity crops such as nutmeg, clove, and pepper, but the weather and soil in Singapore were unsuitable for most commercial crops. The Chinese did, however, find a way to cultivate pepper on the gambier plantations in the jungle of Singapore (Wong 1991: 52–53). When the colonial government tried to collect taxes from these inland plantations, or more precisely, from the Chinese workers there, the revenue farms were the major means.

A revenue farm was a system to outsource the collection of taxes from commodities consumption or business operations. Licenses to manage revenue farms were typically auctioned at regular intervals, with the highest bidder receiving the license and becoming a 'revenue farmer'. The revenue farming system was common in Southeast Asia in the nineteenth and early twentieth centuries (Butcher and Dick 1993).

The revenue farming system was introduced in Singapore in 1820. Opium, liquor and spirits, and gambling farms were initially implemented, but gambling farms, the most lucrative source of revenue at the time, was abolished in 1823 for moral reasons (Turnbull 1989: 15, 23). Subsequently, the opium farms contributed the largest proportion of revenue in Singapore. Throughout the nineteenth century, on average, more than 40% of total revenue was from opium, and sometimes more than half (see Table 5.4).

Table 5.4: Revenue in 19th century Singapore (Spanish $)

Year	Opium Farm	Total Revenue	% of Opium Farm
1820–21	7,345	15,925	46.1
1830–31	39,240	96,331	40.7
1840–41	65,000	142,900	45.5
1849–50	87,567	172,375	50.8
1860–61	266,751	492,853	54.1
1870	360,600	875,690	41.1
1880	600,000	1,277,413	47.0
1890	1,296,000	2,327,795	55.7
1899	1,458,000	3,072,528	47.5

Source: Trocki (1990: 96–97, 188)

The opium farms were controlled by Chinese business elites, who relied on secret societies to suppress smuggling and to promote sales. The biggest consumers of opium were the plantation workers, and it is no coincidence that the secret societies controlled both the plantation labour force and the opium supply on the plantations (Trocki 1990: 77; Wong 1991: 54; Yen 1986: 115, 122).

As long as the colonial government outsourced control of the Chinese population in Singapore to Chinese business elites, the secret societies had to be tolerated as a necessary evil that played important roles in maintaining social order and collecting revenue. In other words, the relatively hands-off approach to policing secret societies reflected the outsourcing practices of the early colonial state. However, after jurisdiction over the Straits Settlements moved from the Indian Office to the Colonial Office in 1867, the colonial government in Singapore took a much more hands-on approach to policing the secret societies.

Control and suppression of 'secret societies'

The attempts to control Chinese secret societies by the colonial government in Singapore started in 1867 when the Straits Settlements became a Crown Colony, under the direct control of the Colonial Office. This change of status was undoubtedly a significant factor in the policy shift from tolerance to suppression, but there were two other important factors.

One was the decreasing inland plantation sector in Singapore. In the 1860s, pepper and gambier plantations inland began moving to the Malay peninsula because of soil degradation and the decreasing productivity of cultivated land in Singapore[5] (Wong 1991: 53). At the same time, access to inland Singapore was rapidly improving by roadworks and deforestation, allowing the colonial government to collect a land tax and thereby reduce its dependence on secret societies[6] (Trocki 1990: 149; Wong 1991: 53).

The other was a change in the nature of the secret societies. From around 1870, following the pacification of the Taiping Rebellion, professional fighters and militants, deemed criminals and outlaws by the Qing government, poured into Singapore from mainland China. Called *samseng*, these professional fighters rapidly joined the secret societies, which in turn became even more violent. The Chinese business elites could not control them, and Singapore experienced incessant riots and violent disputes from the early 1870s (Lee 1991: 34–35, 42; Trocki 1990: 159–160).

These factors, becoming a Crown Colony, the change of socio-economic structures, and the increasingly volatile and violent secret societies, triggered the government's change in approach to the secret societies from the late 1860s.

5 Ibid., Vol. 1, p. 36.

6 Ibid., Vol. 2, p. 106.

In 1867, the governor had the authority to deport undesirables under a state of emergency. The threat of deportation proved to be a highly effective measure as it became widely known that some deportees were arrested and executed by Chinese authorities upon their arrival in mainland China (Lee 1991: 57; Turnbull 1989: 88).

In 1869, an ordinance was passed requiring the registration of societies with ten or more members, which would provide the colonial government with important information about the secret societies. Although initially only a temporary ordinance, it was extended before being made permanent in 1872[7] (Blythe 1969: 151–152; Lee 1991: 57–60).

From 1871 to 1873, the colonial government faced incessant riots in Singapore. In March 1871, a riot broke out among secret societies, and in October, Hokkien and Teochew coolies clashed. In October 1872, an anti-government riot broke out, and there were continuous riots between Hokkien and Teochew secret societies from December 1872 till February 1873. All these disputes were excessively violent because of the participation of *samseng*. The police could not contain them and asked for help from the military and the leaders of Chinese communities. The last of these, from December 1872 till February 1873, were the most severe and violent riots since 1854, and a state of emergency was declared which was not lifted until 1885[8] (Blythe 1969: 155–156, 198; Lee 1991: 35–41; Yen 1986: 197).

Under the state of emergency, another riot broke out in 1876 against the colonial government's decision to set up a Chinese sub-post office to control letters and money sent by the Chinese and to earn revenue from them. The riot started on 15 December 1876, when this post office opened, and continued for four days

7 Ibid., Vol. 2, p. 141.

8 Ibid., Vol. 2, p. 137.

until 18 December, when the police arrested the riot organisers and rounded up some of the leaders of secret societies, put them on a boat, and took them out to sea. This isolation was quite effective, and the riot ended that very evening. Several leaders, including those isolated on the boat, were deported from Singapore after the riot (Blythe 1969: 202; Lee 1991: 43–47).

The colonial government tried to control and suppress Chinese secret societies through legal measures such as deportation and registration, and the riots of 1876 served as a barometer for the effectiveness of these measures. It appeared that while the government had found a highly effective means to stop the riots, if it wanted to prevent future riots, it would have to take further steps to suppress the secret societies. It decided to create an institution that would not only oversee Chinese affairs in the colony but would also fulfil the roles hitherto performed by the secret societies. In 1877, the Chinese Protectorate was established for those purposes.

The main duty of the Chinese Protectorate was protecting Chinese immigrant workers. The Chinese Protectorate tried to weaken the power of *kongsi* and *hoey* by providing alternative protections and controls for Chinese immigrant workers, but to do so, it was essential to understand the Chinese languages and to conduct surveillance not only on *kongsi* and *hoey* but also on the Chinese communities. William A. Pickering, the first Protector of Chinese, had the necessary skills and capabilities. He started his official career in Singapore in 1872 when he was hired as a translator after eight years of doing business in China. He was the first government official who could understand the Chinese languages, speaking several Chinese topolects and reading Chinese. He helped the colonial police with Chinese affairs, engaged in surveillance of secret societies and Chinese communities, and published papers about them (Blythe 1969: 157–158; Pickering [1876] 2000; Turnbull 1989: 85).

After his appointment as the Protector of Chinese, Pickering not only worked hard to protect Chinese immigrant workers by making or checking their labour contracts but also maintained surveillance on *kongsi* and *hoey* by registration, updating information, and personal investigations together with Samuel Dunlop, the Inspector General of Police (Blythe 1969: 205, 207; Lee 1991: 71, 99; Turnbull 1989: 85).

If the colonial government wanted to monitor and control Chinese residents in Singapore, it would have to increase the number of government officials who could understand Chinese. From the 1880s, cadets who would be assigned to work in Chinese affairs were dispatched to Amoy (厦門), Swatow (汕頭), and Canton (広州) to learn Hokkien, Teochew, and Cantonese languages (Turnbull 1989: 84).

The final step to illegalisation began in 1887 when Sir Cecil Clementi Smith became the Governor of the Straits Settlements. Smith had begun his career as a colonial officer in Hong Kong in 1862 where he was in charge of Chinese affairs and had implemented strict policies for dealing with the Chinese. After leaving Hong Kong, he was appointed Colonial Secretary of the Straits Settlements from 1878 to 1885, where he set out to introduce much stricter policies concerning secret societies (Holdsworth and Munn 2012: 398–399; Lee 1991: 151).

In 1888, he drafted a bill to outlaw secret societies, but it was opposed by Pickering and Dunlop, who considered that if the societies were immediately dissolved without prior preparation, the government would lose its mechanisms for monitoring Chinese immigrant workers through the society registration scheme. Pickering had also believed that it was necessary to immediately outlaw the secret societies when he became the Chinese Protectorate, but he changed his mind when he learned the essential roles played by the secret societies in the Chinese communities. He came to understand that the secret societies were useful for controlling the Chinese population. Pickering was acquainted with the members of secret societies through surveillance and registration activities and believed he could collaborate with them to maintain law and order. However, the collaboration worked only when the interests of the two sides aligned. When there was a conflict of interests, the secret societies provided no help and even attacked Pickering. Indeed, in 1887, during an investigation of one of the secret societies' gambling dens, Pickering was physically assaulted and seriously injured (Lee 1991: 92–98, 130, 135–138; Shiraishi 1975: 86).

Cecil Smith, however, did not believe that collaboration worked and introduced his bill to illegalise secret societies to the Legislative Council. The bill passed with several amendments and became effective from 1 January 1890 (Blythe 1969: 225–234; Lee 1991: 98–99, 141–150; Turnbull 1989: 88).

At the same time, Smith established a new institution, the Chinese Advisory Board, consisting of 17 Chinese representatives nominated by the Governor and the Chinese Protectorate. The composition of Chinese representatives reflected the Chinese communities: six from Hokkien, five from Teochew, and two each from Canton, Hakka, and Hainan. The Chinese Advisory Board advised the colonial government on issues related to Chinese communities (Lee 1991: 150; Shiraishi 1975: 93).

From 1867, when the Straits Settlement became a Crown Colony, the colonial government in Singapore tried to control and suppress Chinese secret societies by introducing several measures: registration and surveillance by the Chinese Protectorate, increasing the number of personnel who could manage Chinese languages, providing alternative protections for Chinese immigrant workers, strengthening the police force and legal measures, and deporting arrested secret society leaders and members. Among these measures, surveillance and deportation were the most effective for controlling secret societies. Secret societies were finally outlawed in 1890, and the frequent mass riots and disputes between them came to an end (Turnbull 1989: 88).

The colonial government in Singapore still needed the help of Chinese elites to control the Chinese communities; the Chinese Advisory Board was a step towards controlling the Chinese communities by law, not by secret societies (Shiraishi 1975: 93), formalising the collaboration between the colonial government and the Chinese elites. The opium farms continued in operation until they transferred to the Government monopoly in 1910. However, the secret societies did not disappear after they were outlawed; they just went underground (Yen 1976: 14). And that means that despite the colonial government's strenuous efforts to overcome the linguistic, cultural, and social barriers that had initially rendered them 'invisible', they were once again 'invisible' to the colonial government, albeit in a different way. We can think the secret societies might be seen as analogous to 'chronic diseases' deeply embedded in Singapore's Chinese communities. It may have been impossible for the government to completely 'cure' this disease, but it needed to be contained and prevented from becoming fatal. For prevention, the colonial government needed to deploy effective surveillance of the underground secret societies to identify dangerous and violent members and deport them from the colony.

These procedures – detection and identification through surveillance, detention, and deportation – were developed in response to the struggle to contain secret societies in the late nineteenth century. The colonial government in Singapore established the Chinese Protectorate and the Chinese Advisory Board and expanded the colonial police force. These 'tools' developed to control Chinese immigrants and secret societies were applied to another threat in the 1920s and 1930s, the underground communist movement.

WWI and the political intelligence services

While the Chinese Protectorate was responsible for surveillance of secret societies, surveillance of communist movements was conducted by the political intelligence services. The political intelligence services were needed because political movements, including communist movements, were not limited to Chinese and were run by different kinds of people like intellectuals, agents, and activists who were often in formal positions in legitimate organisations such as night schools, journalism, and unions. Combatting political movements requires detailed and careful surveillance. The first political intelligence service established in the Straits Settlements was the Criminal Intelligence Department of the Straits Settlements Police in 1919, which was tasked with monitoring and collecting information about political and criminal activities in the colony[9] (Onraet 1947: 81).

The Criminal Intelligence Department was established on the initiative of Sir Arthur Young, the Governor of the Straits Settlements during World War I. In a letter to the Colonial Office in London in 1916, he argued the need and outlined a plan for the political intelligence services in the Straits Settlements as follows:

> It is proposed to follow the system in force in India, and to arrange that the Criminal Intelligence Department shall devote itself mainly to work in connection with sedition, with the operations of spies and political agents and with political information generally, whilst also specializing (as in India) to a certain extent upon organized crime, such as the activities of a gang of coiners.
>
> ...

9 Ibid., Vol. 7, p. 302.

> The events which followed the outbreak of war showed that not only was a Criminal Investigation Department needed, but that a Criminal Intelligence Department (which was wholly wanting) was also essential. The present proposals have been drawn up by Captain A. R. Chancellor, Inspector General of Police, and are made in the light of the experience of the past year in dealing with the activities of enemy agents: they have been referred to, and concurred in, by Mr. D. Petrie, C.I.E., a Deputy Director of Criminal Intelligence in the Indian Police Service, who has been visiting the Colony upon duty.[10]

The 'experience ... of enemy agents' mentioned in this letter referred to an incident in 1915 related to the defence of Singapore and British India.

On 15 February 2015, the 5th Light Infantry mutinied in Singapore. The troop was composed of Muslims from the Punjab Province and was responsible for maintaining security in Singapore. The mutiny lasted ten days, and forty Britons (including women and children) and two Chinese residents were killed. The British authorities considered this mutiny to have been manoeuvred by the Ottoman Empire and the Ghadar Party and found it highlighted weaknesses in military and political intelligence in Singapore (Comber 2009: 530–536; Popplewell 1995: 258–262).

The first step toward overcoming this weakness was the establishment of army intelligence in 1917. A naval intelligence service had operated in Singapore since before World War I, so two military intelligence services were in operation in British Malaya to defend not only British Malaya but also British India (Popplewell 1995: 258, 263–264; Yong 1997a: 132).

10 'Creation of Criminal Intelligence and Criminal Investigation Departments', The National Archives, Kew, London, UK, CO273/441/26549.

Second, to improve political intelligence, the Criminal Intelligence Department was established in the Straits Settlements Police in 1919. David Petrie, mentioned in Governor Young's letter, played an important role in setting up this department. Born in 1879, Petrie would become the chief of MI5 during World War II. Beginning his career in the Indian Police Service in 1900, he initially worked in the Criminal Investigation Department of the Punjab Provincial Police and later the Criminal Intelligence Department of the Indian Police Service. In August 1915, he was dispatched to East and Southeast Asia to collect information about conspiratorial activities by Germans and other political activists against British India and to create an intelligence network. Petrie arrived in Singapore in 1916 and advised on the establishment of the Criminal Intelligence Department (Comber 2009: 537–538; Popplewell 1995: 265–268).

From its origin, the Criminal Intelligence Department was expected to collect two kinds of information: on domestic security in the Straits Settlements and on imperial defence, especially of India. This was also true for another intelligence service in British Malaya: the Malayan Bureau of Political Intelligence.

The Malayan Bureau of Political Intelligence was established in Singapore in 1922. It was the first intelligence service placed directly under the Governor of the Straits Settlements. A 1922 report described the duties of this bureau as follows.

> The functions of a Political Intelligence Bureau are, broadly, to keep the Government informed of all political agitation and movements in the country; to be responsible for correspondence with other administrations and consular bodies; to keep the Government advised of such exterior politics as may affect the country; to assist the local authorities in enquiries and investigations, and to publish at regular intervals an Abstract of

> Intelligence containing those items of interest which may have been collected.[11]

The Bureau communicated directly with the Central Security Department in London, the Intelligence Bureau of the Government of India, the Joint Naval and Military Intelligence Bureau in Hong Kong, the British Minister in Bangkok, and the Consul General in Batavia.[12] These duties and connections clearly show that the Bureau was expected to serve both domestic and imperial intelligence.

Until the early 1920s, there were five state surveillance apparatuses in Singapore: the naval and army intelligence services, the Chinese Protectorate, the Criminal Intelligence Department of police, and the Malayan Bureau of Political Intelligence. Out of these five surveillance apparatuses, the last two, the Criminal Intelligence Department of Police and the Malayan Bureau of Political Intelligence, were the most important institutions for combatting anti-British movements.

What the state surveillance apparatuses monitored and collected

According to René Onraet, 'In addition to security work against political movements and suspects the Special Branch concentrated on all racial, religious and social activities, and kept an eye on the trend of events in neighbouring countries' (Onraet 1947: 82). This was clearly evident in the activities of the state surveillance apparatuses in Singapore. For example, the Malayan Bureau of Political Intelligence exchanged information

11 'Report on First Year (1922)', Malayan Bulletin of Political Intelligence (MBPI), *Indian Political Intelligence Files 1912–1950*, Microfiche, Leiden: IDC Publisher, L/P&J/12/103.

12 Ibid.

Table 5.5: Contents of the 'Malayan Bulletin of Political Intelligence'

Year	1922	1923	1924	1925	1926	1927	1928	1929	1930
Number of Issues	10	9	5	10	12	9	11	11	2
Number of Headlines	58	55	28	54	130	48	31	37	3
Contents of Each Headline									
Political Movements									
India	17	16	7	8	15	12	4	11	1
China	8	12	6	17	45	19	23	18	1
Dutch East Indies	3	1	2	5	19	9	4	6	1
Others	–	1	–	1	5	–	2	–	–
Communist Movements	21	17	9	19	52	34	18	16	2
Religious Movements									
Islam	11	15	9	10	25	9	4	2	–
Others	6	5	5	4	7	3	2	6	–
Japan	5	7	4	6	4	2	1	3	–
Singapore Naval Base	–	1	1	4	–	–	–	–	–

Source: Created by author from Malayan Bulletin of Political Intelligence, in *Indian Political Intelligence Files 1912–1950*, Microfiche, Leiden: IDC Publisher.

with India, Hong Kong, Bangkok, and Batavia, was provided with information by the Criminal Intelligence Department of the Straits Settlements Police, the Chinese Protectorate, and the Federated Malay States, and collected information directly from Malay, Indian, and Chinese informants and agents.[13]

The Bureau published a report titled 'Malayan Bulletin of Political Intelligence' from March 1922 to June 1930. Table 5.5 shows the number of issues, the number of headings, and the contents of the bulletin. From this table, it was clear that the Bureau had interests in political movements related to India, China, and the Dutch East Indies, religious movements such as the Pan-Islamic movement, and Japanese activities.

13 Ibid.

Indian political movements included seditious activities by Sikhs, the conditions and activities of the Ghadar Party on the west coast of the United States, and the influence of the Indian nationalist movements over the Indian residents in British Malaya. Political movements related to China were dominated by Kuomintang and communist activities in British Malaya and the activities of Sun Yat-sen until 1925.

The Dutch East Indies, a close neighbouring colony with a large Malay and Muslim population, was a crucial intelligence-gathering target for the Bureau. From the Bulletin's first issue, it reported on political movements and turmoil in the Dutch East Indies, activities and whereabouts of major political leaders, and the suppression measures taken by the colonial government. In 1926 and 1927, the number of headlines mentioning the Dutch East Indies increased in response to communist uprisings.

The Bureau also kept a close watch on the activities of the Pan-Islamic movement in British Malaya, the Dutch East Indies, British North Borneo, and British India, as well as youths who wanted to study abroad at Islamic centres such as El-Azhar University. It also closely monitored the movement's influence on Malay and Indian residents in British Malaya.

Finally, the Bureau also monitored Japanese intelligence activities in British Malaya, especially in Singapore, Japanese commercial activities, Japanese organisations, brothels, and the Japanese navy.

The data in Table 5.5 makes clear that the communist movement was the Bureau's primary focus. The final issue of the Bulletin in 1930 had only one heading, 'Communism', under which it detailed communist attempts to recruit Malay and Indian members, the third representative conference of delegates of the Nanyang Communist Party, strikes and labour unions, and propaganda.[14] The communist movement was also the most reported topic in the monthly *Straits Settlements Police Political Intelligence Journal* (SSPPIJ) published by the Criminal Intelligence Department in the 1930s.

Let us now examine how effective surveillance by the state intelligence apparatus was in suppressing the communist movement in Singapore.

Policing communist movements in Singapore

The communist movement in British Malaya was organised by Chinese communists coming from mainland China. In 1921, agents sent by communist organisations in Shanghai and Canton and migrants seeking jobs as teachers or editors travelled to British Malaya. They created communist cells in night schools, spread propaganda via lectures in night schools and journals, and organised students, women, and workers (Yong 1997b: 9–10, 17–28, 41–44, 53–54).

From 1925 to 1926, activists, radical students, and agents travelled to British Malaya from Shanghai, Canton, and Hainan islands. They organised the Nanyang Communist Youth League, the Nanyang General Labour Union, and the Nanyang Regional Committee of the Communist Party of China in Singapore (Yong 1997b: 62–63, 67, 69, 71–72).

The colonial government's initial step against the communists targeted the night schools and seditious publications. Leaders were arrested and deported. Night schools were closed from 1922 to 1923, and again from 1926 to 1927 (Yong 1997a: 129; Yong 1997b: 33, 36, 57, 74–75).

14 MBPI, No. 79 (1930), *Indian Political Intelligence Files 1912–1950*, L/P&J/12/109.

In 1927, the Criminal Intelligence Department and the Chinese Protectorate raided communist bases in Singapore, rounding up and deporting many suspects. The movement was momentarily weakened, but later that year, scores of Chinese communists fled from China to Southeast Asia after the First United Front in China collapsed in April, and the Canton Uprising failed in December. These exile communists took control of and led the communist movements in British Malaya. In 1928, the Nanyang Regional Committee re-formed as the Nanyang Provisional Committee of the Communist Party of China and the Nanyang General Labour Union and the Nanyang Communist Youth League were rebuilt[15] (Yong 1997b: 76–78).

The Malayan Communist Party was formed in 1930 under the direction of the Far Eastern Bureau of the Comintern (Third International) and the Pan-Pacific Trade Union Secretariat in Shanghai. The Nanyang General Labour Union was reorganised into the Malayan General Labour Union in 1930, and subsequently, the communist movements in British Malaya were controlled by these two organisations (Yong 1997b: 68, 85–86, 91, 101, 113–114, 121, 130–131, 156).

From its inception in 1930, the Malayan Communist Party was suppressed severely by the government. The Criminal Intelligence Department learned communists would be meeting at Nassim Road on 29 April 1930, conducted a raid, and arrested most of the communist leaders in British Malaya. In November 1931, the Central of the Malayan Communist Party was located and searched. From 1932 to 1935, 1,704 suspected communist were arrested in the Straits Settlements, and 882 of them were confirmed to be communists and were deported from the

15 MBPI, No. 48 (1927), *Indian Political Intelligence Files 1912-1950*, L/P&J/12/107.

colony from 1930 to 1935[16] (Hara 2009: 130–131; Yong 1997b: 131, 145, 169).

These raids of communist premises were based on intelligence gathered by the state surveillance apparatuses in British Malaya, especially the Criminal Intelligence Department and the Chinese Protectorate. It was not easy to attain reliable information because the targets, underground communists, knew they were being monitored. They used aliases, cyphers, and invisible ink in correspondence and frequently changed residences and meeting places. They compartmentalised important information, such as organisation structures and the names and locations of leaders and executives, to minimise the risk of exposure to the police. Such 'secrets' were selectively shared among key members. Thus, it was nigh impossible for the Special Branch[17] to acquire crucial information without an agent or a spy in the core of the organisation.

Nevertheless, in 1937, a 'Supplement' published by the Special Branch of the Straits Settlements Police provided not only organisational charts for the Malayan Communist Party, the Singapore Overseas Chinese Anti-Japanese National Salvation Association, the Malayan Proletarian Writers Association, the Malayan Communist Youth Corps, and the Malayan General Labour Union, but also the names of 110 communists, including members of the organisations' central committees. All information was attributed to 'secret sources'.[18]

16 MBPI, No. 79 (1930), *Indian Political Intelligence Files 1912-1950*, L/P&J/12/109; Straits Settlements Police Political Intelligence Journal (SSPPIJ), Supplement No. 4 (1932), Archives nationales d'outre-mer (ANOM), Aix-en-Provence, France, Fonds du GGI (Gouvernement général de l'Indochine), dossier 65560, 65561.

17 Formerly the Criminal Intelligence Department, renamed in 1933.

18 SSPPIJ, Supplement No.5 (1937), ANOM, Fonds du GGI, dossier 65560, 65561.

There were no clues to identify these secret sources, but it is clear evidence that the Special Branch had infiltrated these organisations. And there was one famous agent who infiltrated the centre of the Malayan Communist Party. One of his aliases was Lai Teck. Born in French Indochina in 1903, he joined the Indochinese Communist Party. Arrested by the French Indochinese police in 1925, he agreed to work as an agent of the French police and subsequently became a source of inside information about underground communist activities not only in French Indochina but also in Hong Kong, Shanghai and Tientsin (天津). In 1934, Lai Teck's cover was blown in French Indochina, and he was handed over to the British political police in Hong Kong. He transferred from Hong Kong to Singapore no later than early 1935. Using false documents provided by the British police, he convinced communists in Singapore that he was a representative of the Comintern. He rapidly moved up the party ranks by taking advantage of both factional conflicts among party leaders and police crackdowns. He was elected to the Central Committee of the Malayan Communist Party in 1936 and became Secretary-General in 1939. His power in the party was such that he was seen as the 'Stalin of Malaya' (Akashi 1994: 62–66; Comber 2010: 3–9; Yong 1997b: 145, 169,194).

There was no evidence that Lai Teck was one of the secret sources for the Supplement in 1937 because none of the agents' or informants' names, including Lai Teck, appeared in the police journals. But in 1937, he was already an agent for the political police in British Malaya and a member of the Central Committee of the Malayan Communist Party, and he 'could' have provided information for the Supplement.

The colonial government in Singapore tried to control communists through surveillance: identifying leading and violent members, then arresting and deporting them. Without valuable and reliable information, it was impossible to police underground communist movements. The state surveillance apparatuses, the Special Branch, and the Chinese Protectorate were collecting information from censorship, agents, and informants. Lai Teck was an ideal agent for the Special Branch, which was able to extend its control by collaborating with him.

However, domestic communist movements in Singapore were only one of the communist threats. More difficult targets for the state surveillance apparatuses in Singapore to monitor and contain were travelling agents and activists who tried to penetrate Singapore from outside with funds and directions and did not stay there long.

In the 1920s and 30s, the Comintern, established in Moscow in 1919, supported communist movements around the world. The Comintern established the Far Eastern Bureau in Shanghai in 1926 as its regional headquarters for East and Southeast Asia. The Far Eastern Bureau dispatched agents and couriers to supervise and distribute allocated funds to communist movements throughout East and Southeast Asia (Onimaru 2016).

To monitor these travelling agents, Special Branch in Singapore regularly exchanged information with other political intelligence apparatuses both within the British Empire and in the neighbouring Dutch East Indies and French Indochina, as well as the British Passport Control Offices (Foster 1995: 335–336; Onimaru 2006: 76–77).

In 1931, a French agent named Joseph Ducroux, sent by the Far Eastern Bureau, was arrested in Singapore. He had travelled to Singapore under the alias Serge Lefranc, tasked with creating a regional liaison centre for Southeast Asia in Singapore and making contact with the Indian communist movement. He arrived in Singapore on 27 April 1931, and on 1 May, four days after his arrival, the Criminal Intelligence Department in Singapore knew of his presence via postal censorship. He was located on 16 May and placed under surveillance. His true identity was discovered through the network of colonial political intelligence services across East and Southeast Asia. His activities in Shanghai had been documented by the Shanghai Municipal Police in 1926, and he had been a wanted man in East and Southeast Asia since 1930 when his visa application to British India was rejected by the British Passport Control Officer in France. He was finally arrested in Singapore on 1 June 1931[19] (Metzger 1996: 4).

This was a successful case in which the police could locate and arrest the travelling agent, but of course, it did not always work out like that. For example, in April 1934, the Special Branch in Singapore was informed that an agent of the Far Eastern Bureau in Shanghai had travelled to Singapore from Bangkok by rail and launched an operation to identify and locate him. Initially, the Special Branch only knew that he was a fat Cantonese aged about 40. In June, they received confirmation that he had been in contact with the Malayan Communist Party Central and that he spoke German well. In October, several aliases were revealed, and they learned that he was fluent in French and spoke some English. However, in November 1934, the Special Branch learned that he had departed Singapore for Java. Thus, despite months of effort to identify, locate, and arrest him, the Special Branch had failed.[20] This case highlights the difficulties of detecting travelling agents: he suddenly appeared on the scene and then was gone again.

Belogurova outlined the organizational and functional parallels between Chinese migrant associations and the Communist Party of Malaya (Belogurova 2019: 85–86). We find similar parallels in the control and suppression measures taken against

19 'Serge Norbert Lefranc alias Joseph Ducroux alias Dupont', Shanghai Municipal Police files, The National Archives and Records Administration, College Park, M.D., USA, RG263, D2527/6; 'China Personalities Ducroux or Serge Lefranc', The National Archives, Kew, London, UK, WO106/5814.

20 SSPPIJ, No.4, 6, 10, 11 (1934), ANOM, Fonds du GGI, dossier 65560, 65561.

secret societies and the communist movements: surveillance, detention, and deportation. In both cases, deportation was only effective against migrant agitators and agents, because British citizens and subjects could not be deported. Nevertheless, many people were deported, and surveillance played a crucial role in disclosing, monitoring, and arresting 'dangerous' persons. Arguably, surveillance was more important in policing communist movements than secret societies. If secret societies were analogous to 'chronic diseases', communist movements were more like 'infectious diseases'. If the colonial government failed to contain them, an outbreak of mass communist strikes, uprisings, and revolutions might occur and, in the worst case, destroy the empire. Hence, the colonial government had an existential need to identify, monitor, apprehend, and remove those who were infected with communism from British Malaya. For this, surveillance was essential, as the colonial government and the political police tried to render communists 'visible'. As we have seen, the political police had valuable, well-placed informants like Lai Teck, but that was insufficient to render the communist movements completely 'visible'. Relying on agents and informants means the political police were dependent on what they provided, and it was uncertain that they provided everything they knew. The political police could claim many successes in their efforts to suppress communists, but there were also many cases, such as the fat Cantonese agent in 1934, where there were gaps in the information available, and communists slipped through.

Conclusion

The disputes and riots among the Chinese secret societies in the nineteenth century and the activities of the Chinese communists in the 1920s and 1930s were each in their time regarded by the colonial government as the most serious threats to law and order in Singapore. Secret societies and communist movements were 'invisible' to the colonial government in different senses. The invisibility of secret societies was initially due to the colonial government's ignorance of Chinese languages and cultures, whereas the communist movements were intentionally underground and stealthy. Furthermore, there are no external markers to identify who was a communist and who was not. To control these 'invisible' threats, surveillance was crucial, and the state surveillance institutions scrambled to produce it.

Surveillance of the secret societies was primarily conducted by the Chinese Protectorate, established in 1877. As we have seen, the so-called secret societies were not actually secret, nor were they invisible; they were, in fact, quite open in their performance of important social and economic roles in Chinese communities. However, the colonial government in Singapore could not see the Chinese communities for what they were because no government officials could understand the Chinese languages until the 1870s; and with no understanding of the languages or what the organisations did, their frequent disputes and riots were simply dismissed as dangerous and conspiratorial. After Singapore became a Crown Colony in 1867, measures to control the secret societies began to be implemented, including registration, the declaration of a state of emergency, deportation, and the creation of the Chinese Protectorate. Among these measures, the threat of deportation was a highly effective deterrent because many Chinese in Singapore were afraid of being executed in China. The Chinese Protectorate's surveillance was crucial to making secret societies 'visible'.

William Pickering, the first Protector of Chinese, in cooperation with the police, maintained regular surveillance of the secret societies and revealed their roles and characteristics. He also tried to collaborate with Chinese leaders to control the secret societies, but the collaboration only worked when the interests of the colonial government and those of societies aligned. Secret societies were finally outlawed in 1890, but that did not trigger their immediate dissolution. They simply went underground and continued their activities.

Surveillance against communist movements was mainly conducted by the Criminal Intelligence Department, later renamed the Special Branch of the Straits Settlements Police, established in 1919. The 'tools' developed for controlling and suppressing the secret societies were applied to communist movements: surveillance, arrests, and deportation. Surveillance was the key because communists tried to keep their activities and themselves hidden from the political police. To detect and identify underground communists, especially leaders in the communist movements, reliable information was crucial. In the mid-1930s, the Special Branch in Singapore acquired competent agents in the communist movements. Lai Teck was one of these agents who eventually reached the top of the Malayan Communist Party. The Special Branch received highly valuable information from agents and informants inside the movements, but this did not provide the Special Branch with absolute knowledge of the communist movements. Agents and informants were not searchlights but spotlights through which part of the underground movements came into view. As we saw with the Cantonese agent from Shanghai, even though informed of his presence in Singapore, Special Branch failed to identify and arrest him. He suddenly appeared in the light, then disappeared again.

René Onraet wrote that 'Success against organised violence is not its discovery but its prevention' (1947: 88). On this measure, the colonial state's controlling measures against the Chinese secret societies and the communist movements in Singapore were successful from the 1890s till the 1930s in that they prevented huge riots, disputes, and revolutions. However, the colonial state had to maintain never-ending surveillance to achieve these goals. Secret societies were initially invisible because of the government officials' ignorance of languages, cultures, and societies. Once the Chinese Protectorate overcame these obstacles, secret societies were no longer 'secret' for the colonial government. However, after the illegalisation of secret societies in 1890, they went underground, and the colonial government had to maintain regular surveillance of them and detain and deport those deemed 'dangerous'. Communist movements were 'invisible' because of the underground nature of their activities. The colonial government did not tolerate communist movements because they feared that strikes, uprisings, and 'revolutions' organised by communists would harm and, in the worst case, destroy the colonial state and economy. The key to effective prevention was surveillance. The political police had continued their incessant efforts to find their suspects, and their success depended on developing reliable sources of information, especially from informants within their target groups. Lai Teck was one of these valuable agents, but no matter how much reliable information the Special Branch acquired, it did not mean everything was visible. The colonial state's surveillance was not perfect and was never complete.

References

Akashi, Yoji (1994), 'Lai Teck, Secretary General of the Malayan Communist Party, 1939–1947', *Journal of the South Seas Society,* 49: 57–103.

Ban Kah Choon (2001), *Absent History: The Untold Story of Special Branch Operations in Singapore 1915–1942,* Singapore: Raffles.

Belogurova, Anna (2019), *The Nanyang Revolution: The Comintern and Chinese Networks in Southeast Asia, 1890–1957,* Cambridge: Cambridge University Press.

Blythe, Wilfred (1969), *The Impact of Chinese Secret Societies in Malaya: A Historical Study,* London: Oxford University Press.

Butcher, John G., and Dick, Howard (eds) (1993), *The Rise and Fall of Revenue Farming: Business Elites and the Emergence of the Modern State in Southeast Asia,* New York: St. Martin's Press.

Cheah Boon Kheng (1992), *From PKI to the Comintern, 1924–1941: The Apprenticeship of the Malayan Communist Party,* Ithaca: Southeast Asia Program, Cornell University.

Comber, Leon (2009), 'The Singapore Mutiny (1915) and the Genesis of Political Intelligence in Singapore', *Intelligence and National Security,* 24(4): 529–541.

Comber, Leon (2010). '"Traitor of all Traitors" – Secret Agent Extraordinaire: Lai Teck, Secretary-General, Communist Party of Malaya (1939–1947)', *Journal of Malayan Branch of Royal Asiatic Society,* 83(2): 1–25.

Foster, Anne (1995), 'Secret Police Cooperation and the Roots of Anti-Communism in Interwar Southeast Asia', *The Journal of American-East Asian Relations,* 4(4): 331–350.

Gillis, E. Kay (2005), *Singapore Civil Society and British Power,* Singapore: Talisman Publishing.

Hara, Fujio (2009), *Mikan ni owatta Kokusai Kyouryoku: Maraya Kyousantou to Kyoudaitou* (Unfinished International Cooperation: The Malayan Communist Party and its Brotherhood Parties), Tokyo: Fukyousha.

Hara, Fujio (2017), *The Malayan Communist Party as Recorded in the Comintern Files,* Selangor: Strategic Information and Research Development Centre.

Holdsworth, May, and Munn, Christopher (eds) (2012), *Dictionary of Hong Kong Biography,* Hong Kong: Hong Kong University Press.

Kobayashi, Atsushi (2013), 'The Role of Singapore in the Growth of Intra-Southeast Asian Trade, c.1820s–1852', *Southeast Asian Studies,* 2(3) December: 443–474.

Lee, Edwin (1991), *The British as Rulers: Governing Multiracial Singapore 1867–1914,* Singapore: Singapore University Press.

Mak Lau Fong (1981), *The Sociology of Secret Societies: A Study of Chinese Secret Societies in Singapore and Peninsular Malaya,* Kuala Lumpur: Oxford University Press.

Makepeace, Walter, Brooke, Gilbert E., and Braddell, Roland J. (1991), *One Hundred Years of Singapore,* vol. 1, Singapore: Singapore University Press.

Metzger, Laurent (1996), 'Joseph Ducroux, a French Agent of the Comintern in Singapore (1931–1932)', *Journal of the Malayan Branch of Royal Asiatic Society,* 69(1): 1–20.

Morrah, Patrick (1968), *The History of the Malayan Police,* Kuala Lumpur: Rajiv Printers.

Onimaru, Takeshi (2006), 'Nūran Jiken: Senkanki Asia ni okeru Kokusai Kyousansyugi Unndou to Igirisu Teikoku Tianiji Sisutemu (Noulens Case: International Communist movement and British security system in Asia)', *Kokusai Seiji* (International relations), 146: 70–87.

Onimaru, Takeshi (2016), 'Shanghai Connection: The Construction and Collapse of the Comintern Network in East and Southeast Asia', *Southeast Asian Studies,* 5(1): 115–133.

Onraet, René (1947), *Singapore: A Police Background,* London: Dorothy Crips.

Pickering, William Alexander ([1867] 2000), 'The Chinese in the Straits of Malaca', in Kingsley Bolton and Christopher Hutton (eds), *Triad Societies,* vol. 1, London: Routledge.

Popplewell, Richard (1995), *Intelligence and Imperial Defence: British Intelligence and the Defence of the Indian Empire 1904–1924,* London: Frank Cass.

Shiraishi, Takashi (1975), 'Kamin Goeisyo no Seturitu to Kaitō: Jyūkyū Seiki Singapōru Kakyō Syakai no Seiji teki Henka (Establishment of the Chinese Protectorate and secret societies: Political change in Chinese societies in nineteenth century Singapore)', *Ajia Kenkyu* (Asia Studies), 22(2): 75–102.

Shiraishi, Takashi (2021), *Empire of the Seas: Thinking about Asia,* Tokyo: Japan Publishing Industry Foundation for Culture.

Trocki, Carl (1990), *Opium and Empire: Chinese Society in Colonial Singapore, 1800–1910,* Ithaca: Cornell University Press.

Turnbull, Constance Mary (1989), *A History of Singapore 1819–1988,* Singapore: Oxford University Press.

Wong Lin Ken (1991), 'Commercial Growth before the Second World War', in Ernest C.T. Chew and Edwin Lee (eds), *A History of Singapore,* Singapore: Oxford University Press, pp. 41–65.

Yen Ching-hwang (1976), *The Overseas Chinese and the 1911 Revolution: With special reference to Singapore and Malaya,* Kuala Lumpur: Oxford University Press.

Yen Ching-hwang (1986), *A Social History of the Chinese in Singapore and Malaya 1800–1911,* Singapore: Oxford University Press.

Yong Ching Fatt (1994), *Chinese Leadership and Power in Colonial Singapore,* Singapore: Times Academic Press.

Yong Ching Fatt (1997a), 'Law and Order: British Management of Malayan Communism during the Interwar Years, 1919–1942', in Brook Barrington (ed.), *Empires, Imperialism and Southeast Asia,* Australia: Monash Asia Institute, pp. 126–148.

Yong Ching Fatt (1997b), *The Origin of Malayan Communism,* Singapore: South Seas Society.

Yong Ching Fatt (2002), 'Modern Transformation of Chinese Political Leadership in Colonial Singapore', in Leo Suryadinata (ed.), *Ethnic Chinese in Singapore and Malaysia: A Dialogue between Tradition and Modernity,* Singapore: Times Academic Press, pp. 85–107.

Chapter 6

Political Management, Policing, and Nationalist Politics in the Dutch Indies

Takashi Shiraishi[1]

Benedict Anderson defines the state as 'an institution' which 'ingests and excretes personnel' in 'the steady rotation out of their top leaders' (Anderson 1990: 95). The state, he argues, 'has its own memory' in the forms of 'files, dossiers, archives, laws, financial records, censuses, maps, treaties, correspondence, memoranda, and so on'. Anderson likens the state to 'the complex electrical system in any large mansion' (1991: 160). This perspective seems to assume that the state is able to see the population through the maps and optics it creates, a capacity that James Scott cogently terms 'legibility' (1998: 2).

The problem with this perspective, however, is that the state is not monolithic, but, rather, a collection of departments and agencies run by different sets of officials with diverse interests, career prospects, and ways of seeing and reading things. Rather than an electrical system in a mansion, a better metaphor might be a village lighted by many candles in the gathering dark. The state's capacity to render social and natural landscapes legible cannot be taken for granted because the state often struggles to see and read, owing to its inadequate optics and its lack of resources. To understand 'the process of state-making', it is not sufficient, as Scott (2010) argues, 'to follow the conquest of

1 This chapter is a revised version of Chapters 4 and 5 of *The Phantom World of Digul: Policing as Politics in Colonial Indonesia, 1926–1941* (Kyoto and Singapore: Kyoto University Press and NUS University Press, 2021), initially drafted in 2020.

illegibility' per se. We must also understand the ways in which state-making is fundamentally driven by a diverse collection of desires, aspirations, interests, wishes, and designs for the conquest of illegibility. Arguing that the state sees through a glass darkly means taking seriously the fact (and consequences) of state apparatuses and officials being unable to see, seeing only what they want to see, and drawing different conclusions about what should be done about what they thought they saw. Among other things, this means recognising that policy outcomes are not always determined by what the state sees.

This chapter is an attempt to reexamine modern colonial state formation at the time when the Dutch Indies government was confronted with popular politics in the twentieth century. Fearing that the rise of popular nationalist politics could trigger wild forces in the colony, and deeply concerned about its ability to maintain colonial peace and order, officials debated how to interpret what they 'saw' as they tried to formulate a strategy for surveillance and containing nationalist politics.

Nationalism emerged in the Dutch Indies in the 1910s with the rise of the *pergerakan* (movement). It was expressed in newspapers and journals, rallies and meetings, trade unions and strikes, associations and political parties, novels, songs, theatres, and revolts. It signified the arrival of something new, exciting, and revolutionary, because the new forms and languages the *pergerakan* introduced allowed people to 'say' what they could not and unleashed popular radicalism (Shiraishi 1990).

Modern surveillance politics arrived in the Indies as a twin of modern popular nationalism, beginning with the establishment of the Algemeene Recherche Dienst (ARD., General Investigation Service) in the attorney general's office (*hoofdparket*) in 1919. The ARD developed a regional intelligence apparatus that spread across the Indies and penetrated deeply into the native world during the 1920s. It grew up with the Indonesian Communist

Party (PKI, Partai Komunis Indonesia) as its enemy before destroying it in 1926–1927, and then watched, spied upon, and shaped the *pergerakan* in major ways in the 1930s (Shiraishi 2003: 47–74).

The Dutch Indies surveillance state expanded its reach in the wake of the communist revolts of 1926–1927, achieving an age of normalcy (*zaman normal*) through regulation and repression of what the Dutch termed 'wild' forces. Even though the government was successful in containing the movement in a terrain it shaped, however, it was never certain that these wild forces could be tamed. The revolts marked the beginning of a new era in the history of the Dutch Indies native policy. The government was determined to destroy the PKI and made sweeping arrests, imprisoning and interning thousands of people who participated in the revolts: 13,000 arrested, 4,500 imprisoned, and 1,140 interned in Boven-Digul in Dutch New Guinea. While the immediate objective of these actions was to destroy the core of PKI, it also wanted to teach Indonesians that there were limits beyond which they risked internment. Words such as PKI, Communist International, Moscow, and Tan Malaka were effectively declared 'out-of-bounds', and their association with arrest, imprisonment and internment was impressed on popular consciousness. The strategy worked. The communist underground remained minute and never threatened the peace and order of the post-revolt Indies (Shiraishi 1997; Shiraishi 2021).

Managing and policing nationalist politics, however, was more complicated. A small but increasing number of university-educated native intellectuals emerged in the 1920s who, supported by secondary-school educated youth, took leadership in nationalist politics. Senior Dutch officials were divided over how to deal with them, but the government eventually decided the political intelligence apparatus should police native politics.

This chapter examines how and why the government came to this decision; what thinking informed its policies; and how and to what end the political policing apparatus was deployed.

Soekarno, the PNI, and the demise of the liberal strategy

Soekarno and the PNI

The historical contours of Indonesian nationalist politics following the communist revolts are well-known. A new, secular, nationalist movement arose in the mid-1920s, driven by an emerging cohort of intellectuals who called for *Indonesia Merdeka*, Free Indonesia, and spearheaded the creation of the PI (Perhimpoenan Indonesia, Indonesian Association) in the Netherlands as well as study clubs in the Indies. The significance of school education in the rise of nationalism is well understood (Anderson 1991), but it is important to note that university education came late to the Indies. The first engineering faculty was established in Bandung in 1924. The law school became a faculty of law in 1924. The first faculty of medicine was established in 1927. During this period, it became possible for a small number of Indonesians to receive professional education in the Indies for the first time. Until this time, Indonesians went to the Netherlands for higher education. Relatively few Indonesians, mainly from aristocrat-turned-bureaucratic elite families, studied in Dutch universities. The Dutch authorities called this group the 'intellectuals'. Their numbers were small: 109 in 1929, including Indies Chinese, Dutch and Indo-Europeans. There were also relatively few native students passing through the institutes of higher education in the Indies: a mere 230 had graduated from these schools by 1940. Intellectuals constituted a very small elite of the native society, who were conscious of their status, and seen as such by the Dutch, who accorded them special treatment (Ingleson 1975: 2; Abeyasekere 1972: 3–4).

The PI's brief glory in 1925–1927 was the fruit of these developments in higher education. Indonesian students travelled to the Netherlands for professional degrees, especially law degrees at Leiden University. Originally called Indies Association (Indische Vereeniging), it was renamed Indonesian Association (Indonesische Vereeniging) in 1922. It became primarily concerned with nationalist issues in 1925 when Mohammad Hatta served as chairman. Its membership was a mere 38 in 1926 and 26 in 1929 (Ingleson 1975: 3–5).

Hatta was the central figure in the PI and was in close contact with two leading PKI members then in the Netherlands: Semaoen and Darsono. The PI radicalized under Hatta, who called for a national united front to fight for Indonesian independence from the Dutch. His strategy was non-cooperation, self-help and mass action organized and led by politically articulate intellectuals (Ingleson 1979: 5 and 9). PI representatives attended the Comintern sponsored International Democratic Congress for Peace in France in August 1926. Hatta and others also attended Brussels Congress of the League Against Imperialism and Colonial Oppression (Ingleson 1975: 33–34).

In the wake of the revolts, Hatta tried to create a new party in the Indies to provide a leadership in the movement. Seeing a chance to revive the PKI in a new form, Semaoen produced an 'Organizational Plan' for the new party. Hatta and Semaoen also signed a 'convention' in December 1926, agreeing that PKI henceforth would accept PI's leadership in the nationalist movement. Semaoen's organizational plan, however, did not provide the base for Hatta's planned party – he saw it as unfeasible – and Semaoen terminated the convention two weeks after the signing as he was instructed to do by the Comintern (Ingleson 1975: 33–34). Alarmed at its radicalization, the police raided the residences of PI activists in June 1927 and confiscated Semaoen's organizational plan, the convention, and other PI documents as evidence that the PI was under communist influence. In September 1927, Hatta and three others were arrested. Their trial began in March 1928 (Ingleson 1975: 55–56).

In the meantime, other PI activists returned from the Netherlands (Ingleson 1975: 63). Some joined established parties. Some established study clubs. Before Hatta began trying to create a new party, however, there was an initiative to establish a new party among intellectuals in Bandung. In July 1927, the Bandung General Study Club transformed into a party, the Perserikatan Nasional Indonesia (PNI, Indonesian National League) under the leadership of Soekarno, an engineer, and Sartono, a Leiden trained lawyer. It called for 'a free and independent Indonesia' through 'a conscious nationalist mass action' and the creation of 'a state within the state' (Ingleson 1979: 32–34).

The General Study Club also established a youth association which was soon renamed Pemoeda Indonesia (Indonesian Youth). Its driving force was law students in Batavia who were active in the Perhimpoenan Peladjar Peladjar Indonesia (PPPI, Indonesian Students' Association) (Ingleson 1979: 35; Kwantes 1981: 1–9). By the time of its inaugural congress, held in Surabaya in May 1928, the PNI, though small, had emerged as a major force in nationalist politics. It was renamed the Partai Nasional Indonesia (PNI, Indonesian National Party) and had four branches (Batavia, Bandung, Yogyakarta, and Surabaya) with about 550 members. The congress decided to publish its party organ, Persatoean Indonesia (Indonesian Unity) with Soekarno as editor and Sartono as administrator (Kwantes 1978: 54–55, 79–85).

Dealing with intellectuals

The government watched the PI and PNI carefully. The central question senior government officials asked was what to do with this new group of intellectuals. Two different approaches were offered by senior officials.

W.P. Hillen, Governor of West Java, represented one position in his letter to Governor General de Graeff on 20 January 1927 (Kwantes 1978: 527–532). He was concerned that 'native' trust in the administrative officials had disappeared. He blamed the movement leaders for the development: 'the rally man [*vergaderingsman*, i.e., movement leader] could criticize the government and the administration, normally unpunished'. This development brought about an enormous change 'in the thought world of a simple native'. 'In the past he might once in a while talk pleasantly with his district chief ... at a village meeting' and he did what he was ordered to do. Now came non-officials, who disapproved whatever the government had decreed. Yet 'district chief ... sat by [at a rally] and did not shut up the speakers, [let alone] arrest them!' '*Kromo* [uneducated native]' may not understand what was going on, but eventually he would conclude that his district chief was not such a powerful man as he had thought. A 'class of professional leaders [*beroepsleiders*]' were attacking 'the loyal administrative official' and undermining his authority. 'The governors will be alienated further from the governed'. Hillen did not believe any dialogue with 'intellectuals' of study clubs would be politically useful.

Resident of Palembang J. Tideman expressed a more liberal position in his letter to de Graeff dated 2 March 1927 (Kwantes 1978: 552–558). He also located 'the movement' in a larger context, but he cautioned against equating 'the large native movement' with 'this excess, which locally went into revolt' and 'leaders' with 'instigators'. It was important, he argued, to 'give faith' in 'the movement', if the government wanted to restore native trust. In his view, any effort for improvement should start with 'ourselves'. With 'the dismissal of ringleaders and the help of disciplinary means', the teacher might succeed in restoring surface order in the classroom. But:

> eventually his inability to win the trust of the youth will take its own revenge. Neither his own interest nor that of his pupils is served this way. It is not enough that he is just and gives good education. If the boys in the classroom do not accept him as their teacher, there [will] develop fatal alienation for all.

This was also the case with the government and the population, especially in a colony, because he said 'the task of administration has a pedagogical side with it'. For the administration to be effective, not only had it to be just and good, but also to make the population understand it was in their interest to accept the administration. This meant, in his view, the government should work on 'those who exercise influence on people's development'.

He classified the 'leaders' into three groups: the full-fledged educated intellectuals, the 'half-educated' journalists and speakers at rallies who styled themselves as leaders, and the demagogues or misleaders. Tideman immediately wrote the third group off. He admitted the need for the 'European' administration to work closely with *volkshoofden* (people's chiefs) or traditional chiefs, but he argued that 'anyone who wants to devote his energies to the development of the Indies has to turn to the leaders of the first group, the so-called intellectuals'. If they were to accept the government offers and lead 'the youth and the mass of people' 'along the just path of cooperation with the Netherlands', it should be possible to work in a constructive sense.

As we can see, both the conservative and the liberal position in the government in 1927 were equally paternalistic to natives (*kromo* for Hillen and *jongen* for Tideman). They disagreed whether there was any hope of cooperation with intellectuals for native development. Hillen held little hope of cooperation from native intellectuals. Tideman believed in native evolution, but his liberal optimism was hedged by his notion of 'leaders'. If he were logical in his classification, his third category should have been 'non-intellectuals' or 'fake intellectuals', not 'demagogues and misleaders'. The beauty of his classification was precisely there, for if any intellectual turned out to be a trouble-maker for the government, he/she would be reclassified as a demagogue or misleader. And if there were not very many in the first category, his position in effect would be the same as Hillen's.

Governor General de Graeff's position was closer to that of Tideman's (Kwantes 1978: 559–569). At the conference in March 1927, he stated his position on the study clubs thus:

> [He is aware] that these study clubs are watched with distrust by the administration. This is understandable, because those associations are left-oriented and do not hesitate to admit communist leaders in their midst. In his opinion, however, it does not mean that such associations, especially [Soetomo's] Surabaya Study Club, are moving in the communist direction. One should rather see in it an outcome of the idealistic plan of such debating clubs to give each [school of] thought an opportunity to express its views. Since this centre for the native political life looked more important for the moment than the organized parties, he urged the administrative chiefs not to take them negatively with distrust and to promote contact [with them]. (Kwantes 1978: 568–569)

The PNI was established in July 1927. As we have seen, soon after the inaugural PNI conference, the CID (Dutch Central Intelligence Service) raided Hatta's residence and confiscated

Semaoen's documents, arresting Hatta and other PI activists. These developments strengthened the position of the attorney general's office which had been arguing that there was no point making 'a sharp distinction between communists and nationalists', that study club intellectuals were closet communists, and that PI activists were working 'to unite elements of the industrial proletariat and revolutionary intellectuals in an anti-imperialist bloc'. Semaoen's organizational plan provided the attorney general with a powerful piece of evidence for its case (Kwantes 1978: 509–510).

Since Semaoen's organizational plan is available in English, we do not need to dwell on it. Briefly, Semaoen defined the goal of a new party as creating 'a state within the state' based on 'self-help'. He argued that 'a revolution will only succeed if it is well organized' (Ingleson 1975: 80–84; See Kwantes 1978: 884–888 for the Dutch text). In fact, it was a plan for building a revolutionary organization in the political void. It contained no political or economic analysis of the Indies. Hatta testified at his trial that Semaoen had given him the original Malay language text in November 1926. Although he had translated it into Dutch, he claimed to have thought it unfeasible and that he had never submitted it to the PI executive. It was sitting somewhere in Hatta's apartment, without getting his serious attention, until it was discovered by the CID, but it was written by Semaoen, the former PKI chairman and Communist International agent. It contained such key concepts as 'self-help' and 'a state within the state' that informed PI and PNI visions. And, conveniently, it was available in Dutch (Kwantes 1981: 51; Ingleson 1975: 80).

Semaoen's organizational plan provided clear evidence, according to the attorney general's office, of the true nature of nationalist politics. Attorney General J.K. Onnen happily interpreted 'the nature and development' of the PNI in terms of the PI and the organizational plan in his letter to de Graeff dated

18 June 1928 (Kwantes 1978: 639–647; Kwantes 1981: 51–57). J.J. Schrieke, government representative to the Volksraad, shared the attorney general's view and understood the establishment of the PNI in light of the convention and the Organizational Plan and argued that the PNI signified the creation of 'a national-communist bloc' in the Indies (Kwantes 1978: 630–639).

The policy implications were clear. According to the attorney general, the enemy was 'a relatively small core of determined members' intent on overthrowing 'the established Western authority', and the only thing the government could do was to ensure they understood the impossibility of achieving independence with violence.[2] The governor general, however, continued seeking a way to engage nationalist intellectuals for 'constructive cooperation'. Charles O. van der Plas, an official for native affairs, was tasked with conducting 'field investigations and discussions' and reporting to the governor general what the government could do either directly or indirectly 'to neutralize and fight the revolutionary propaganda among the native population'.[3]

Van der Plas submitted his report to the governor general in April 1928.[4] He accepted the attorney general's thesis on the communist strategy of establishing an anti-imperialist bloc with nationalist intellectuals. He also accepted its argument about the PI and its Communist International connections. But he was more nuanced about former PI members in the Indies. He noted that they organized study clubs, including the Surabaya Indonesian Study Club and the Bandung General Study Club. He reported that the Indonesian Study Club was moderate, but the

2 PG to GG, July 17, 1927, Mr. 1060x/1927.

3 First government secretary to deputy adviser for native affairs, Aug. 29, 1927, Mr. 1060x/1927. See also PG to GG, July 17, 1927, Mr. 1060x/1927.

4 Now available in Mr. 457x/1928.

Bandung General Study Club 'consistently strives for the implementation of the PI program, that is the Organizational Plan'. He interpreted the rise of the PNI in this light and concluded that its organizational development – as well as the establishment of Jong Indonesia/Pemoeda Indonesia and National Scouting Organization – clearly demonstrated 'the Moscow-PI program is implemented systematically', calling for the creation of a people's party and the organization of 'a state within the state'. He further noted that numerous associations were being infiltrated by former PI members through 'the formation of cells'. Van der Plas concluded that 'the second offensive of Moscow has started' in accordance with the guidelines determined at the 5th World Congress of the Communist International, as 'a national liberation struggle' under the leadership of nationalists with the 'PNI as the centre'.

The question was how to meet this communist offensive. Van der Plas mapped out the political terrain in the Indies and located 'counter forces' in: the Moehammadijah, a modernist Islamic education and social association which opposed both communism and the Sarekat Islam; the Nahdatoel Oelama, an association of orthodox Muslims, which 'sought the support, at least the friendship of the government'; autonomous administrations (*zelfbesturen*), princely courts of Java's *Vorstenlanden* (principalities), and *priyayi* (aristocrats-turned-bureaucrats); Javanists, 'the local patriots', such as the Boedi Oetomo and the Pasoendan; and the Indonesian Study Club led by Dr. Soetomo in Surabaya, 'a counter force of far more importance', whose members' nationalism is 'beyond any doubt as much as that of the extremists in Bandung and Batavia'. Van der Plas understood that Dr. Soetomo was no rival to Soekarno in charismatic leadership and oratory, but argued, nonetheless, that his energy, pragmatism, and knowledge of Java's countryside could be highly valuable for Java's 'social construction'.

Van der Plas also noted two groups in the PNI: 'the group of engineers with Dr. Tjipto Mangoenkoesoemo as the spiritual father' and the group of lawyers, represented by Sartono and others. Soekarno was the most influential figure in the first group, 'a very gifted speaker, an upright and courageous man, who carries the heart on his tongue, is often incautious, and if he gives his trust, goes very far in it'. 'I regard him as a perfectly sound figure, no doubt [...] revolutionary of temperament and seized by a firm belief in the liberation of Asia in the near future, but by his disinterestedness, his sensitivity and sunny openness, someone who in the future, when he has become a bit older and has learnt to work for a distant future, may be hoped to be ready for fruitful cooperation'.

Having thus assessed the central intellectuals of nationalist politics, van der Plas proposed a two-pronged strategy. The government should 'meet all constructive work with sympathy' and strive to make sure native intellectuals understand that it was possible to work for national construction under the current regime. The government should 'meet every self-motivation in social and economic fields with sympathy', and government subsidies should be given to Soetomo's Indonesian Study Club and Soewardi Soerjaningrat's Taman Siswa. At the same time, the government should 'forcefully combat destructive action' and guarantee 'the peaceful development' of the peoples in the Indies. He proposed establishing a bureau for political affairs to implement this strategy.

Van der Plas' strategy was built on his fine understanding of Indonesian nationalist politics, its terrain, its major forces, their political and ideological positions and their leaders. His analysis of 'counter forces' was the best available in the government. He became personally acquainted with nationalist intellectuals, who he approached from the perspective of political management.

The governor general made a statement in the Volksraad on 15 May 1928 to communicate the government's desire for constructive engagement.[5] He expressed hope that 'the healthy sense of self-preservation' would be 'a strong dam against nationalism that moves in the extremist direction and against the invasion of false slogans'. He continued:

> One should not think that I am blind to the great difficulties which are in the way of those nationalists who, without denying their future ideals, show the insight that the realization [of their ideals] can be approached [in cooperation] with the government. Their position in the political struggle is delicate and difficult…, but the government is certain that in the long run the exchange will be fully honoured. With genuine sympathy, the government continues to watch their efforts and work. It [will be] also vigilant – against those who, because of their utterly unfruitful position of non-cooperation, stand aloof to the government and to the fulfilment of its task.

Clearly de Graeff had Soetomo's Indonesian Study Club in mind for cooperation, but it was the PNI that emerged as the focus of the government's engagement. The reason was simple. As van der Plas put it, his strategy was predicated on two possibilities. If the PNI remained small and marginal, nationalists such as Soetomo and Soewardi would have more influence on the course of nationalist politics. If not, it would depend on what direction Soekarno and the PNI took. It was too early to write off Soekarno as a recalcitrant (*onverzoenlijk*) revolutionary (see Shiraishi 2021: 57–60) nor was it yet time for immediate action against

5 'Bijeenkomst tot opening van de zitting 1928–1929, May 15, 1928, Rede van Zijne Excellentie den Gouverneur-Generaal,' Handelingen Volksraad 1928–1929, pp. 4–5.

the PNI. The government had to wait and see whether the PNI under Soekarno would get to the masses through 'destructive practical politics' (Kwantes 1981: 51–57).

This seems to be what de Graeff had in mind when he explained his position to his officials on 20 August 1928 (Kwantes 1981: 101–106). His message can be summarized as below. The government decided to 'check' the PKI and 'immobilize its core leadership' by means of internment and imprisonment, because it was 'fed' from abroad. The situation created by PNI action is more serious and complicated. One should have no illusion that nationalist feelings among 'the thinking part of the masses' can be suppressed by government intervention... 'The government should let PNI action uncurbed under all circumstances' and 'in assessing if and what measures are needed, he (de Graeff) will consider carefully what should be achieved with them and if and to what extent the opposition should be weighed against the possible useful effect expected of them'. The government has two instruments for the PNI, criminal prosecution and internment. But the PNI leadership has been careful not to provide any excuse for prosecution. Internment is the only instrument available to the government, but it should be the last resort. Enough evidence needs to be marshalled 'to justify internment decisions'. It should also be the internment of a relatively small number of people which is enough to destroy the PNI leadership. A second massive internment as applied to the PKI ... is out of the question. And it should achieve its expected effect in a larger circle to exorcise any potential danger in PNI action. He does not believe all these conditions are there for now... He does not preclude the future possibility of interning Soekarno and others, but it should be under an 'entirely different' situation.

PNI mass action

The government's position on the PNI was to wait and see. The PNI held its first national congress in May 1928 in Surabaya, when it was still a very small party. At the end of 1928 its membership was 2,787 (Ingleson 1979: 58–61; Kwantes 1981: 51–57). The party leadership was aware that it had to keep tight control over local action. Regular courses were held to train second echelon leaders and propagandists. It also began organizing its own trade unions. As PNI propaganda gained momentum, it started to develop into a mass party (Ingleson 1979: 62–68).

The government monitored the PNI closely. In October 1928, van der Plas wrote to the governor general: 'the influence of the PNI will steadily grow'; 'Its propaganda would take a deeper root in the long run than the communist without any real resistance from those educated and well-to-do, and given its influence on students, there would be a real danger'; 'that a great part of intellectuals would join the recalcitrant nationalists in the future' (Kwantes 1981: 115–120). Local government and police officials also became increasingly alert to PNI propaganda. What was at issue was the question of authority inherent in the very theatricality of the rally itself, the effect on the audience of what Soekarno and other PNI leaders said at rallies and of police intervention or non-intervention there (See Shiraishi 1990: 65–68, 159–165).

The PNI leadership then decided to transform the PNI from a cadre to a mass party at its May 1929 congress (Ingleson 1979: 90). It decided to establish trade unions and organize reading clubs. Its membership reached 1,700 in Batavia and 2,800 in Bandung. Cadre training courses held in Bandung and presided over by Soekarno attracted 800 to 1,000 members (Kwantes 1981: 282–289; Ingleson 1979: 94–96).

PNI propaganda action alarmed the government. The government warned the PNI leadership not to go beyond the limits it could tolerate. In July 1929, the government representative stated in the Volksraad that it would not hesitate to intervene if the PNI leadership did not meet three conditions: to use its forces for socially constructive work and guard against destructive actions, to maintain sufficient discipline over its party and to prevent any active resistance movement of its members, and to exercise caution in its recent involvement in trade unionism. In August 1929 he warned the PNI about its relationship with the PI and the Liga, stating that the government would expect popular leaders to demonstrate a sense of responsibility and warning that if excessive disturbances resulted from their propaganda, the government would have to take severe measures.[6]

Yet PNI continued organizing open rallies, meetings, and cadre training courses. Regional governors and residents demanded the government take tougher measures against the party. In November 1929, the advocate general instructed regional chiefs to report on rumours about disturbances and strikes, which generated more rumours about PNI-led disturbances. Rumours of imminent disturbances reminded the governor general and the advocate general of the communist revolts and prompted a decision to intervene in PNI. The attorney general instructed regional chiefs on 24 December 1929, to conduct searches of PNI offices, its leaders' residences, and other premises on 29 December, to confiscate all important documents, to interrogate PNI leaders and propagandists, and to report to him by telegraph about any revolutionary action, contacts with abroad, and who should be considered for internment. Soekarno was arrested along with other PNI leaders and propagandists (Kwantes 1981: 317–318).

The governor general wrote to the minister of colonies on 9 January 1930 that since mid-December there had been a sudden

6 *Handelingen Volksraad*, Aug. 6, 1929.

increase in rumours of imminent disturbances reported to the attorney general, and that both authorities and private persons had received anonymous warnings toward the end of December. His conclusion, as he wrote, was that revolts were in the making, to prevent which he had to act (Kwantes 1981: 318, 323–325).[7] But he also wanted to make it clear publicly that his policy remained unchanged. The government representative to the Volksraad made a statement to underline that there were no policy changes concerning PNI:

> The government policy toward the people's movement – I am authorized to make this announcement expressly – is and remains unchanged... There always is a line drawn between evolutionaries and revolutionaries, between socially useful constructive work and socially dangerous destructive activity. The government has always warned that it shall not tolerate the revolutionary inclination swelling into serious threats. It has always put it as its duty to protect the seeds of sound growth in the native society against harm by popular violence. What is socially productive must be encouraged or at least permitted and what is socially destructive must be assailed and destroyed.[8]

The government, he said, would not destroy PNI, nor ban it, nor be hostile to the 'well-intentioned, at least reformable, currents in PNI'.

The demise of liberal policy

Although the attorney general was certain that the PNI was organizing unrest, no evidence was found in the searches to

7 See also Van der Most, Voorloopig Rapport, Jan. 3, 1930, Mr. 30x/1930.

8 *Handelingen Volksraad*, Jan. 16, 1930.

support his contention. In a few days, all but seven PNI leaders were released from prison. In his report dated 13 May 1930, L.J.A. Roskott, who led the investigation, said that even though Soekarno and three other PNI leaders could be prosecuted, there was no convincing evidence to support the case. The attorney general proposed the governor general intern the four. On 16 June 1930, the governor general announced that the government would prosecute Soekarno and three others.[9] Their trial lasted from 18 August to 29 September 1930. On 22 December 1930, Soekarno was sentenced to four years imprisonment, while three others were sentenced to 24, 20, and 15 months respectively. The sentences were confirmed on appeal by the Batavia court of justice on 17 April 1931.

On 5 May 1931, the governor general reaffirmed his policy of constructive engagement at an administrative conference (Kwantes 1981: 551–555). He once again noted 'the increasing notion of national desires and consciousness in all strata of the native population' and said that whether 'one might deplore it or applaud it', 'one cannot but accept this course of affairs'. His policy would remain unchanged: 'within the limits determined by the law and the government, any effort of the native population for "self-realization" would be unhindered and meet government sympathy... He told senior officials that the native administration has to listen to the voices that come from the population'.

De Graeff thus retained his policy of constructive engagement. He hoped there would be a transition in the movement for 'self-reform' and 'reorientation'. But this hope was based on the

9 Hoofdambtenaar ter beschikking van den procureur-generaal bij het Hooggerechtshof van Nederlandsch Indie, Geheim Verslag van het Vooronderzoek inzake de PNI leiders, May 13, 1930, Mr. 501x/1930; Chief of the ARD, Geheim Rapport over the Partai Nasional Indonesia (PNI), May 13, 1930, Mr. 501x/1930; Kwantes 1981: 371–381, 394–416.

proposition that nationalist intellectuals should be allowed to pursue their political ideals and plans for social and economic construction, as long as they remained within the limits set by the law and the government, did not attempt popular mobilisation, did not threaten peace and order, and therefore remained insignificant and need not be taken seriously by the government. Soekarno would return and challenge this position with mass revolutionary action: he was determined to be taken seriously by the government.

On 31 August 1931, de Graeff remitted the sentences of Soekarno and three others in anticipation of his imminent replacement by de Jonge on 12 September 1931. This was the last signal he sent native intellectuals that he still hoped for constructive cooperation. But it was most likely not read as such. Soekarno by this time had come to be seen by Indonesians as a martyr for the nationalist cause and the remission a personal triumph. Hillen called it 'a certificate of approval' for extremism.

Shaping the native political terrain

Bonifacius C. de Jonge replaced de Graeff as governor general in September 1931. A protégé of Minister of Colonies H. Colijn, he was critical of de Graeff's liberal approach and was determined to give more powers to the native officials to deal firmly with revolutionary endeavours. Van der Plas, de Graeff's adviser for native affairs, was sent to Blitar, East Java, and de Jonge turned to Attorney General R.J.M. Verheijen and Dr. A.D.A. de Kat Angelino, chief official at the general secretariat, for native political affairs. De Kat Angelino believed in 'retraditionalisation', saw the purpose of colonial policy as producing a 'fruitful synthesis' of the East and the West, and regarded nationalism as 'sterile' (Sutherland 1979: 132). The centre of gravity of native policy making shifted towards the attorney general's views.

The new administration coincided with the deepening of the Great Depression, which dealt a crippling blow to the Indies' export economy. The sugar industry in Central and East Java suffered huge losses as demand disappeared, forcing cutbacks in production. The area under sugarcane cultivation declined from 200,000 hectares in 1930/31 to 34,000 in 1933/34. The number of sugar factories in operation fell from 179 to 45 in the same period. Land-owning peasants and agrarian workers were badly hurt (Elson 1984: 233–235; Ingleson 1979: 175–176). De Jonge recognised that this was fertile ground for nationalist propaganda, and was in no mood to tolerate any sign of unrest being stirred up by 'irresponsible Indonesian political leaders' (Wal 1968: 114–116). Under these circumstances, maintaining social order was the highest priority in government deliberations on native policy, which in turn favoured tougher measures on nationalist politics.

Nationalist politics, 1932–1933

The nationalist upon whom Governor General de Graeff relied most for 'purifying' and 'reorientating' the native movement was Soetomo, leader of the Surabaya Indonesian Study Club. After the government raids on the PNI at the end of 1929, Soetomo met with Sartono and other PNI leaders and called for the dissolution of PNI and the creation of a new party. In July 1930, several Leiden trained lawyers moved to Surabaya and joined *Soeloeh Rajat Indonesia*, a newspaper published by the Indonesian Study Club. In November 1930, Soetomo's Indonesian Study Club became the Persatoean Bangsa Indonesia (PBI, Indonesian National Union). Its stronghold was in East Java, but it rapidly expanded its influence in Central Java (Ingleson 1979: 122–125; Kwantes 1981: 575–577).

The PNI central leadership, however, did not go along with Soetomo. After Soekarno's arrest, Sartono assumed leadership of the PNI and on 25 April 1930, the party decided to disband under his leadership. Twelve of 14 branches supported Sartono and established a new party, Partai Indonesia (Partindo, Indonesian Party), on 1 May (Kwantes 1981: 575–577). PNI members who had opposed the party dissolution established their own associations: Golongan Merdeka (Free Group). Hatta and his most trusted lieutenant Sjahrir, who were still in the Netherlands, were behind the group (Ingleson 1979: 144–154; Kwantes 1981: 589–590, 649–650).

When Soekarno was released from prison at the end of 1931, he was almost immediately a dominant figure in the movement again. He returned to centre stage at the Great Indonesia Congress (Congres Indonesia Raja) held in Surabaya 1–3 January 1932, where he announced he would join neither the Partindo nor Golongan Merdeka, but would instead work to restore the unity of the old PNI. He was convinced that 'national spirit' was there in the people's mind. His 'message' was to forge a 'national will' out of 'national spirit', to restore unity between the Partindo and Golongan Merdeka and achieve unity in the national movement under his leadership (Kwantes, 1928: 609–616).

Whatever possibility there had been for a 'reorientation' of the movement under Soetomo dissipated with Soekarno's return. Soekarno, however, was not successful in unifying the Partindo and Golongan Merdeka. In March 1932, Golongan Merdeka established the Pendidikan National Indonesia (Indonesian National Education) or the New PNI (PNI Baru) under Sjahrir's leadership. It called for 'power formation' through non-cooperation and mass action and announced its plan to establish a nation-wide association 'as soon as the suitable leader for it is found'.[10] The leader it had in mind was Hatta. In a letter to the governor general in July 1932 the attorney general reported a perceived threat in the New PNI, arguing that Sjahrir and Hatta would try to reignite the revolutionary movement which had been moribund since the PNI had disbanded (Kwantes 1981: 647–648). Hatta returned to the Indies in August 1932 and assumed the New PNI leadership from Sjahrir (Kwantes 1981: 647–648; Legge, 1988: 21–38).[11]

Partindo, meanwhile, had increased its membership to 3,000 with strongholds in Batavia, Yogyakarta, Surakarta, and Surabaya by February 1932. While the PNI had been led by Tjipto's proteges and Leiden-trained lawyers, student activists from the Faculty of Law in Batavia now formed Partindo's backbone. Active in the PPPI (Indonesian Students' Union), they were the driving force behind the unification of youth organisations such as Jong Java, Pemoeda Indonesia, and Pemoeda Soematera into Indonesia Moeda in December 1930. By the time of the Partindo congress in Batavia in May 1932, PPPI activists such as Amir Sjarifoeddin had emerged as leaders alongside Sartono and others (Kwantes 1981: 489–491, 647–648).

At the first Partindo congress in May 1932, Sartono announced that it was a political party seeking to achieve Free Indonesia on the principles of the 'right of self-determination, Indonesian nationalism, self-help, and democracy'. By the second congress in Surabaya in April 1933, Partindo membership had reached more than 20,000, with 43 branches in Java and Madura alone (Kwantes 1981: 635–638).

The New PNI and Partindo were threats to PBI's dominance of the private sector trade unions. The trade union federation Soetomo had established in Surabaya in May 1930 was trans-

10 Adviser for native affairs to GG, March 12, 1932, Mr. 303x/1932.

11 Adviser for native affairs to GG, March 12, 1932, Mr. 303x/1932.

formed into Centraal Perhimpoenan Boeroeh Indonesia (Centre for Indonesian Workers Unions) in May 1933 under the influence of Soekarno and Sjahrir. Despite Soetomo's warning against 'bringing politics in[to] the trade union movement', the federation adopted self-help and nationalism as its guiding principles (Kwantes 1981: 766–769).

Reshaping the terrain: The wild school ordinance

The government became increasingly alarmed at the influence of the Partindo and the New PNI in the movement. The wild school ordinance became a major issue in this context. The ordinance was first introduced in 1923 to bring the non-subsidized, private, native education under government supervision. It required teachers of private schools to report to local authorities and prohibited teaching anything perceived to be a threat to peace and order. The government tightened the regulation in 1925. granting powers to local authorities to prohibit anyone from teaching who could be expected 'to educate his pupils in a spirit harmful for peace and order'. Hit by the depression, in 1932 the government drastically reduced its educational spending, which led to increased enrolments at private, unsubsidised schools in the early 1930s. The government tried to regulate such schools, called 'wild schools', with a revised ordinance which stipulated that all teachers in private schools should have permission from local authorities before they could begin teaching, and that to qualify for a permit they should have a certificate from a government or a government-subsidized private school. The ordinance was a direct threat to unsubsidised private schools and their teachers (Surjomihardjo 1986: 39–45; Ingleson 1979: 205).

Popular resistance to the new regulation began on 1 October 1932, the day it was enacted. Ki Hadjar Dewantara (Soewardi

Soerjaningrat), the leader of Taman Siswa schools, sent a telegram to the governor general warning of the strongest possible non-violent opposition. Three days later, he called for passive resistance. Indonesian parties and associations participated in protest action. The Partindo called for resistance. The PSII (Indonesian Party of Islamic Association) issued a statement for 'spontaneous' protest meetings. The Moehammadijah announced its total disagreement with the ordinance. The BO (Boedi Oetomo) announced if the ordinance was not withdrawn by 31 March 1933, it would pull all its members from representative bodies. Local committees were established with representatives from the Taman Siswa, the Partindo, the New PNI, the PSII, the BO, the Moehammadijah, and other parties and associations. Protest rallies were held in many places, often simultaneously.

The widespread popular protest alarmed the government. Kiewiet de Jonge, government representative to the Volksraad, met with Ki Hadjar Dewantara in October 1932 and assured him that 'bona fide private educational institutions need not worry about their position'. The governor general was ready to drop the ordinance if an initiative came from the Volksraad and wild schools were not 'misused'. R.A.A. Wiranatakoesoema, regent of Bandung and Volksraad member, offered the government a way out. In January 1933, he introduced a proposal in the Volksraad for a temporary suspension of the ordinance. In February 1933 the governor general suspended the ordinance.

The government yielded on this issue because de Jonge did not want to make Ki Hadjar Dewantara 'a Gandhi-figure' and because it could have a 'contagious' effect, encouraging popular resistance on other issues (Wal 1968: 152). It was not, however, an unalloyed victory for the movement. The government yielded to the movement on condition that Taman Siswa and other schools police themselves and not allow their teachers and students to be active in 'practical' politics. But it was an important victory, for the government did agree to allow a space for the movement in education.

Reshaping the terrain: Rural action

Another arena in which the government negotiated the limits of tolerance for the movement was rural action.

In West Java, the government was alarmed at Partindo and New PNI action in Batavia, Cirebon, and Indramayu. The governor of West Java reported to the governor general in December 1932 that the situation in Batavia was 'not that good'. The major force there was the Partindo, with its membership reaching 8,000 in the city and private estates in the vicinity. With terrible economic conditions in private estates, there could be a possibility, he wrote, that 'as in 1926 the political agitation finds a fertile soil here ... for direct extremist action'. The situation was worse in Indramayu, he reported, where economic hardships combined with administration and police understaffing. The New PNI was very active there. Resident of Cirebon van der Plas was of the opinion, the governor reported, that if its activity expanded, it would pose a direct threat to peace and order (Kwantes 1981: 669–671).

Van der Plas applied the strategy he had outlined in his 1928 report and mobilized 'counter forces' to contain and neutralize revolutionary forces. As he wrote in December, he 'carefully as well as consciously' rallied the support of 'trustworthy and order-loving elements, above all adat elders and kyais' to fight the New PNI. This 'counter action' proved successful, he said, and there were signs of New PNI members returning their membership cards to local authorities (Kwantes 1981: 671–674).

In Surakarta, Pakempalan Kawoela Soerakarta (PKS, Association of Surakartan Subjects) was the greatest concern. Its central figure was Singgih, a leader in the PBI. PKS's first branch formed in Polanharjo, a sugar plantation region, in November 1932 and focused on rallying popular support in the countryside. In 1933 it expanded its activity into the territory of the Mangkunegaran royal house. Its rallies attracted huge crowds, with villagers walking 'miles' to see 'Goesti (Lord) Singgih'. As its name suggests, the PKS was an association of royalists. Singgih sought to cooperate with an association of princes from the Surakarta royal house.[12] Yet the local authorities were alarmed at its members looking to the PKS branch leaders rather than village officials for guidance, many 'recidivists' had been appointed as branch leaders, and its activists advocated for the refusal to perform village corvee duties and pay taxes.[13] The resident of Surakarta warned Singgih to tone down its propaganda.

The situation in Yogyakarta was similar, where the Pakempalan Kawoela Ngajogjakarta (PKN, Association of Yogyakartan Subjects), established by Pangeran (Prince) Ario Soerjodiningrat, a half-brother of Sultan Hamengku Boewono VII, in 1930, emerged as a major influence. Its stated purpose was to work for the good of the Yogyakartan principality and its royal house, the welfare of its subjects, harmony of the native population of different statuses, and the achievement of self-rule on a democratic basis. It was royalist and anti-revolutionary. It organised congresses, open rallies, member meetings, and cadre training courses. It established cooperatives and schools, purchased rice milling machinery, motor vehicles (for taxi and rental) and a printing firm, and published its own organ. With a membership of 34,000 within six months of its establishment in late 1930 and more than 200,000 by May 1932, it was far larger than any other comparable organization of its day.

---

12 Ibid.

13 Ibid.

According to William O'Malley (1977), peasants joined the PKN knowing that it had spoken out against the head tax and felt that they therefore did not need to pay it. Local leaders, sensing the emergence of a new source of authority, challenged village officials. Incidents took place time and again in which Pangeran Soerjodiningrat was mentioned as *ratu adil* (just king) and there were rumours that those who were not PKN members would not be part of the new kingdom when it was established. By 1933, the governor of Central Java had called Pangeran Soerjodiningrat 'an untrustworthy socialist in duplicity' and officials began pressuring villagers to resign from the PKN. Its membership rapidly declined, its revenue stream from dues dried up, and its cooperatives collapsed almost completely (O'Malley 1977: 309–334).[14]

In East Java, the PBI was the major presence in the countryside where the most acute issue was over the contracts between sugar factories and peasants for land which they could no longer use for sugarcane cultivation. Factories sought to annul or revise these contracts and relied on village chiefs and local government officials to find in their favour in negotiations with peasants. The PBI actively represented the peasantry in these negotiations. Its peasant organization, Roekoen Tani (RT, Peasants' Association), encouraged the peasants to unite to press their claims against the sugar factories. By 1933, according to the governor of East Java, it had 'annexed the whole political terrain of East Java' (Elson 1984: 234–238; Kwantes 1981: 802–809).

PBI/RT activities were centred in Sidoarjo. PBI leaders regularly visited the region, consulted with local RT leaders, and attended RT meetings. Those meetings discussed not only the reduction in sugar cane planting area, but also issues such

---

14 See also Chief of the ARD, Overzicht van de Politieke Beweging in de Gouvernementen Soerakarta en Jogjakarta, May 10, 1936, Mr. 602x/1936.

as land taxes, salt and kerosene prices, dismissal of village officials, establishing rice barns, and changes in land tenure (Kwantes 1981: 804). In the village of Sukorame, local RT executive members were called '*loerah*' (village chief), '*tjarik*' (secretary), and '*kebajan*' (messenger), as if they were village officials. The resident of Surabaya argued that RTs were led by 'entirely unfavourable elements (dismissed village heads and foremen [*mandoer*] of sugar factories)' and that those peasants who were willing to renegotiate the terms of contracts with factories were afraid of being accused of being 'spies' by RT (Kwantes 1981: 803–804). With the resident's approval, the assistant resident of Sidoarjo intervened to suppress unrest and 'restore ... the peasants' peace of mind'. The PID (i.e., *Politieke Inlichting Dienst*, or Political Intelligence Service) was deployed to watch PBI and RT rallies and meetings. Native officials were instructed to maintain 'the right standpoint'. The resident of Surabaya said that the PBI was 'hostile to authority', much like the Partindo and the New PNI (Kwantes 1981: 806). 'The inland [*binnenlanden*] can tolerate no political agitation', he argued, because of the economic 'debacle', the population was 'emotional, primitive and easy to incite', and there were 'no proper intelligence services and power instruments' available (Kwantes 1981: 809).

The resident of Surabaya clearly expressed a view widely shared among Dutch officials about the policy the government should take vis-à-vis rural action. Whether in West Java, the principalities, or East Java, they agreed that rural areas should be off limits to any organizational activity – loyalist, royalist, constructive, evolutionary, bona fide, destructive, revolutionary, and *mala fide* – because whatever the stated intentions were, parties and associations would create a space for 'recalcitrant', 'wild', and 'criminal' elements to act, people were 'emotional, primitive, and easy to incite', and there were 'no proper intelligence services' there.

The policy shift

The 1932 wild school ordinance proved to be an excellent opportunity for Indonesian parties and associations to unite and resist the government. Organized rural action often prompted unintended resistance to the authority. Partindo membership expanded from 4,300 in May 1932 to 20,000 in July 1933 (Ingleson 1979: 189), alarming the governor general, who worried the situation might get out of control. It was under these circumstances that the crew of the Dutch warship de Zeven Provincien mutinied on 4–10 February 1933 (Wal 1968: 158–160).

The governor general convened an extraordinary meeting of the Council of the Netherlands Indies on 8 February 1933 (Kwantes 1981: 684–693), worried about the potential for the mutiny to 'infect' the native society (Wal 1968: 162). The attorney general argued that political freedom for natives should be restricted to such an extent that any undesirable consequences could not happen. Governor General De Jonge did not agree; although he recognised that it 'is attractive for its simplicity, its easy handling, and its underlying rational thought', he believed that there would be objections to those measures in the Netherlands (Kwantes 1981: 684–693). By the end of March, however, he had decided that he needed to handle the matter more systematically.

In a letter to Minister of Colonies de Graaff on 11 April 1933, de Jonge spelled out his position (Kwante1981: 721–25). All civil servants were prohibited from membership in any society with either revolutionary or non-cooperation principles (such as the Partindo, the New PNI, and the PSII). Neither membership nor participation in societies with social-democratic principles was allowed for any members of the state coercive apparatuses (army, fleet, and police). Civil servants should be required to take an oath of allegiance. And all the executive members of trade unions who were civil servants should be required to declare their loyalty to the government.

There was a broad consensus in the government that it should not tolerate any risk of disturbances. Government representative to the Volksraad Kiewiet de Jonge said in late April 1933 that as in the 1923 railway strike, the 1926–1927 communist 'disturbances', and the 1929 PNI-led unrest, 'today, in 1933, the course of events' was coming to a point of disjunction and that as the popular movement evolved, 'the general attitude of leading figures [was] getting increasingly irreconcilable'. This was a frank admission that the memories of past events haunted the government, that constructive engagement was not working, and that the government would not allow the movement to develop in such a way that might lead to disturbances (Kwantes 1981: 729–737).

On 27 June 1933, the government banned civil servants from joining or working with associations that actively or passively acted against the Indies state. The Partindo and the New PNI were designated as such associations. The decree allowed civil servants to remain as members of a trade union if its executive had at least a civil servant among its members. For a civil servant to serve on the board of a trade union, he was required to sign a declaration of allegiance to the Indies state (Kwantes 1981: 729–737).

De Kat Angelino, however, did not think the government had gone far enough and, when Colijn came to power in the Netherlands as prime minister and colonial minister in May 1933, thought the timing was right for taking stronger measures. He submitted a note to de Jonge in late June 1933, arguing that the very nature of organized mass action would create problems, that Partindo and New PNI revolutionary propaganda was creating trouble and dangerous trends in all sectors of the population, that the government was being made a scapegoat, that moderates, weak in the first place, were being further weakened by rising radicalism, and that even though the fanatic revolutionary associations were small in membership, people would join in as initial timidity wore off (Kwantes 1981: 819–833). He further argued that banning civil servants from joining these parties and imposing tougher control on public meetings would not be enough to prevent Partindo and the New PNI growing in influence. He predicted that without further government measures there would be another '*deraillement*' in the near future. He concluded that 'some simple guidelines' were needed to cleanse the movement and to force it to change from revolutionary to evolutionary nationalism, from the destructive to the constructive, and from the disloyal to the loyal. The government should make it clear, he suggested, that it would not allow any association with a non-cooperation principle to take political action.

On 18 July, the governor general asked Deputy Attorney General G. Vonk for his opinion about banning the meetings (*vergaderverbod*) of Partindo and the New PNI (Kwantes 1981: 850–851). On 31 July, the attorney general proposed banning the meetings of Partindo and the New PNI along with interning their leaders as a preventive measure (Kwantes 1981: 855–857). On the same day, Soekarno was arrested in Batavia. On 1 August, the Council of the Netherlands Indies met and endorsed the attorney general's proposed measures of banning meetings and selective internment. The governor general imposed the meeting ban on the Partindo and the New PNI on the same day, to take effect immediately (Kwantes 1981: 858–859). On 29 August, the governor general decided to monitor the press more closely and to muzzle (*persbreidel*) the PNI newspapers *Soeara Oemoem* (public voice) and *Persatoean Indonesia* (Kwantes 1982: 21–36).

In the meantime, de Kat Anglino sent another note to the governor general in August 1933 to explain his view on government policy to the native political movement (Kwantes 1982: 1–20). In his view nationalism as represented by the Partindo, the New PNI, and others was 'anti-Western, anti-kafir, anti-capitalist, anti-imperialist, anti-Dutch and anti-regime' and as a matter of principle the government should ban all these parties on the grounds that they conflict with peace and order. Trade unions should be 'free' from political influence. The right of association and assembly should not be allowed, not only for the sake of peace and order, but also for the sake of the 'healthy and balanced' development of native communities. To that end, he wrote, it would suffice to revise the legal provisions concerning exercising the right of assembly to require prior notification to the local administration for holding political meetings (both open and closed).

By the end of August 1933, the governor general decided to take action as de Kat Angelino had suggested (Kwantes 1982: 21–36). In the meantime, the attorney general had proposed internment of Soekarno in a letter to the governor general on 19 August 1933 (Kwantes 1982: 870–882). It was a foregone conclusion, but the reasoning offered by the Council of the Netherlands Indies on 13 October clearly expresses the government's foremost concern about Soekarno. The Council was convinced that Soekarno was a man of 'weak and uncontrolled nature' and that even if he promised to moderate himself in the future, 'he would be unable to resist the charm of the applauding audience' (Kwantes 1982: 44–49). To put it differently, the Council in effect concluded that it was not only his ability to mobilize the masses but also his inability to resist being carried away with popular radicalism that was a threat.

The attorney general offered different reasons for his proposal to intern Hatta, Sjahrir and other New PNI leaders in a letter to the governor general dated 22 December 1933 (Kwantes 1982: 189–206). In his view, Hatta, a proponent of the cooperation between revolutionary nationalists and communists, was culpable beyond any doubt. He also noted that New PNI leaders were preparing to go underground and that Sjahrir was the head of the revolutionary trade union federation. It should not be a cause for alarm for now, he said, but cautioned that in the long run it could become impossible to fight revolutionary propaganda and agitation if the movement became 'anchored' in trade unions. The history of the 1926–27 revolts 'taught us', he wrote, that the longer the government allowed 'criminals' to grow, the more disturbing and extensive they would become and that the government in the end would have to intervene. Something similar was going on, which 'according to my firm conviction' would eventually lead to similar mass internments, 'unless main troublemakers are eliminated in time'. He proposed Hatta, Sjahrir, and other New PNI executive members be interned. The Council endorsed his proposal on 16 February 1934 (Kwantes 1982: 217–220). In its opinion, the New PNI had been 'walking right along the barbed wire', and intervention would clearly demonstrate that the government had 'moved the barbed wire'. Hatta, Sjahrir, and others were arrested on 24 February 1934 for internment.

The 'barbed wire' metaphor the Council employed sheds light on how senior officials understood the policy shift, but it does not capture the precise nature of that shift. The 'No trespass' signs, which the Council called the barbed wire, were not moved. Instead, the government decision to intern Soekarno, Hatta and others created a grey zone where those who ventured into it might risk being arrested, imprisoned and interned. This zone was not clearly marked, yet it was obviously there, because it was watched intensely by the police. Partindo, the New PNI, and their substructures were not treated as harshly as the PKI and the Pari, but people were aware – and the police made them aware – that they were being watched and that their actions risked arrest, imprisonment, and internment. The grey zone was also capable of expanding or shifting: Partindo and the New PNI were banned; trade unions, youth organizations, reading clubs, and other substructures associated with the parties were suffocated; and Soekarno, Hatta, and other New PNI leaders were arrested and interned. No one who led a party or one of its substructures, whether cooperationist or non-cooperationist, could be certain they would not be arrested, imprisoned or interned. Under these conditions 'politics' came to be equated with 'policing'.

It should be no surprise, then, that the government took further measures in the following months. In September 1933, it banned all teachers at government and government-subsidized schools from being members or attending meetings of Indonesia Moeda. In October it banned state employees from joining the PBKI (Indonesia Railway Workers Union) (Ingleson 1979: 222–223). In November 1933 de Kat Angelino made a case for a series of 'desirable political measures' the government should take 'to influence the political situation' and to 'combat excesses in the press and printed materials' (Kwantes 1982: 103–109). He reasoned that once the government banned party newspapers, journals, and periodicals, they would publish pamphlets; if the government banned associations, they would hold meetings and gatherings; if the government interned revolutionary party leaders, a new generation of leaders, already active in student and youth associations, would take over their positions; if the government required any association to obtain permission to hold an open public rally, they would organize a closed meeting; if the government allowed activists to keep teaching at schools, they would influence school children. His conclusion was that 'the [entire] terrain be surveilled completely'.

The Council of the Netherlands Indies endorsed de Kat Angelino's proposal on 13 April 1934 that the government toughen 'the legal arsenal against popular politics' such as extraordinary powers, muzzling the press, banning associations, requiring associations to obtain government permission to hold open public meetings, possible travel bans and teaching bans (Kwantes 1982: 226–235).

politics=policing

In his final days as governor general, de Jonge gave a speech at a conference of governors, residents, and regents of Java on 18 August 1936:

> The governor general has little to say about the political situation. In general there is enough reason to be satisfied. Although a small upswing of unrest can be expected here and there [...], vigilance and if necessary deliberate and calm intervention can no doubt manage it. When he looks back at the past five years, he is surprised how little he has to do to maintain peace and order. But when he is here [in the conference] and finds himself among all the regents, this surprise disappears. After all, the good, quiet, patient people, administered by men of position and standing as regents, must be able to live in peace, if only one manages to curb the few malicious elements. (Kwantes 1982: 349–356)

De Jong had good reasons to be complacent about the movement. The governor of East Java observed that even though student, youth, and scouting organizations still constituted a major base for Partindo, the government ban on the SBKA (Railway Workers

Union) had a devastating effect on the party.[15] ARD chief van der Most reported about the situation in the Vorstenlanden that the arrest of New PNI leaders in Surakarta in June 1933 and the ban on meetings had crippled the party, that youth groups remained active, but not Partindo and the New PNI.[16] The regent of Bandung Wiranatakoesoemah reported in 1936 that the Partindo and the New PNI were reduced to a small group of core members and that there was not much to say about trade unions and youth movements. He also said that religious associations in Bandung were largely under his control and that although some politicians joined religious associations, it should not be a concern, because any attempt at political infiltration into religious associations would be resisted by their members (Kwantes 1982: 349–356).

It should be clear by now how the Indies government's policy on the movement evolved following the 1926–1927 revolts. 'Mapping' (a word the Dutch used) the native world to learn how best to mount a counter-offensive against the PNI, van der Plas identified 'counter forces' in the Moehammadijah, the Nahdatoel Oelama, autonomous administrations (*zelfbesturen*), the princely courts of Java's *Vorstenlanden*, *priyayi*, 'the local patriots' such as the BO and the Pasoendan, and Soetomo's Indonesian Study Club in Surabaya. He was well disposed to Soetomo, but did not see him as a rival to Soekarno. This was the reason he pinned his hopes on Soekarno to guide the movement onto a constructive path. The governor general granted Soekarno a remission to signal his desire and willingness for constructive cooperation.

This liberal approach, however, did not work as de Graeff had hoped. De Jonge, de Kat Angelino and others adopted a more

15 Governor of East Java to GG, Nov. 9. 1933, Mr. 1403x/1933.

16 Chief of the ARD, Overzicht van de politieke beweging in de Gouvernementen Soerakarta en Jogjakarta, May 10, 1936, Mr. 602x/1936.

hardline approach that not only relied on the political policing mechanism to place the native population under surveillance, but also adopted van der Plas' map of the native world and built its strategy accordingly. The government made deals with the Taman Siswa, the Moehammadijah and other 'bona fide' educational institutions to allow them freedom within their own space, on the condition that they avoid nationalist politics, self-police their teachers and students, and in effect work as de facto 'counter forces' to nationalist politics. The government opted to rely on *volksleiders* (traditional leaders) as represented by Wiranatakoesoemah and no longer hoped much for cooperation with – and sometimes was outright hostile to – moderate, bona fide, cooperationist forces (such as Soetomo's PBI, BO, and Pasoendan), because the latter's rural action tended to attract 'bad elements' and provoke unintended consequences. The terrain thus hedged, the remaining space was left for nationalist politics and political policing. De Jonge and his lieutenants were confident of the state's capacity to police and control the space. Political policing measures adopted under de Jonge effectively denied Indonesian nationalists any form in which popular politics manifested – holding rallies and meetings, publishing newspapers and journals, organizing trade unions and youth, women and scout associations for nationalist politics, while banning government employees from membership in any nationalist parties and organizations and interning a select few party leaders.

Memories of the 1926–1927 'disturbances' continued to haunt the government, driving government policy in a particular direction. Governor General de Graeff understood that the government had to create a space for nationalists to make his constructive engagement work, but was compelled to intervene in the PNI and arrest Soekarno out of fear of the wild forces and imminent disturbances that popular politics might unleash. The more reactionary Governor General de Jonge introduced much tougher policies for dealing with the popular movements in the hopes of quelling disturbances triggered by the economic hardships of the Great Depression. Anything that might induce disturbances was deemed 'revolutionary'. In this respect the distinctions between revolutionary/evolutionary, non-cooperation/cooperation, mala fide/bona fide, radical/moderate became largely irrelevant. It was not that the government was not confident in its capacity to police and control nationalist politics. The government was haunted by wild forces and had no other option but to do its best to contain those forces. It forced all the nationalist parties to be cooperationist, but did not allow rural action in social and economic fields for fear of unleashing the wild forces that Soekarno had set loose in PNI and through Partindo propaganda, the same forces that had carried away Soekarno and mobilized the PKI in 1925–1927. The Indies state in the 1930s placed the native population under much closer surveillance than in the 1910s and '20s. Its historical and ever-present fear of popular forces running wild and threatening the highly treasured colonial peace and order drove the state to adopt a hardline approach of clamping down on native popular movements. The Dutch thought they had conquered illegibility, but they could not read Indonesian minds and hearts, certainly not of those activists who moved in-and-out of the underground.

References

Abeyasekere, Susan (1972), 'Relations between the Indonesian Cooperating Nationalists and the Dutch, 1935–1942', Ph.D. dissertation, Monash University.

Anderson, Benedict (1990), *Language and Power*, Ithaca: Cornell University Press.

Anderson, Benedict (1991), *Imagined Communities*, Ithaca: Cornell University Press.

Elson, Robert E. (1984), *Javanese Peasants and the Colonial Sugar Industry: Impact and Change in an East Java Residency, 1830–1940*. Singapore: Oxford University Press.

Ingleson, John (1975), *Perhimpunan Indonesia and the Indonesian Nationalist Movement, 1923–1928*, Melbourne: Monash Centre for Southeast Asian Studies.

Ingleson, John (1979), *Road to Exile: The Indonesian Nationalist Movement, 1927–1934*, Singapore: Heinemann.

Kwantes, R.C. (ed.) (1978), *De Ontwikkeling van de Nationalistische Beweging in Nederlandsch-Indie, Bronnenpublikatie 2e Stuk Medio 1923–1928*, Groningen: Wolters-Noordhoff.

Kwantes, R.C. (ed.) (1981), *De Ontwikkeling van de Nationalistische Beweging in Nederlandsch-Indie, Bronnenpublikatie 3de Stuk 1928–Aug. 1933*, Groningen: Wolters-Noordhoff.

Kwantes, R.C. (ed.) (1982), *De Ontwikkeling van de Nationalistische Beweging in Nederlandsch-Indie, Bronnenpublikatie 4de Stuk Aug. 1933–1942*, Groningen: Wolters-Noordhoff.

Legge, J.D. (1988), *Intellectuals and Nationalism in Indonesia: A Study of the Following recruited by Sutan Sjahrir in Occupation Jakarta*, Ithaca: Cornell Modern Indonesia Project.

O'Malley, William J. (1977), 'Indonesia in the Great Depression: A Study of East Sumatra and Jogjakarta in the 1930's', Ph.D. dissertation, Cornell University.

Scott, James C. (1998), *Seeing Like a State: How Certain Schemes to Improve the Human Condition Have Failed*, New Haven and London: Yale University Press.

Scott, James C. (2010), 'The Trouble with the View from Above', *Cato Unbound*, https://www.cato-unbound.org/2010/09/08/james-c-scott/trouble-view-above/

Shiraishi, Takashi (1990), *An Age in Motion: Popular Radicalism in Java 1912–1926*, Ithaca and London: Cornell University Press.

Shiraishi, Takashi (1997), 'Policing the Phantom Underground', *Indonesia* 63, April.

Shiraishi, Takashi (2003), 'A New Regime of Order: The Origin of Modern Surveillance Politics in Indonesia', in James T. Siegel and Audrey R. Kahin (eds), *Southeast Asia over Three Generations: Essays Presented to Benedict R. O'G Anderson*, Ithaca: Cornell Southeast Asia Program.

Shiraishi, Takashi (2021), *The Phantom World of Digul*, Kyoto and Singapore: Kyoto University Press and National University of Singapore Press.

Surjomihardjo, Abdurrachman (1986), 'Taman Siswa and the "Wild Schools"', in Colin Wild and Peter Carey (eds), *Born in Fire: The Indonesian Struggle for Independence*, Athens, Ohio: Ohio University Press, pp. 39–45.

Sutherland, Heather (1979), *The Making of a Bureaucratic Elite: The Colonial Transformation of the Javanese Priyayi*, Singapore: Heinemann.

Wal, S.L. van der (ed.) (1968), *Herinneringen van Jhr. Mr. B. C. de Jonge met brieven uit zijn nalatenschap*, Groningen: Wolters-Noordhoff.

Chapter 7

Independence and Public Health: Technologies of Rule in the Colonial Philippines, 1900–1930s

Ma. Mercedes G. Planta

Introduction

While scholars often describe the United States (US) as an empire, citing its global military presence, economic influence, and political interventions, the US has consistently refrained from identifying itself as such, due to a combination of ideological, historical, and political factors. Central to the US identity is its commitment to democracy, liberty, and self-determination – values that are at odds with the nature of empire, which typically involves domination and control over other peoples. This contradiction is evident in the nation's founding, as outlined in the US Declaration of Independence, where the thirteen American colonies explicitly rejected British imperial rule in favour of independence. The colonies' desire to break free from British control was a clear rejection of imperial authority, marking the beginning of the US' quest for self-governance and sovereignty, establishing the philosophical and political foundation for American independence.

The concept of the US as an empire, nevertheless, has long been embedded in its history and rhetoric (Immerwahr 2019). George Washington in a letter to John Hancock, American founding father and hero of the American Revolution described the US as uniquely founded during an era of enlightenment, when human rights were better understood and knowledge more accessible. He envisioned Americans as 'sole Lords and Proprietors' of a vast, resource-rich continent, with the 'foundation of our Empire' offering unparalleled opportunities for political happiness, intellectual advancement, and societal refinement (Sparrow 2019: 339).[1]

In the late nineteenth century, particularly around the time of the 1898 Spanish-American War, Americans frequently referred to the US as an empire, regardless of their stance on overseas expansion. Across this period policymakers and intellectuals largely supported the ideals of territorial growth, statehood integration, resistance to foreign influence, and economic prosperity, reflecting a shared vision of the nation's imperial trajectory (Sparrow 2019: 39).

This study aims to contribute to the genealogy of the state through a specific geographical setting and historical context: the American colonial administration in the Philippines during the early twentieth century. By examining the technical workings of the American colonial public health system within the broader Filipino campaign for independence, this study aims to add to the scholarship on state formation and societal development (See, for example, Arendt 1958; Claessen and Skalnik 1978; Hobson 2004; Tilly 1990; Burns 2017).

In 2009, Alfred W. McCoy and Francisco A. Scarano's *Colonial Crucible: Empire in the Making of the Modern American State* presented a pivotal thesis on the profound influence of US colonial experiences in shaping the domestic formation of the modern American state. Their work highlights how innovations in public health, environmental management, and prison reform, among other policies introduced in the colonies, were later

1 George Washington, 'George Washington to John Hancock (Circular)', 11 June, Head Quarters Newburgh, New York, Washington Papers, The University of Virginia (1783), retrieved from: https://washingtonpapers.org/documents/george-washington-to-john-hancock-circular-11-june-1783/.

integrated into US governance. This process reveals the ways in which the colonial experience influenced state-building beyond the confines of the empire.

Similarly, Ann Stoler and Frederick Cooper's 1997 *Tensions of Empire: Colonial Cultures in a Bourgeois World*, expands on this notion by exploring the intricate relationships between colonial powers and their colonies. Their work focuses on how European imperial projects, particularly in the eighteenth through early twentieth centuries, contributed to the development of bourgeois societal structures both in the metropole and in the colonies. *Tensions of Empire* shows how the imperial context not only redefined ideas of modernity, welfare, and inclusion but also sparked the contestation of these concepts within the colonial sphere, revealing the fluid and dynamic boundaries between coloniser and colonised.

These two works complement each other by offering a broader understanding of how imperial governance shaped both the colonies and the metropole, highlighting the reciprocal nature of this relationship. Where *Colonial Crucible* illustrates the transference of colonial innovations to the metropole, *Tensions of Empire* contextualises the broader political and cultural dynamics that enabled such exchanges, providing a broader perspective on how imperialism influenced both state formation and societal values across time and space.

Building on these works, this study shifts the focus to the Philippines, exploring how American colonial public health strategies shaped both governance and everyday life in the colony. The study draws on Michel Foucault's concept of governmentality – those techniques, codes, and rationalities that direct human behaviour and create conditions for certain norms and practices to emerge (Foucault 1997: xvii; Burchell, Gordon and Miller 1991; Foucault 1991; Gordon 1991). Through public health policies, the colonial government shaped Filipinos' health and hygiene practices as both a disciplinary mechanism and a means of fostering a sense of self aligned with colonial objectives. These 'regimes of truth and power' (Rabinow 1997: xvii) not only conditioned individual behaviour but also structured the broader social order, as seen in the context of the Philippines under American colonial rule at the time.

This study identifies public health as a colonial crucible that not only directed behaviour and mediated the relationship between Filipinos and Americans but also shaped Filipino responses to political and social conditions. Public health measures functioned as a tool for structuring patterns of governance during the early twentieth century, moulding both individual behaviours and the broader social order. Through targeted initiatives in health, hygiene, nutrition, sanitation, and medical education, the American colonial administration aimed to transform Filipinos into subjects who embodied the rationalities of colonial governance. These measures served a dual purpose: they were tools for assessing the capacity of Filipinos for self-rule and mechanisms for promoting 'responsible' behaviour that aligned with the ideals of the American civilising mission. In this way, public health was not only a means of controlling and disciplining the population but also an instrument that reinforced American colonial authority and bolstered Filipino support for American colonial rule during a period when aspirations for Filipino independence were gaining momentum.

Technicians of rule: School children, education and public health

The American rhetoric of civilising mission in the Philippines framed the development of formal knowledge, political freedom, healthy bodies, and improved living conditions as interlinked goals, with the promise of independence central to the rationale for American public health efforts. While the Spanish colonisers remade Filipino society through religion, the Americans sought to prepare Filipinos for self-rule and democracy through education, the English language, and public health reforms. This aspect of the American civilising mission transformed the Philippines not only into a 'laboratory of modernity' but also placed Filipinos at the centre of colonial policy and scientific research subject to discipline, surveillance, and reform (Stoler and Cooper 1997: 4–5). Public health and education thus became the arenas in which the drama of Filipino 'progress' towards democracy was played out, with the colonial public health system serving as a crucial tool in the American project of state-building and governance in the archipelago.

William Howard Taft, the first American governor-general of the Philippines (1901–1904), firmly believed that the education system was critical in promoting a healthy lifestyle, a perspective he emphasised in his correspondence with Secretary of the Interior Dean Worcester (1901–1913). Taft saw the school system as not just an educational tool but a means of fostering public health, with a 'sanitary' role that was as important, if not more so, than its educational function.[2] Director of the Bureau of Health Victor G. Heiser (1905–1915) shared this view, arguing that educating Filipinos about hygiene, alongside the 'effort, example, and practice of sanitary officials', was vital to the success of public health in the colony.[3]

Under this framework, primary schools became instrumental in the spread of hygiene practices. The curriculum incorporated

2 William Howard Taft, 'Letter to the Honorable Dean C. Worcester enroute Trans-Siberian Railway', 30 November, Correspondence File, Worcester Collection, University of Michigan Ann Arbor, Bentley Historical Library, USA (1907), p. 3.

3 Edward C. Carter, 'Report of the Commissioner of Public Health for the Year 1905', *Annual Report of the Commissioner of Public Health for the Year 1905–1906* (Manila: Bureau of Public Printing, 1906), p. 15.

lessons on personal hygiene, house sanitation, and the prevention of contagious diseases. Schools across the Philippines were tasked with conducting medical inspections in Manila and in the provinces.[4] Health records for each child were compiled, and physical markers of health, such as a well-formed body, clean hair, clear skin, and amiable disposition, were emphasised as signs of 'healthiness'.[5] In this process, schoolchildren were not merely passive recipients of health knowledge but active participants in its dissemination, especially when it came to teaching their families these practices at home.

The Bureau of Education mandated the inclusion of hygiene, physiology, and sanitation in the Grade VII curriculum, embedding public health principles into the education system. Children were taught fundamental practices such as washing their hands before meals and after using the toilet. During the cholera epidemic of 1913, Heiser recognised the Filipino custom of eating with their hands and introduced the use of a 1–1000 bichloride solution, along with other disinfectants for handwashing before meals.[6] Schools also emphasised the vital connection between personal hygiene, waste management, drainage, and overall sanitation to prevent diseases such as smallpox and cholera (Racelis 2001: 9).

In 1913, the first school health clinic was established, marking a significant milestone in public health education. Hilario D. G. Lara, often referred to as the 'father of the modern public

4 Jacobo Fajardo, *Report of the Philippine Health Service for the Fiscal Year from January 1 to December 31, 1929*, 2 volumes (Manila: Bureau of Printing, 1931), p. 12.

5 Bureau of Education and Philippine Health Service, *Health: A Manual for Teachers* (Manila: Bureau of Printing, 1928), 49.

6 Victor G. Heiser, 'Cholera in the Philippines during 1913, *Medical Record*, Paper Read at the Manila Medical Society on 2 March, bMS AM 1364.4, Box 7/8, William Cameron Forbes (WCF) Papers, Houghton Library, Harvard University, USA (1914), p. 8. Hereafter WCF Papers.

health movement' in the Philippines for his pioneering work in epidemiology and training under American public health experts, designated the Grade VII curriculum as the formal inception of health education in the country.[7] This integration of health education in schools played a foundational role in shaping public health initiatives and practices across the archipelago.

Beyond promoting hygiene, American colonial authorities addressed the widespread lack of toilets, especially in impoverished areas where people often relied on rudimentary methods, such as digging holes and covering waste with lime or fresh earth. To address this concern the construction of latrines was introduced as a school project primarily assigned to boys.[8] This initiative proved highly effective, as schoolchildren played a critical role in encouraging their families to adopt these new sanitary technologies.

By the 1920s the 'Antipolo toilet', a standardised model latrine, had become a common feature in Filipino households.[9] Schoolchildren not only learned the principles of hygiene but also became the conduits for disseminating these practices to their parents and communities. In this way, children emerged as key agents of public health, bridging the gap between colonial reforms and everyday domestic life.

Heiser's emphasis on schoolchildren as agents of public health was well-founded, reflecting a strategic approach to community engagement in the early twentieth-century Philippines. The focus on children as vectors of change capitalised on their

---

7 Hilario D. G. Lara, 'Development of Hygiene and Preventive Medicine (Public health)', *Philippine National Research Council Bulletin*, 4 February 1935

8 Bureau of Education and Philippine Health Service, p. 49.

9 Asuzano Marcelino, 'The Problem of the Disposal of Human Excreta with Special Reference to the Antipolo Closets', *Monthly Bulletin of the Philippine Health Service* 5 (2) (1925), pp. 56–58; Julio Ruiz 1925, 'A Brief Historical Sketch of the Antipolo System of Privy', *Monthly Bulletin of the Philippine Health Service* 5 (2) (1925), pp. 59–60.

curiosity, adaptability, and influence within their households. In a letter to Walter Tiedeman of the Rockefeller Foundation, Francisco Baisas, an engineer in Pampanga, highlighted the enthusiasm among schoolchildren for public health initiatives and proposed a novel strategy to harness their potential. Baisas suggested organising mosquito-catching competitions to raise awareness about sanitation, a creative method that linked education, public health, and community participation.[10] This approach not only empowered children by positioning them as active participants in health campaigns but also illustrated how American public health programs leveraged education to foster grassroots support for sanitation initiatives. By targeting children, these programs aimed to instil lifelong habits of hygiene and sanitation and directly influence older generations. Baisas' proposal reflected a broader colonial strategy to overcome resistance to modern health practices by embedding them in the educational system, thus creating a ripple effect through families and communities. The letter reveals the ingenuity and adaptability of local public health workers, like Baisas, who sought to align global public health strategies with the cultural and social realities of Filipino communities. His insights underscore the dual role of children as learners and teachers, capable of bridging the gap between modern health knowledge and traditional practices. Baisas wrote:

> I have for some time been thinking of some way by which we can awake the interest (and enlist, if possible, the cooperation) in our work of the townspeople in Florida and Porac. The response I received from those with whom I talked gave me the opinion

10 Francisco Baisas, 'Letter to Walter D. Tiedeman, 28 July, Record Group 5.1.2 (Projects), Box 184, Folder 2387, Rockefeller Archive Center (RAC), Tarrytown, New York, USA (1924). Hereafter RAC.

> that the matured folks, with few exceptions, cannot be won without imposing upon ourselves efforts which we cannot so far afford. The school children, however, show so much of curiosity in this, which I believe can be transformed into interest in some manner like this: Some arrangements with the principal in each locality may be made by which selected or volunteer pupils may compete in mosquito-catching with the understanding that the one (or three) catching the most mosquitoes in say either a month or two months' time will receive some prizes. This can be so arranged as not to interfere with or any way be a detriment to the pupil's [schoolwork]. The competition may be continued till the beginning of the busiest school month, and prizes should be given in less but not more than two months' time. My idea is to keep the pupils' enthusiasm in it so that some valuable impressions may be left upon their young mind. This will also be a help to us in some degree. If my observation does not fail me, the present trend of things – the pupils enlightening the old folks about new and modern things – is the most effective means of eliminating some of the factors that handicap us in this work, namely, people's ignorance and indifference.[11]

In a broader sense, these efforts were linked to a sense of political duty. By engaging schoolchildren in public health initiatives, colonial authorities and local collaborators such as Baisas framed health education as an essential aspect of civic responsibility. Children were not merely passive recipients of health knowledge; they were moulded into active participants in the governance of their communities. This approach aligned with the colonial government's broader agenda of fostering a disciplined and modern citizenry, one that internalised the

---

11 Ibid.

values of hygiene and sanitation as markers of progress and civic virtue.

The mosquito-catching competition, for instance, exemplified how public health campaigns were designed to cultivate a sense of collective responsibility while simultaneously addressing pressing health concerns such as malaria and dengue. Such activities served dual purposes: they reinforced the colonial narrative of 'upliftment' through education and modernisation and encouraged communities to view health not as a private concern but as a public duty intertwined with the well-being of the nation.

Moreover, these initiatives reflected the shifting dynamics of power and knowledge in colonial society. By positioning children as agents of change, public health campaigns sought to bypass the resistance and indifference of older generations, effectively using the younger population to challenge traditional practices and promote new ways of thinking. This strategy highlighted the role of education not only in individual development but also as a tool for societal transformation, embedding the ideals of health and hygiene within the framework of nation-building.

As part of their health education, children in the early twentieth-century Philippines were taught the 'Ten Precepts for Disease Prevention', a set of guidelines that merged public health practices with moral and civic instruction. Framed as civic duties, these precepts reflected the influence of American colonial public health policies, which sought to instil a sense of collective responsibility for community well-being. By embedding health practices within a framework of ethical conduct and national responsibility, the precepts underscored the interdependence of individual actions and public health outcomes. Drawing on the language of both religious commandments and civic duty, the Ten Precepts – sometimes referred to as the 'gospel of health' – aimed to shape a hygienic and disciplined citizenry. They addressed a range of issues, from environmental sanitation to personal hygiene, and reflected contemporary concerns about urban cleanliness, disease prevention, and the role of education in promoting public health. Below are the 'ten precepts' or the 'gospel of health' for disease prevention:[12]

I. Honor your city and keep its sanitary laws.

II. Remember your cleaning day and keep it holy.

III. Love your children, and provide for them decent homes, good food, and playgrounds.

IV. Keep fresh air in your house day and night.

V. Keep clean and in order, your alleys, your back yard, your halls and stairways.

VI. You shall not kill your own, nor your neighbor's bodies, with poisonous air and disease breeding filth.

VII. You shall not let the filthy fly live.

VIII. You shall not steal your children's happiness from them by neglecting their health.

IX. You shall not carry filthy, decayed teeth in your mouth nor tolerate them in the mouths of those about you.

X. You shall not spit on the sidewalks, nor on the floor, nor in the street car, nor in any public place whatsoever.

Compliance with sanitary measures was framed not merely as a personal responsibility but as a patriotic duty, intertwining

12 G. Mamerto Tianco, *Philippine Health Service Sanitary Almanac for 1919 and Calendars for 1920 and 1921* (Manila: Bureau of Printing, 1928), RG350,

public health with notions of political identity and civic responsibility. This framing aligned public health with broader colonial efforts to instil discipline, order, and modernity in Filipino society, emphasising that personal hygiene and sanitation were integral to the nation's progress. The convergence of health and civic duty culminated in 1914, with Heiser's inauguration of the first 'Clean-Up Week', a landmark event aimed at fostering community-wide engagement in improving sanitation.[13] By positioning hygiene as a collective effort, *Clean-Up week* transformed sanitation from a private obligation into a public demonstration of civic pride and national solidarity. Children were rigorously taught the importance of daily bathing, regardless of their health status, a practice that reflected deeper ideological underpinnings. This emphasis on cleanliness as a daily ritual reinforced the belief that hygiene was not merely a personal or family concern but a visible marker of modern, responsible citizenship. It also served as a way to embed colonial values within Filipino households, ensuring that public health principles were disseminated and practised across generations.

This integration of health into the civic sphere had broader implications for how individuals understood their roles within the community and the state. Cleanliness became a metaphor for moral and civic virtue, suggesting that a clean body and environment signified a disciplined, orderly, and progressive citizenry. These campaigns thus went beyond addressing immediate health concerns; they sought to reshape cultural practices and redefine what it meant to be a 'modern' Filipino under colonial rule. Interestingly, these health reforms and the

---

Entry 95, Box 372, folder 150/56/18/3, United States National Archives Records Administration (NARA), USA, p. 2. Hereafter NARA.

13 Victor Heiser, 'Report of the Director of Health', Report of the Secretary of War to the Philippine Commission (Washington: Government Printing Office, 1906a), p. 73.

American emphasis on hygiene contradicted earlier Spanish observations, which noted the Filipino habit of bathing and their general cleanliness, despite their low regard for the local population.[14] This contrast underscores how the American colonial administration imposed its own standards and practices on Filipinos, using public health as a key tool to shape both the body and the mind according to its imperial vision. In this regard, American interventionism went beyond a mere misunderstanding of Filipino hygiene practices – it involved a broader effort to impose their own standards, particularly in public health. While the Spanish, despite their prejudice, acknowledged the Filipinos' cleanliness, the Americans, driven by different priorities and assumptions about 'modern' hygiene, sought to reshape Filipino behaviour according to American ideals of sanitation and health. By introducing disinfectants, sterilising measures, and a rigid health regimen, the Americans were not simply addressing public health issues – they were reinforcing a broader narrative of 'civilising' Filipinos by imposing their own cultural standards of cleanliness. The assumption that American methods were superior to traditional Filipino practices exemplifies the colonial mindset: the idea that intervention was necessary to 'improve' Filipinos, even in areas where their cultural practices were already integral to their notions of health and well-being. Ultimately, through the establishment of public health and educational programs, schoolchildren became the central figures in the American colonial mission, serving as conduits for the dissemination of hygiene and sanitation practices. These programs positioned children not merely as passive recipients of colonial education

14 See Antonio de Morga, *Sucesos de las Islas Filipinas, con anotaciones del Dr. Jose Rizal* (Quezon City: R. Martinez and Sons, 1958) and Pedro Chirino, *Relacion de las Islas Filipinas: The Philippines in 1600*, translated by Ramon Echevarria (Manila: Historical Conservation Society, 1969).

but as active participants in reshaping societal norms. By internalising the principles of cleanliness and public health, children were transformed into extensions of the state's authority within their families and communities, embodying what can be described as 'technicians of rule'.

This strategy was not only practical but profoundly ideological, as it leveraged the perceived malleability of children to instil values that aligned with the colonial agenda of modernization and discipline. By engaging children as intermediaries, the colonial government effectively bypassed traditional hierarchies and resistance from older generations, embedding public health practices into the fabric of everyday life. In this way, public health education became a tool for broader societal transformation, where the act of bathing, cleaning, or eradicating mosquitoes transcended its immediate utility and became a symbol of civic virtue and modern citizenship. The colonial project thus succeeded in linking individual behaviour with national progress, using children as both the subjects and agents of this transformation. While these initiatives aimed to uplift Filipino society under the guise of benevolence, they also reinforced the dynamics of power and control, embedding colonial values in ways that would persist long after the end of American rule in the Philippines.

Diet

Colonial health officials also emphasized the importance of good nutrition and diet as part of public health efforts, particularly in response to widespread beriberi outbreaks and high infant mortality rates in the early twentieth century. Thomas R. Marshall, Chief Health Inspector for Manila, identified the persistently high infant mortality rate as a key factor contributing to the relatively slow population growth in the Philippines.[15] Improper care and feeding of infants were considered the primary cause of these high mortality rates. At a 1911 meeting of the Philippine Islands Medical Association (PIMA), Heiser highlighted the government's decade-long efforts to combat beriberi by encouraging the inclusion of more meat, vegetables, and mangoes in the typical Filipino diet.[16]

School officials observed that Filipino children, particularly those from rural areas, often brought a week's supply of food provisions when staying in rented accommodations near their school in urban areas. Their diet – consisting primarily of rice, corn, sweet potatoes, yams, salted fish, and dried meat – was not only limited in nutritional quality but also lacked variety (Racelis 2001: 7). As Worcester noted:

> It is obviously of very great importance that the common people should be able to obtain an inexpensive but adequate diet, and the ability to furnish such a diet is also of great importance to the Government, which has to feed the inhabitants of its leper colony, the inmates of its contagious-disease hospitals and insane hospital, its prisoners, and many other persons. It is needless to say that proper and inexpensive diet is fundamentally necessary in connection with the cure, upon a large scale, of persons in the early stages of tuberculosis.[17]

15 Carter, 1906, p. 71.

16 Victor G. Heiser, 'Practical Experiences with Beriberi and Unpolished Rice in the Philippines', Paper read at the Eight Annual Meeting of the Philippine Islands Medical Association, 23 February, Reprinted from *Journal of the American Medical Association* 56: 1237–1238, bMS Am 1364.4, Box 7/8, (WCF) Papers, (1911), pp. 1237–1238.

17 Dean Worcester, *Annual Report of the Bureau of Health for the Philippine Islands for the Fiscal Year Ended June 30, 1910* (Manila: Bureau of Printing, 1910a), p. 43.

In promoting a balanced diet for school children, officials stressed the importance of regular meal schedules. They issued guidelines prohibiting children from attending school without having breakfast, and discouraged eating between meals, particularly sweets, as it was believed to spoil the appetite for regular meals. Undernourished children with poor appetite were advised to have longer meal intervals between meals to stimulate appetite.[18]

Guidelines for a balanced diet, tailored to the available food in the Philippines, were developed and distributed, alongside recommendations for regular meal schedules. Breakfast, served between 6:30 AM to 7:00 AM, might include a ripe banana, a soft-boiled egg, rice, and milk, or alternatively, papaya, smoked fish, rice, and milk. Lunch or dinner around 11:30 AM, could consist of rice, fried fish, sautéed mung beans with onion, garlic, and shrimp, or rice, fried beef with onions, boiled potato, and fried banana with syrup or sugar. A tea break around 4:30 PM featured options such as biscuit bread with milk or boiled yam with coconut and sugar. Supper, served around 7:00 PM, included dishes such as rice, fried or dried roast beef and boiled sweet potato, or rice with chicken soup, winter melon, and banana.[19]

It is worth noting that the 'recommended diet' reflected the average Filipino diet in adjusted quantities based on common local consumption patterns. However, the prescribed meals appeared imbalanced, as they include limited green vegetables. This raises questions about the ideal diet that American officials envisioned for Filipinos.

In 1910, Hans Aaron of the Philippine Medical School (PMS), supported by Harry Drake Gibbs, food chemist from the Bureau of Science and Associate Professor of Chemistry at the University

18 Fajardo, p. 41.

19 Ibid.

of the Philippines, and George F. Richmond, chief chemist from the Bureau of Science, conducted a study on the appropriate diet and nutrition for Filipinos. Their findings suggested that a varied and satisfactory diet could be achieved for just ten centavos (PHP 0.10) per day.[20] Subsequently, health officials announced plans to promote corn as a staple food for Filipino children. In 1912, this initiative culminated in nationwide corn festivals, with thousands of school children and their parents participating. As author Edwin Schell described:

> There were six different dishes of corn prepared and sold, and probably four thousand ate one or more of these prepared dishes. What a side show the corn-germinating box was, and how the thousands looked at the selected seed-ears!... A swarm of boys, some of them dressed as fat, husky clowns, wore placards 'I eat corn,' others, dressed as lean clowns, wore other placards, 'I eat rice'... Rice is the Oriental food... But corn and corn pone, and corn cakes, like science and the English language, and the Christian faith belong to the Occidental civilization. It is suggestive of fat swine, thick beefsteaks, butter, and cheese, and the introduction of corn to the Philippine Islands is naturalization, revolution, and revelation.[21]

Schell further remarked: 'corn is king in the United States, and will be in the Philippines' (Cannell 2005: 175). However, the corn campaign was more than just a nutritional initiative – it also conveyed undertones of American material and cultural superiority, positioning corn as a symbol of progress and modernity aligned with American values. This framing not

20 Worcester, 1910a, p. 43.

21 Edwin Schell, *In Ports Afar* (New York and Cincinnati: The Abingdon Press, 1914), p. 177.

only reflected colonial efforts to reshape Filipino agricultural practices but also subtly reinforced hierarchies of power and civilization under the guise of dietary reform.

Public schools also introduced a comprehensive and affordable lunch system, initially launched in Manila and later adopted in other provinces.[22] For an average of four or five centavos (PHP 0.4/0.5) for a more expensive meal, students could enjoy a typical lunch that included a bowl of soup or stew, a buttered sandwich, a slice of cake, and ice cream or ice.[23] Other items included fritters, tarts, cookies, pies, hot biscuits, and muffins. Students could also purchase donuts, chicken pie, devilled crabs, cheese straws, fried salmon and bread, baked potato and salmon, Johnny cake, Washington pie, and macaroni and cheese.[24] Students, under supervision of their teachers in Home Economics class, were responsible for preparing these meals. This system not only taught them how to prepare nutritious food in a sanitary way, but also encouraged a simple, healthy lifestyle (Racelis 2001: 7). However, while this diet may have seemed appealing to Filipinos it also reflected a distinctly American, carbohydrate-heavy food culture.

To further enhance the diet of Filipino children, American health officials introduced gardening into the school curric-

22 Worcester, 1910a, p. 33.

23 In this context, 'ice' likely refers to a frozen dessert, similar to what is now called 'shaved ice' or 'ice slushy'. In the early twentieth century, 'ice' could have been a simple treat made from finely crushed ice, often sweetened with syrup or flavoured water, much like snow cones today. It could also refer to ice cream, which was becoming more popular at the time, although this would have typically been noted specifically as 'ice cream'.' Given the context of the lunch offerings, it is reasonable to assume that the 'ice' mentioned here was an inexpensive, ice-based dessert that was a common refreshment at the time. This would make sense, especially in tropical regions like the Philippines, where ice-based treats were a refreshing option in the heat.

24 Worcester, 1910a, p. 33.

ulum.[25] This initiative was spurred by the establishment of the Office of Hygiene and Industrial Development of the Bureau of Health on 16 July 1915, which aimed to reduce infant mortality and increase the overall population through improved public health practices.[26] Hygiene officials took note of the limited vegetable consumption among Filipinos and discovered that adequate quantities were often unavailable in markets, and when available, had prohibitive costs. In response, the Office of Hygiene launched a campaign to promote vegetable gardens in every Filipino home. As G. Mamerto Tianco, acting chief of the Bureau, explained:

> The purpose of the house vegetable garden is to induce the people to eat more legumes which when added to the ordinary Filipino diet will provide all the essentials of a well-balanced diet, thus increasing the vitality of parents and their resulting children and enabling mothers to nurse their babies as otherwise they would not be able to do, thus effecting an important reduction in infant mortality.[27]

This initiative to encourage Filipinos to establish vegetable gardens in their homes was also largely driven by American health officials' realisation that:

> if, therefore, we can provide a proper diet, or take steps which will lead to an increased and improved diet for the poorer

25 G. Mamerto Tianco, 'Report of the Office of Hygiene and Industrial Development', in John D. Long (ed.), *Report of the Philippine Health Service for the Fiscal Year from January 1 to December 31, 1916* (Manila: Bureau of Printing, 196), p. 154.

26 John D. Long, *Report of the Philippine Health Service for the Fiscal Year from January 1 to December 31, 1915* (Manila: Bureau of Printing, 1916), p. 154.

27 Tianco, 1916, p. 154.

> Filipinos, we will not only improve their physical condition, but will indirectly provide a better quality and increased quantity of breast milk for infants, thus increasing their strength, resistance, and chances for life. In other words, we will be attacking the problem of mortality, both adult and infant, and aiding in another way to increase the population.
>
> It has been decided, therefore, to endeavour to establish vegetable gardens in as many homes in the Philippines as possible, such gardens to contain foods which will furnish all the elements necessary for a well-nourished body.[28]

Due to the perceived health benefits of a vegetable-rich diet, gardening was considered a matter of national importance. Gardening eventually expanded into industrial arts for boys, which included skills such as furniture-making using bamboo and coconut shells, among other materials.

On a broader scale, health officials viewed gardening as fostering industry and self-reliance, teaching families to adopt both economical and healthy lifestyles. It was believed that gardening not only contributed to physically strong and robust bodies but also cultivated a more disciplined and methodical way of living. Interestingly, gardening was also framed as a patriotic duty, as self-sufficiency in food production was seen as vital to national resilience, especially in the event of war.[29] This emphasis on food sufficiency mirrored American wartime mentalities during World War I and may have been further fuelled by long-standing American concerns over the threat of a Japanese invasion.

Thus, Filipinos were educated in health and hygiene practices, as well as consumption habits, which Americans deemed

28 Ibid., 1916, p. 156.
29 Ibid., p. 40.

essential for cultivating 'good citizens' and improving public health standards in the Philippines. By 1916, about 6,000 Antipolo-style sewage systems had been installed, and nearly 15,000 families were maintaining vegetable gardens.[30] As health became intertwined with citizenship, being a 'good citizen' was defined by one's ability to promote personal health, prevent illness, and regulate one's diet. Personal goals and desires were thus aligned with public and state objectives. Over time, as the importance of diet and hygiene in American colonial governance became more recognised, these principles also came to be regarded as vital for effective state administration.

Relevant and scientific education

As Filipinos were being developed 'physically', the establishment of medical institutions and the professional training of Filipinos were crucial not only as parallel efforts for their 'physical establishment' but also as key criteria for assessing their capacities for self-rule. For Americans, education and science were seen as the primary solutions to what they perceived as the Spanish-imposed barriers to Filipino development. These 'remedies' revived the rhetoric of the civilising mission, which was increasingly criticized both in the Philippines and among the anti-imperialist factions in the US. As the reinforced ideology of the civilising mission became the driving force for American colonial officials, its core categories – public health and its operationalization – became prerequisites for developing Filipino capacities for self-rule and a civilised life. Fuelled by belief, purpose, and renewed vigour, Americans consistently argued that Filipinos were unfit for self-rule, claiming Spain had failed to prepare them for self-governance despite three centuries of

30 Long, 1916, p. 8.

Spanish rule. What began as a defence of the civilising mission ultimately evolved into deliberate efforts to justify the long-standing view of Filipinos as backward and inferior.

From the American perspective, the absence of a proper medical school in the Philippines exacerbated the situation. While there were Filipino doctors, such as Trinidad Pardo de Tavera, Ariston Bautista, and Manuel Gomez, their scientific qualifications were considered by Americans to be below 'more modern' standards.

Until the second half of the nineteenth century, the Philippines lacked an accredited medical school, exacerbating an already significant shortage of medical doctors.[31] Most physicians had to be imported from abroad, and those available primarily served the Spanish population, as local medical practitioners were few (de la Cruz 1984: 33). The University of Santo Tomas (UST), established by the Spaniards and deeply influenced by the Catholic Church, opened its College of Medicine and Pharmacy in 1871. However, it initially offered only a Licentiate in Medicine rather than a full medical degree. This system underscored not only the Church's significant role in shaping education but also in maintaining control over access to professional training, including medicine.

In contrast, medical schools in countries such as France, Germany, and the United Kingdom had long granted full medical degrees and offered more advanced, secular curricula, fostering a scientifically rigorous approach to medicine and emphasising broader academic freedom. As a result, medical practice in the Philippines during the Spanish colonial period was deeply intertwined with religious control, and healthcare was often shaped by the priorities of the colonial church rather

---

31 Joseph Ralston Hayden, *The Philippines: A Study in National Development* (New York: The Macmillan Company, 1942), p. 639.

than secular or scientific advancement. The system of medical education, limited in scope and controlled by the church, played a significant role in maintaining the colonial status quo and curbing the development of a more modern, independent healthcare system. In other words, the limited number of physicians available to the local population, combined with the colonial context, meant that healthcare services were often focused on the Spanish elite, further marginalising the broader Filipino population from adequate medical care.

Moreover, while the Americans found the overall educational system in the Philippines to be deficient, they regarded the San Jose Medical College at the UST, then considered the foremost medical school in the country, as a particularly 'hopeless affair'.[32] For example, pathology was taught directly from textbooks, and diagnoses were made without actual autopsies or any pathological specimens. In anatomy classes, over a hundred students shared a single cadaver, and those who wished to study dissections had to independently arrange access to additional cadavers or anatomical material, often seeking it from private sources such as local doctors or hospitals. Given the difficulty of convincing American physicians to relocate to the Philippines, the need to train Filipino doctors was urgent.[33]

On 21 January 1905, the Committee on Public Policy and Legislation of the PIMA, sent a letter to Governor-General Luke E. Wright (1904–1906), requesting the establishment of a medical school in the proposed university in the Philippines. Heiser was particularly enthusiastic about the prospect of advancing medical education and the 'science' that Americans

---

32 William S. Carter, 'Status of Medical and other Scientific Activities in Manila on his Visit', 4–8 May, Record Group 1.1, Series 242.242a, Box 2, Folder 14, RAC (1921), p. 2.

33 Ibid., p. 2; 101.

were introducing to the Philippines. In a speech at a meeting of the Philippine Medical Association (PMA), Heiser stated:

> The microscope has supplanted the sword, the material spirit gave place to the research habit, and the status of social and political prominence, to self-sacrificing obscurity, until today the medical man of the Philippine Islands, like the medical man the world over, is struggling on in the race of life, with no hope beyond that of being granted the sacred privilege of helping his fellow man.[34]

On 10 June 1907, Act No. 1415 was passed and the Philippine Medical School (PMS) in Manila was formally opened to both male and female students. According to Heiser:

> The establishment of this school will mark a new era in the progress of medicine in the Philippine Islands. In time, it will prove to be the best investment that the commission could have possibly made. The Philippines, with an educated native doctor for every 1000 inhabitants, would be a different country, with a different history.[35]

Modelled after the medical school of Johns Hopkins University in the US, the PMS prioritised practical teaching. To execute this plan, American professors were recruited to instruct Filipino students.[36]

---

34 Victor G. Heiser, 'The Progress of Medicine in the Philippine Islands', Address delivered at the *3rd Annual Meeting of the Philippine Islands Medical Association* in Manila, 28 February, Reprinted from the *Journal of the American Medical Association* 47: 245–247, bMS Am 1364.4, Box 6/8, WCF (1906b), p. 3.

35 Ibid., 3.

36 Carter, 1906, p. 91.

On 18 June 1908, the first Philippine Legislature passed Act 1870, establishing the University of the Philippines (UP) as a state university. On 8 December 1910, the Philippine Medical School (PMS) was incorporated into the university, becoming the University of the Philippines College of Medicine and Surgery (UPCMS). The UPCMS also included the School of Pharmacy and the School of Dentistry. As with medicine, dentistry and pharmacy were regulated by their respective professional bodies. By the time the school opened in 1908, the faculty consisted of 21 professional males, 14 of whom were Americans and seven were Filipinos.[37] This may suggest that the Americans hired Filipinos who had been trained under the Spanish colonial system, most likely at the UST.

American colonial officials lauded the emphasis on laboratory and practical training methods, which they believed modernised medical education and improved medical service in the country. Full of optimism, Heiser declared, 'We do not need American, European, or other foreign physicians, but educated [Filipino] sanitarians'.[38] The role of doctors in the Philippines was thus viewed with great hope and expectation. Heiser further remarked:

> Medical science holds the key to the prosperity of the Philippine Islands, and on every doctor here rests an individual responsibility so great that its magnitude [cannot] be measured. Whatever may be the relative importance of the medical man in other parts of the world, he, and the profession he represents, stands first in this country. To be healthy is an economic asset of the highest possible value, contributing to the economic

37 Letter from William S. Carter to Richard M. Pearce, Director of the Division of Medical Education, Rockefeller Foundation, 13 December 1922, p. 19, Record Group 1.1, series 242.242A, box 2, folder 14, RAC.

38 Heiser, 1906, 1.

> strength of the people, furnishing the foundation on which the entire superstructure of municipal credit and life is built. A strong people, relieved of unnecessary burdens caused by sickness and death, can bear other and larger burdens, which will give them a commanding lead in this age of commercialism.[39]

The Philippine Health Service (PHS) also considered sending several of its Filipino officers to the US for post-graduate studies. In 1920, three PHS officers were sent to the US to specialise in contagious diseases. As part of the long-term plan to prepare Filipinos for self-rule, these officers were expected to assume key positions at the PHS upon their return to the Philippines.

Spirits were high at the PHS, especially with the frequent visits of other sanitarians and medical men from around the world. Representatives from China, Japan, Java, and Siam (Thailand) inquired about the organisation of public health work in the Philippines and its various activities. The head of the Civil Medical Service in India and the Netherlands, and the Commissioner of Health in Java, who conducted a study of public health work in Manila, all praised the public health achievements in the Philippines.[40]

By 1927, the Graduate School of Hygiene and Public Health was established at the University of the Philippines.[41] According to William Carter, representative of the Rockefeller Foundation's International Health Division for the East who taught at the UPCMS, the work of the UP School of Public Health would

---

39 Ibid.

40 Vicente de Jesus, *Report of the Philippine Health Service for the Fiscal Year from January 1 to December 31, 1920* (Manila: Bureau of Printing, 1921), p. 56.

41 William S. Carter, 'Letter to Dr. William B. Wherry, Medical School, University of Cincinnati', 20 February, Record Group 1.1, Series 242.242A, Box 4, Folder 45, RAC (1929).

be crucial in training staff for the PHS, many of whom were UST graduates in need of further education in bacteriology, parasitology, and public health.[42] Worcester also observed that as more Filipinos became involved in public health campaigns and the number of well-trained Filipino physicians and surgeons grew, American health officials had successfully altered the sentiments of Filipinos toward public health measures.[43] By the second decade of American rule, public health in the Philippines and its symbols – doctors, nurses, midwives, medical and sanitary inspectors, and various hospitals and dispensaries – had become recognised as symbols of relief and benevolence.

Scientific research

Parallel to these efforts was the establishment of a scientific laboratory in the Philippines. For Worcester, the creation of such a laboratory also meant centralising all scientific research and service functions in one bureau, allowing for more efficient allocation of government resources for research and development (Sullivan 1991: 115). Worcester had high hopes for the laboratory, envisioning it as a cornerstone for American administration in the Philippines. He remarked, 'The day has passed when any government can afford to attempt to get on without laboratories for scientific investigation and the need of such laboratories has long been urgent in the Philippine Islands'.[44]

---

42 William S. Carter, 'Letter to Richard M. Pearce, School of Public Health in the Philippines', 15 April, Record Group 1.1, Series 242.242A, Box 2, Folder 15, RAC (1928).

43 Ibid., pp. 22–23.

44 United States Philippine Commission, *Report of the Philippine Commission, 1900–1903* (Washington: Government Printing Office, 1904), p. 55.

To realise this vision, Worcester drafted Act No. 156, which established the Government Laboratories for the Philippine Islands, passed by the Philippine Commission on 1 July 1901. In 1905, this became the Bureau of Science. The Bureau's well-equipped library contained all the scientific books held by the colonial government, aside from those privately purchased by the bureau, leading its first director, Paul Freer, to remark, 'No one need fear a lack of literature' in Manila.[45] The Bureau of Science, the PGH, and the institutions of health and medical training were all integral to Worcester's broader vision of safeguarding the health of Filipinos and 'make the tropics not only habitable but healthful for men of every race'.[46]

To garner further support for public health initiatives and scientific research, Worcester encouraged American doctors and scientists to engage with local medical knowledge, explore its potential integration into medical practices, and generate interest by publishing their findings. In 1906, the Bureau launched the *Philippine Journal of Science* (PJS), which not only received favourable recognition within the international scientific community but also emerged as a significant primary resource for the development of Philippine science in the twentieth century.

The success of the education and health initiatives led by American colonial officials was not solely a result of their dedication, hard work, or of the cooperation of the Filipinos. It was also tied to the overarching agenda of preparing the

45 Paul Freer, *Fourth Annual Report of the Director of the Bureau of Science, 1904–1905* (Manila: Bureau of Printing, 1905), p. 4.

46 Dean Worcester, 'A Brief Review of the Movement for the Establishment of the Philippine General Hospital at Manila at the Laying of the Cornerstone of the Hospital', 28 February, Box 1, Lecture and Speeches, 1908–1913 Folio, Dean Conant Worcester Papers, Harlan Hatcher Worcester Collection, Harlan Hatcher Graduate Library (now the University Library), University of Michigan Ann Arbor, USA (1908), p. 18.

Filipinos for self-rule. As these efforts became integrated into the broader project of Philippine independence, the goals of Americans and Filipinos began to converge. However, Filipinos had a far greater stake in ensuring their success.

Reorganising public health

In 1913, the American promise of independence brought about the policy of Filipinization, enabling Filipinos to assume positions within the bureaucracy. This policy allowed Filipino health and medical personnel to take prominent roles in the PHS, the PGH, the UPCMS, and the Bureau of Science. However, Heiser and Worcester were sceptical about the continuity of public health achievements under Filipino leadership. They believed the progress made in public health would falter once Filipinos assumed control of the government. As Filipinization advanced, both Worcester and Heiser resigned – Worcester in 1913 and Heiser in 1915. Heiser departed convinced that Filipinos lacked the dedication required to sustain public health initiatives, asserting that they had:

> a difficult time comprehending that anybody should want to do anything for him without expecting something in return; he was always looking for a concealed motive. Service without expectation of reward, in the Anglo-Saxon sense, was outside his cosmogony, and he regarded giving for the sake of giving as absurd.[47]

On 1 March 1915, John D. Long assumed the position of Director of Health. By 1917, more than 30,000 people were using sanitary

---

47 Victor Heiser, *An American Doctor's Odyssey: Adventures in Forty-five Countries*, reprint of the 1936 Edition (Quezon City: GCF Books, 1988), p. 9.

sewage disposal systems, a significant improvement over the previous lack of such infrastructure.[48] Filipinos were also beginning to realise that while many health problems were inevitable, many were preventable and treatable. Reflecting on the achievements of the health service at the end of his first year as director and the first year after Heiser's departure, Long noted in his annual report: 'A marked change has been brought about in the attitude of the people generally toward sanitation, and a renewed interest has been aroused'.[49]

Despite the accomplishments of the PHS, given its limited funding, Long reported that these successes seemed unrecognised by the insular government. He noted the ongoing difficulty of securing financial support for public health initiatives, even when requesting minimal amounts. Long also mentioned concerns that there might be no funds allocated to the service for the fiscal year 1918.[50]

The lack of funding was not a new issue for public health work; however, the persistent failure of health officials to secure the necessary resources highlighted the colonial government's ambivalence toward public health and welfare in the Philippines. While the Americans continually acknowledged the importance of promoting health in the colony, they were unwilling to allocate the funds needed to achieve these goals.

Evaluating Filipino capacities

As part of the Filipinization process, Long resigned as Director of Health on 31 December 1918. The following day,

48 John D. Long, *Report of the Philippine Health Service for the Fiscal Year from January 1 to December 31, 1916* (Manila: Bureau of Printing, 1917), p. 7.

49 John D. Long, *Report of the Philippine Health Service for the Fiscal Year from January 1 to December 31, 1917*, (Manila: Bureau of Printing, 1918), p. 69.

50 Long, 1917, p. 8.

1 January 1919, Vicente de Jesus became the first Filipino to head the PHS, assuming office at an exceptionally challenging time.[51] The year 1919 was marked by the simultaneous outbreaks of cholera, influenza, and smallpox epidemics. De Jesus described the public health crisis that year as nearly comparable to the cholera epidemics of 1902, in terms of the demands it placed on the PHS.

Exacerbating these challenges were several factors: the mass resignation of PHS staff in protest of the 1914 Salary Law, which equalised the salaries of American and Filipino personnel; the repatriation of medical staff to the US due to the demands of World War I; and the scrutiny of Americans who had already formed critical opinions about Filipino capabilities. These factors aggravated the difficulties de Jesus faced during a particularly turbulent period in Philippine public health administration.

Americans opposed to Filipinos taking over the health service were convinced Filipino inadequacies would soon become apparent. Charles Moriarty of the Rockefeller Foundation expressed this sentiment, stating, 'constructive work in the Philippines can only be secured under responsible direction; this removed, and the work will cease'.[52] Such perceptions are difficult to reconcile with American declarations of improving conditions in the colony, particularly in public health.

It is noteworthy that the newly trained Filipino medical personnel were educated in American institutions, while those trained in the Philippines received their education under the guidance of American professionals through American-led educational and medical institutions. Many of these Filipinos also worked closely with pioneering American health officials

51 de Jesus, 1921, p. 3

52 Charles F. Moriarty, 'Outline for a Demonstrable Unit, 11 April, Record Group 1.1, Series 242 (Project Files), Box 7, Folder 94, RAC (1928).

and scientists such as Freer, Richard Strong (Head of the Philippine Biological Laboratory, 1905), Heiser, Frank Bourns (Head of the Philippine Board of Health, 1901), Louis Mervin Maus (Commissioner of Public Health, 1901), and Worcester – all of whom had led distinguished careers in public health and science in the Philippines.

As these bureaucratic changes posed challenges for the largely Filipinized PHS, outbreaks of cholera, influenza, and smallpox occurred. In 1921, cases of diphtheria, dysentery, malaria, tuberculosis, and typhoid were also reported. Among these, only tuberculosis presented a notably high death rate, with recorded fatalities rising from 17,411 in 1916 to 17,882 in 1917, and peaking at 20,498 in 1918. By contrast, the other diseases did not reach levels that caused significant alarm. De Jesus explained that the outbreaks and the spread of various diseases were aggravated by the influenza pandemic, which was worsened by the effects of the war. The general population's resistance to other diseases was also generally weakened, facilitating the transmission and spread of cholera, which had been intermittently present in the Philippines since 1913. The overall low resistance of Filipinos made them more vulnerable to new epidemics. In addition, improved transportation networks contributed to the rapid movement of viruses and infections, further aiding the spread of diseases. De Jesus noted that while the complete eradication of cholera was a 'possibility for the future', current measures were only sufficient to prevent and control its spread.[53]

Heiser, who had been away from the Philippines for three years and was actively involved with the Rockefeller Foundation's International Health Board (IHB) projects in other parts of Asia, became aware of the widespread epidemics in the

53 de Jesus, 1921, p. 10.

Philippines. He found de Jesus's explanation for the transmission and spread of these epidemics unacceptable. Between 1918 and 1920, Heiser pointed out, 'the Philippines had lost twice as many lives from smallpox as the United States had lost from casualties in the World War'.[54] Heiser viewed this incident as evidence of Filipino incompetence.

The push for Filipinization

On the Filipino side, the perceived unequal treatment from their American superiors had led to a push for Filipinization years before it was officially implemented in 1913. In a letter to Secretary of War Jacob Dickinson, F. Quintes, Vicente Rodriguez (a pharmacist), and an unnamed signatory claimed to represent the Filipinos of the College of Physicians and Pharmacy. Quintes and Rodriguez expressed their concerns about the 'lack of consideration, anomalies, and injustice' faced by Filipino personnel at the Department of Sanitation.[55] Despite their longer service and comparable competence to their American colleagues at the College, they stated, Filipino employees were paid much lower salaries. For example, they cited G. Intengan of La Union and Vicente Rivera of Tayabas, Quezon, who each earned only PHP 120, while American sanitary inspectors – who were not physicians – received PHP 150. Filipino physicians were also denied leave of absence or vacation, privileges granted to Americans. They further resented the fact that higher sanitary positions and the offices of supervising physicians were reserved for American physicians. Moreover, the civil service had not called for examinations for Filipino medical inspectors

54 Heiser, 1988, p. 140.

55 F. Quintes and Vicente Rodriguez, 'Letter to the Secretary of War, Jacob Dickinson', in *Monthly Report of the Board of Health to Dean C. Worcester, September 1905* (Manila: Bureau of Printing, 1905), p. 1.

since 1905, nor for Filipino district sanitary inspectors since 1906. These positions appeared to be reserved for recently graduated American physicians, while vacancies for district health officers were often temporarily filled by unqualified American substitutes, who were paid the full salary of district health officers. Adding to the frustration were young American doctors who came to the Philippines to gain experience, received substantial salaries for two or three years, and then returned to the US.

The letter also recounts how Filipino medical examiners were pressured to change their diagnoses of deaths after performing autopsies when an American doctor disagreed with them. One such case occurred in July 1905, when a professor from the PMS examined the body of a woman in Barangay Palumpong, Tondo, Manila, and diagnosed her death as caused by eclampsia. However, the American medical inspector from the Sanitary Station of Tondo objected, classifying the death as due to post-partum haemorrhage. Quintes and Rodriguez further explained that the Department of Sanitation commonly ordered bodies to be moved immediately to the morgue, disregarding the medical examiner's diagnosis unless the examiner was American. Worse still, they noted that American doctors often took bodies of the recently deceased to study diseases they were unfamiliar with. While cadaver study was standard in the medical profession, these American doctors, after drawing lots to determine which corpses they would take, would transfer them to the morgue without the consent or knowledge of the attending physician or the deceased's family. This occurred even when the cause of death was determined not to be infectious or suspicious.

When this issue was brought to Worcester's attention, he quickly stated that there was no need to pay 'the best Filipino physicians as much as we pay the best American physicians'.[56] He explained this 'discrepancy' by citing the higher cost of living for Americans in the Philippines compared to Filipinos. Worcester also expressed confusion as to why Filipinos would complain, given that they were 'drawing eight times as much pay as they had ever received under the Spanish government'.[57] Clearly, Worcester either missed the point of the Filipinos' complaint or chose not to acknowledge it. In either case, his attitude did little to foster positive relations between Americans and Filipinos. Ironically, the proposals put forth by the Filipino doctors to address their grievances revealed that, while they were aware of the inequality between American and Filipino doctors, they were still willing to accept subordinate positions.

Meanwhile, the Filipinization process being implemented at the Bureau of Science drew significant criticism from American personnel. At this time, the International Health Commission for Asia, under Heiser and the Rockefeller Foundation, was involved in health and scientific research on hookworm and malaria in the Philippines. During a visit to Manila to assess the status of medical and scientific activities, Carter noted that the staff at the Bureau were 'perturbed' by the actions of the Harrison administration. Once considered one of the most advanced American scientific research institutions in Asia, the Bureau had become an arena of conflict.[58] As the Bureau was being Filipinized, American scientists complained that the terms of their employment were not being upheld. Specifically, the Salary Law passed by Harrison allowed the administration

56 Dean Worcester, 'Report of the Secretary of Interior', *Bureau of Health for the Philippine Islands* (Manila: Bureau of Printing, 1910b), p. 2.

57 Ibid., p. 17.

58 William S. Carter, 'Status of Medical and other Scientific Activities in Manila on his Visit', 4–8 May, Record Group 1.1, Series 242.242a, Box 2, Folder 14, RAC (1921), p. 2.

to renege on the salary and contract promises made to them. In addition, there was growing concern among American scientists that the government intended to curtail research and tailor it to the immediate needs and problems of the Philippines. To make matters worse, they felt that Filipinos eager to take over the Bureau were making their work increasingly difficult. George Lacy, Assistant Director of the Bureau of Science, shared his experience, stating:

> When I first came to the Bureau of Science it seemed to me as though I could never get things done. The natives were so notoriously slow and deliberate in everything they did that it was quite useless to think of asking for even the simplest things one day hoping to get them the same day. So the things I wanted in a hurry I had to get by myself. Of course, I was not accustomed to their ways, and they were not accustomed to mine. There was only one thing I could count on being done on time and that was that every time the whistle blew all work stopped immediately. This condition applied not only to the laborers but to all of the employees including the doctors. In addition to this, I was met with more or less antagonism due, I think, to the fact that *there is undoubtedly a certain amount of anti-American feeling among the natives since the political turmoil has set in*. It was, therefore, very difficult for me to get anything accomplished for several weeks after my arrival. There is, too, a certain disadvantage of coming into a place where the employees do not exactly understand your status and where they do not understand your motives. These are things with which I had to be content for some weeks. [emphasis added][59]

59 George Lacy, 'Report on the Conditions in Bureau of Science to the Director of IHB, International Health Division', Rockefeller Foundation, Record Group 5, Series 2.24e, Special Reports, Box 20, Folder 21, RAC (1924), pp. 2–3.

Earl B. McKinley, Director of the Bureau of Science, further aggravated the already strained relations between Americans and Filipinos at the Bureau. It appeared that he was not consulting the Filipino staff on policy matters related to general laboratory work or issues concerning their respective departments, which led to divisiveness among the chiefs of various divisions. Given McKinley's views on Filipinos, this strained relationship was not surprising. He writes:

> All will agree that the mass of the Filipinos represent an inferior race. They are not in the position to know what is best for them. The [local Filipino] politicians may know but for political reason does not care to admit that they need further help from any source. They do not want more Americans out here and for the most part, they are able to see to it that government funds will not be used for the purpose of bringing any out.[60]

Moreover, McKinley believed that while the training and education of Filipinos were adequate, sending them abroad for further studies would lead to the development of a 'superiority complex', making it difficult to work with them. He argued that it would be better to train and educate Filipinos locally in the Philippines.[61] Ironically, according to Lacy's observations, Americans at the Bureau were not making significant efforts to train Filipinos who might eventually succeed them.[62]

For Selskar Gunn, Vice-President of the Rockefeller Foundation, Filipinization had led to the deterioration of the Bureau,

60 Earl B. McKinley, 'Views about Filipinos and Filipino Doctors and their Training', Manila, Record Group 1.1, Series 242 (Project Files), Box 1, Folder 1, RAC (1927), p. 15.

61 Ibid., p. 13.

62 Lacy, 1924, p. 3.

diminishing its prospects as a research institute.[63] Gunn's disappointment with the Philippines was so profound that he became convinced Filipinos were not yet ready for independence. Ultimately, his disillusionment led him to recommend ending Rockefeller's involvement with the Philippines.[64]

At the UPCM, Carter asserted that replacing American staff with Filipinos 'has wrecked efficient teaching and practically abolished research'.[65] He pointed to the lack of courses over the past two years due to the absence of American faculty at the Graduate School of Tropical Medicine and Public Health at the UP. By replacing American faculty with Filipinos, the government had failed to allocate funds for teaching and research, leaving the graduate school without teachers, researchers, public health administrators, laboratory officers, or practitioners in tropical diseases.[66] American officials who opposed Harrison's Filipinization policy also argued that it overlooked critical institutional needs. They believed that in the rush to implement reforms, the complexities of local governance, cultural contexts, and the infrastructure necessary to support such a policy were insufficiently addressed. Critics felt that while the policy aimed to empower Filipinos, it failed to recognize the existing limitations within key sectors such as education, healthcare, and the civil service, which were still deeply influenced by colonial legacies. This oversight, they contended, hindered the potential for meaningful and sustainable progress.[67] In his

63 Selskar M. Gunn, 'Letter to Max Mason, Report on the Visit to the Philippines, 26 August to 4 September, Record Group 1.1, Series 242 (Project Files), Box 1, Folder 4, RAC (1933), pp. 4–6.

64 Ibid., p. 6.

65 Carter, 1922.

66 Carter, 1921, p. 4.

67 See for example: Heiser, 1988, p. 9; Sullivan, 1991, p. 182; Dean Worcester, 'OUR NEW POLICY IN PHILIPPINES IS ATTACKED; Dean Worcester Points Out the Evils of Substituting Ignorant Filipinos for Americans. NATIVES

Intramural Committee Report to Richard M. Pierce, Director of the Division of Medical Education of the Rockefeller Foundation, Carter wrote:

> Filipinization has gone on rapidly in this institution and the elimination of Americans has taken place to a greater extent in the laboratory than in the clinical branches. As a result, the department is far from what it should be, probably as a result of not having the guiding influence of American ideals, training, and experience for the past three years. Equipment is insufficient, methods are unsatisfactory and teaching is not as effective as it should be in a first class medical school.[68]

Carter was of the opinion that 'the best Filipino teachers in the College of Medicine were those who had completed both their undergraduate and graduate training in the US'.[69]

Independence unfulfilled

In 1921, a new Republican administration under Warren G. Harding succeeded the Democratic administration of Woodrow Wilson. With this change in leadership, the Filipino readiness for independence, particularly the Filipinization policy vigorously implemented by Harrison, was reassessed. An evaluation was conducted by the Wood-Forbes Mission, a committee composed of former American colonial officials: Governor-General William

---

NOW IN CONTROL Dismissal of Bureau Chiefs Threatens Efficiency of Land, Health, and Printing Bureaus. NATIVE HEADS LAND BUREAU And Admits He Knows Nothing About the Work; Poor Landholders Likely to Suffer. OUR NEW POLICY IN PHILIPPINES IS ATTACKED,' *New York Times*, November 18 (1918), retrieved from: https://www.nytimes.com/1913/11/18/archives/our-new-policy-in-philippines-is-attacked-dean-worcester-points-out.html

68 Carter, 1921, p. 1920.

69 Ibid., p. 21.

Cameron Forbes and Leonard Wood, Governor of the Moro Province. From the outset, Filipinos criticized the selection of Forbes and Wood for the mission. Both were seen as biased against the Harrison administration and the Filipinization policy, with Forbes having a reputation for being anti-Filipino and opposed to independence, while Wood was also seen as having a low opinion of Filipinos.

The Commission's report highlighted the lack of hospitals and dispensaries, as well as inadequate funding for sanitary work and medicine. It also pointed to a shortage of doctors, nurses, and trained sanitary personnel. Assessing the state of public health in the country, the report noted that 'the excellent health service which previously existed has become largely inert; much of the personnel remains, but it has lost the zeal and vigour which formerly characterized it'.[70] Joseph Ralston Hayden, former Vice-Governor and Secretary of Public Instruction under Governor-General Frank Murphy (1931–1935) and a leading authority on Philippine affairs, affirmed this assessment, stating, 'This was part of the cost of demonstrating what will happen in the Philippines should there be a brief relaxation of the precautionary and preventive measures dictated by modern public health practice'.[71]

Shortly after the mission's conclusion, Harding appointed Wood as Governor-General of the Philippines, signalling his agreement with the mission's evaluation and recommendations. Largely opposed to Filipinization, Wood's appointment exacerbated his already strained relationship with Filipino politicians, who had long felt his lack of sympathy for Philippine independence. As Filipino health and medical capacities became

---

70 United States Special Mission to the Philippines, *Report of the Special Mission to the Philippine Islands to the Secretary of War* (Washington: Government Printing Office, 1927), pp. 73–75.

71 Hayden, 1942, p. 578.

tied to the country's right to self-rule, the evaluative role that public health played provides a lens through which to examine the development and transformation of Philippine society and culture in the years leading up to independence.

Conclusion

As an American 'strategy of governance', public health and medicine came to embody the broader colonial ideals that Americans sought to impose on the Filipino population. Filipinos were urged to adopt these ideals – virtue, patriotism, and self-sacrifice – reflecting American hopes of remaking the Filipino national character. The American belief that they were the rightful architects of Filipino development was rooted in the assumption that the US could shape a 'civilised' Filipino identity, one that had already been largely influenced by Spanish colonial rule. Americans viewed the structural, cultural, and social changes brought about by their governance as natural and necessary steps in the evolution of Filipino society.

During the first decade of American colonial rule, as public health campaigns took root, Americans scrutinized Filipino practices and lifestyles, which they deemed unsanitary and unhealthy. However, these assessments ignored the broader context of health conditions in Manila, which had been heavily influenced by the economic, demographic, and infrastructural changes under Spanish rule, as well as the disruptions caused by the Spanish-American War and the Philippine-American War. When American officials first entered Manila, the unsanitary conditions they encountered were immediately attributed to Filipino hygiene practices, with little recognition of the historical and colonial factors that contributed to these issues.

The Americans, believing they were acting in the best interests of the Filipinos, assumed that public health and medicine were the definitive solutions to the social, economic, and environmental problems plaguing the country. In addition to promoting sanitation, American health officials emphasized proper hygiene, diet, and nutrition, especially among schoolchildren, who were envisioned as the future carriers of the 'gospel of public health'. Health, hygiene, and nutrition became entwined with ideas of citizenship, encouraging children to see their personal health as a form of national service. These values became deeply embedded in the Filipino psyche, imparting a sense of duty and patriotism.

By linking sanitation and health with Western ideals of education, discipline, hard work, moral duty, and selflessness, American colonial rule sought to cultivate qualities they perceived as lacking in the Filipino character – qualities they believed were necessary for self-rule.[72] For Americans, the transformation of the body through health reforms was not just a physical change but also a moral one, signalling the broader cultural and ideological shifts they hoped to instil in their colonial subjects. This process reflected the core of the American 'civilising mission', which aimed to reshape not only Filipino society but also the individual Filipinos, aligning them with Western notions of progress and governance.

The success of colonial rule was viewed as dependent on incorporating and transforming Filipino ways of life, and the role of local agencies – particularly the Filipino elite – was crucial in this process. The Americans sought the cooperation of the Filipinos by making public education accessible, which many saw as tangible proof of the 'civilising mission'. For those

72 I use the term 'West' to refer to the group of European and American countries, primarily led by the United States, that have played a major role in shaping Filipinos' Anglophone worldview, and by extension, the Western influence that has dominated the Philippines' major interests and concerns.

who had been deprived of education under Spanish rule, the American educational system provided a concrete opportunity for advancement. According to American logic, education would prepare Filipinos to eventually take over the institutions they had created, fulfilling the goal of Filipinization, the final stage of Filipino tutelage.

In public health, as Filipino doctors, nurses, and other health personnel were trained to inherit the responsibility of managing the nation's health system, the Americans found it easier to implement their public health campaigns. Filipinos increasingly volunteered for these campaigns or took the initiative to promote health within their own communities. Over time, Filipino support and cooperation strengthened the foundation for the ultimate goal of Filipinization. However, as the Filipinos gained the skills and knowledge to take over their health institutions, they began to challenge the colonial narrative about their capacities. With their growing competence in managing public health, they demanded equal treatment and recognition, asserting that they could handle the welfare of their countrymen.

Despite the growing competence of Filipinos in managing public health and their increasing ability to take charge of health institutions – evidenced by their participation in health campaigns and initiatives to promote public health in their communities – some American colonial officials were recalcitrant, being fully convinced that Filipinos were not yet ready for self-rule. As Americans continuously revived the idea that Filipinos lacked initiative and were irresponsible, it became obvious that whether Filipinos complied with what was required of them, the Americans would never be entirely satisfied. Apparently, however much colonial institutions fostered changes in Filipino life, which could be read as evidence of progress, Americans would always remain doubtful of Filipino capacities. In the end, the measure of Filipino capacities remained subjective and dependent on American personalities. While Filipinos embraced the idea of 'civilisation', the state of being 'civilised' could only be learned, but never truly earned – at least for this period in Philippine history.

References

Arendt, Hannah (1958), *The Origins of Totalitarianism*, New York: Meridian.

Baisas, Francisco (1924), 'Letter to Walter D. Tiedeman, 28 July, Record Group 5.1.2 (Projects), Box 184, Folder 2387, Rockefeller Archive Center, Tarrytown, New York, USA.

Burchell, Graham, Colin Gordon, and Peter Miller (eds.) (1991), 'Preface', *The Foucault Effect: Studies in Governmentality with Two Lectures by and an Interview with Michel Foucault*, Chicago: University of Chicago Press, pp. ix–x.

Bureau of Education and Philippine Health Service (1928), *Health: A Manual for Teachers*, Manila: Bureau of Printing.

Burns, Adam (2017), *American Imperialism: The Territorial Expansion of the United States, 1783–2013*, Oxford: Oxford University Press.

Cannell, Fenella (2005), 'Immaterial Culture: "Idolatry" in the Lowland Philippines', in Andrew Wilford and Kenneth M. George (eds.), *Spirited Politics: Religion and Public Life in Contemporary Southeast Asia*, Ithaca, New York: Southeast Asia Program Publications, pp. 159–184.

Carter, Edward. C. (1906), 'Report of the Commissioner of Public Health for the Year 1905', *Annual Report of the Commissioner of Public Health for the Year 1905–1906*, Manila: Bureau of Public Printing.

Carter, William S. (1921), 'Status of Medical and other Scientific Activities in Manila on his Visit', 4–8 May, Record Group 1.1, Series 242.242a, Box 2, Folder 14, Rockefeller Archive Center, Tarrytown, New York, USA.

Carter, William S. (1922), 'Letter to Richard M. Pearce, Director of the Division of Medical Education', Rockefeller Foundation, 13 December, Record Group 1.1, Series 242.242A, Box 2, Folder 14, Rockefeller Archive Center, Tarrytown, New York, USA.

Carter, William S. (1928), 'Letter to Richard M. Pearce, School of Public Health in the Philippines', 15 April, Record Group 1.1, Series 242.242A, Box 2, Folder 15, Rockefeller Archive Center, Tarrytown, New York, USA.

Carter, William S. (1929), 'Letter to Dr. William B. Wherry, Medical School, University of Cincinnati', 20 February, Record Group 1.1, Series 242.242A, Box 4, Folder 45, Rockefeller Archive Center, Tarrytown, New York, USA.

Chirino, Pedro (1969), *Relacion de las Islas Filipinas: The Philippines in 1600*, translated by Ramon Echevarria, Manila: Historical Conservation Society.

Claessen, Henri J.M. and Peter Skalnik (eds.) (1978), *The Early State*, New York: De Gruyter Mouton.

de Jesus, Vicente (1921), *Report of the Philippine Health Service for the Fiscal Year from January 1 to December 31, 1920*, Manila: Bureau of Printing.

de la Cruz, Eduardo (1984), *History of Philippine Medicine and the PMA*, Quezon City: PMA Printing Press.

de Morga, Antonio (1958), *Sucesos de las Islas Filipinas, con anotaciones del Dr. Jose Rizal*, Quezon City: R. Martinez and Sons.

Fajardo, Jacobo (1931), *Report of the Philippine Health Service for the Fiscal Year from January 1 to December 31, 1929*, 2 volumes, Manila: Bureau of Printing.

Foucault, Michel (1991), 'Governmentality', in Graham Burchell, Colin Gordon, and Peter Miller (eds.), *The Foucault Effect: Studies in Governmentality with Two Lectures by and an Interview with Michel Foucault*, Chicago: University of Chicago Press, pp. 87–104.

Foucault, Michel (1997), *Subjectivity and Truth: The Essential Works of Michel Foucault, 1954–1984*, edited by Paul Rabinow, translated by Robert Hurley, Paul Rabinow, and James D. Faubion, New York: New Press.

Freer, Paul (1905), *Fourth Annual Report of the Director of the Bureau of Science, 1904–1905*, Manila: Bureau of Printing.

Gordon, Colin (1991), 'Governmental Rationality: An Introduction', in Graham Burchell, Colin Gordon, and Peter Miller (eds.), *The Foucault Effect: Studies in Governmentality with Two Lectures by and an Interview with Michel Foucault*, Chicago: University of Chicago Press, pp. 1–52.

Gunn, Selskar M. (1933), 'Letter to Max Mason, Report on the Visit to the Philippines, 26 August to 4 September, Record Group 1.1, Series 242 (Project Files), Box 1, Folder 4, Rockefeller Archive Center, Tarrytown, New York, USA.

Hayden, Joseph Ralston (1942), *The Philippines: A Study in National Development*, New York: The Macmillan Company.

Heiser, Victor G. (1906a), 'Report of the Director of Health', *Report of the Secretary of War to the Philippine Commission*, Washington: Government Printing Office.

Heiser, Victor G. (1906b), 'The Progress of Medicine in the Philippine Islands', Address delivered at the 3rd Annual Meeting of the Philippine Islands Medical Association in Manila, 28 February, Reprinted from the *Journal of the American Medical Association* 47: 245–247, bMS Am 1364.4, Box 6/8, William Cameron Forbes Papers, Houghton Library, Harvard University, USA.

Heiser, Victor G. (1911), 'Practical Experiences with Beriberi and Unpolished Rice in the Philippines', Paper read at the Eight Annual Meeting of the Philippine Islands Medical Association, 23 February, Reprinted from *Journal of the American Medical Association* 56: 1237–1238, bMS Am 1364.4, Box 7/8, William Cameron Forbes Papers, Houghton Library, Harvard University, USA.

Heiser, Victor G. (1914), 'Cholera in the Philippines During 1913, *Medical Record*, Paper Read at the Manila Medical Society on 2 March, bMS AM 1364.4, Box 7/8, William Cameron Forbes Papers, Houghton Library, Harvard University, USA.

Heiser, Victor G. (1988), *An American Doctor's Odyssey: Adventures in Forty-five Countries*. Reprint of the 1936 Edition, Quezon City: GCF Books.

Hobson, John M. (2004), *The Eastern Origins of Western Civilisation*, Cambridge, UK: Cambridge University Press.

Immerwahr, Daniel (2019), *How to Hide an Empire: A History of the Greater United States*, New York: Farrar, Strauss, and Giroux.

Lacy, George (1924), 'Report on the Conditions in Bureau of Science to the Director of IHB, International Health Division', Rockefeller Foundation, Record Group 5, Series 2.24e, Special Reports, Box 20, Folder 21, Rockefeller Archive Center, Tarrytown, New York, USA.

Lara, Hilario D. G. (1935), 'Development of Hygiene and Preventive Medicine (Public Health)', *Philippine National Research Council Bulletin*, 4 February.

Long, John D. (1916), *Report of the Philippine Health Service for the Fiscal Year from January 1 to December 31, 1915*, Manila: Bureau of Printing.

Long, John D. (1917), *Report of the Philippine Health Service for the Fiscal Year from January 1 to December 31, 1916*, Manila: Bureau of Printing.

Long, John D. (1918), *Report of the Philippine Health Service for the Fiscal Year from January 1 to December 31, 1917*, Manila: Bureau of Printing.

McCoy, Alfred W., Francisco A. Scarano, and Courtney Johnson (2010), 'On the Tropic of Cancer: Transitions and Transformations in the U.S. Imperial State', in Alfred W. McCoy and Francisco A. Scarano (eds.), *Colonial Crucible: Empire in the Making of the Modern American State*, Quezon City: Ateneo de Manila University Press, pp. 3–33.

McKinley, Earl B. (1927), 'Views about Filipinos and Filipino Doctors and their Training, Manila, Record Group 1.1, Series 242 (Project Files), Box 1, Folder 1, Rockefeller Archive Center, Tarrytown, New York, USA.

Moriarty, Charles F. (1928), 'Outline for a Demonstrable Unit', 11 April, Record Group 1.1, Series 242 (Project Files), Box 7, Folder 94, Rockefeller Archive Center, Tarrytown, New York, USA.

Quintes, F. and Vicente Rodriguez (1905), 'Letter to the Secretary of War, Jacob Dickinson', in *Monthly Report of the Board of Health to Dean C. Worcester, September 1905*, Manila: Bureau of Printing.

Rabinow, Paul (1997), 'Introduction: The History of Systems of Truth', in *Subjectivity and Truth: The Essential Works of Michel Foucault, 1954–1984*, edited by Paul Rabinow, translated by Robert Hurley, Paul Rabinow, and James D. Faubion, New York: New Press, pp. xi–xlvii.

Racelis, Mary (2001), 'Introduction: Bearing Benevolence in the Classroom and Community', in Racelis, Mary and Judy Celine Ick (eds.), *Bearers of Benevolence: The Thomasites and Public Education in the Philippines*, Pasig City: Anvil Publishing, pp. 3–20.

Schell, Edwin (1914), *In Ports Afar*, New York and Cincinnati: The Abingdon Press.

Sparrow, Bartholomew H. (2019), 'Becoming an American Empire', *Tulsa Law Review* 54 (39): 339–352.

Stoler, Ann Laura and Frederick Cooper (eds.) (1997), 'Between Metropole and Colony: Rethinking a Research Agenda', in *Tensions of Empire: Colonial Cultures in a Bourgeois World*, Berkeley: University of California Press, pp. 1–56.

Sullivan, Rodney (1991), *Exemplar of Americanism: The Philippine Career of Dean C. Worcester*, Ann Arbor, Michigan: Center for South and Southeast Asian Studies, University of Michigan.

Taft, William Howard (1907), 'Letter to the Honorable Dean C. Worcester enroute Trans-Siberian Railway', 30 November, Correspondence File, Worcester Collection, University of Michigan Ann Arbor, Bentley Historical Library, USA.

Tianco, G. Mamerto (1916), 'Report of the Office of Hygiene and Industrial Development', in John D. Long (ed.), *Report of the Philippine Health Service for the Fiscal Year from January 1 to December 31, 1916*, Manila: Bureau of Printing.

Tianco, G. Mamerto (1928), *Philippine Health Service Sanitary Almanac for 1919 and Calendars for 1920 and 1921*, Manila: Bureau of Printing, RG350, Entry 95, Box 372, folder 150/56/18/3, United States National Archives Records Administration, USA.

Tiglao, Teodora (1975), *Seven Decades of Public Health in the Philippines, 1898–1972*, Tokyo: Southeast Asia Medica Information Center (SEMIC).

Tilly, Charles (1990), *Coercion, Capital, and European States, AD 990–1992*, Cambridge: Basil Blackwell.

United States Philippine Commission (1904), *Report of the Philippine Commission, 1900–1903*, Washington: Government Printing Office.

United States Special Mission to the Philippines (1927), *Report of the Special Mission to the Philippine Islands to the Secretary of War*, Washington, D.C.: Government Printing Office.

Washington, George (1783), 'George Washington to John Hancock (Circular)', 11 June, Head Quarters Newburgh, New York, Washington Papers, The University of Virginia, retrieved from: https://washingtonpapers.org/documents/george-washington-to-john-hancock-circular-11-june-1783/.

Worcester, Dean (1908), 'A Brief Review of the Movement for the Establishment of the Philippine General Hospital at Manila at the Laying of the Cornerstone of the Hospital', 28 February, Box 1, Lecture and Speeches, 1908–1913 Folio, Dean Conant Worcester Papers, Harlan Hatcher Worcester Collection, Harlan Hatcher Graduate Library, University of Michigan Ann Arbor, USA.

Worcester, Dean (1910a), *Annual Report of the Bureau of Health for the Philippine Islands for the fiscal year ended June 30, 1910*, Manila: Bureau of Printing.

Worcester, Dean (1910b), 'Report of the Secretary of Interior', *Bureau of Health for the Philippine Islands*, Manila: Bureau of Printing.

Worcester, Dean (1918), 'OUR NEW POLICY IN PHILIPPINES IS ATTACKED; Dean Worcester Points Out the Evils of Substituting Ignorant Filipinos for Americans. NATIVES NOW IN CONTROL Dismissal of Bureau Chiefs Threatens Efficiency of Land, Health, and Printing Bureaus. NATIVE HEADS LAND BUREAU And Admits He Knows Nothing About the Work; Poor Landholders Likely to Suffer. OUR NEW POLICY IN PHILIPPINES IS ATTACKED,' *New York Times*, November 18, retrieved from: https://www.nytimes.com/1913/11/18/archives/our-new-policy-in-philippines-is-attacked-dean-worcester-points-out.html

Chapter 8

Surveillance, Policing and Filtration: Quarantine for Repatriates in Busan after WWII

Jeong-Ran Kim[1]

On 15 August 1945, Korea was liberated from Japan after the latter's unconditional surrender in World War II. However, liberation from Japan did not mean independence as the United States and the Soviet Union, two of the victorious nations of World War II, now confronted each other in Korea and the peninsula was divided into North and South along the 38th parallel. A week before Japan surrendered, on 8 August, the Soviet Union declared war on Japan and invaded the northern part of the peninsula the following day. This alarmed the US military and on 12 August 1945, a draft agreement to divide Korea along the 38th parallel was drawn up by US military officers. The Soviet's accepted the proposal, and after the liberation from Japan, a US-oriented regime was established in the South and a communist regime (under Soviet influence) was established in the North.

General Douglas MacArthur, Supreme Commander of the Allied Powers (SCAP) had ultimate responsibility for the occupation of South Korea but he delegated this responsibility to General John Reed Hodge, Commander of the United States Army Forces in Korea (USAFIK, September 8, 1945–August 15, 1948). In the immediate postwar period, the American occupation of East Asia was designed to minimise Soviet influence, and South Korea

1 I generously acknowledge the support of the Wellcome Trust for this research (Grant: 106874/Z/15/Z).

was at the forefront of this struggle (Lee 1995: 12). As a defeated country, Japan was also placed under Allied occupation. The US led the implementation of occupational policies under the command of General MacArthur with support from the British Commonwealth Occupation Forces. The US initiated a self-assigned mission to mould Japan into a stable democracy, conforming to Western and capitalist norms (Guthrie-Shimizu 2010). Japan was designated as the main regional ally in the competition between the two Cold War rivals, assisting the US's Far Eastern strategies. The United States thought that strengthening economic cooperation between South Korea and Japan would help to prevent further Soviet penetration in East Asia (Lee 1995: 13). These US policies in the Asia-Pacific region impeded the decolonisation of South Korea (Augustine 2017).

As such, South Korea and Japan were incorporated into the American sphere of influence in East Asia in the formative period of the Cold War. For the United States' geopolitical strategies, it was necessary to stabilise the occupied areas as quickly as possible. Moreover, it was essential to remove vestiges of the Japanese imperial system and entrench Western control. To this end, one of the most urgent missions for the US occupation forces was to disarm the Japanese military abroad and repatriate them to Japan. The repatriation of Japanese civilians followed. In addition, there was a pressing need to repatriate Japan's former imperial subjects back to their countries from Japan and its overseas possessions, as well as from the battlefields.

After Japan's surrender, a massive movement of people ensued, heralding the dismantling of the Japanese empire. In this process, Japanese in liberated Korea rushed to return to their homeland via the south-eastern port of Busan, the nearest port to Japan. At the same time, many Koreans returned from Japan to Korea through the same port. As such, masses of people had flooded Busan before the US occupation forces arrived. US forces soon recognised that this unprecedented number of repatriates might carry many diseases to their respective countries unless proper preventive measures were taken (Sams 1998: 89–91). Outbreaks of epidemic diseases could cause social unrest and threaten soldiers' health and morale in the occupied areas. Therefore, the US military government instituted quarantine at repatriation ports in their occupation zones, and Busan was the first repatriation quarantine station. To implement quarantine effectively, the occupation forces used data from disease surveillance in Japan and its former colonies, which was collected towards the end of the war.

These repatriation programs have been extensively studied by scholars. Lori Watt has shown how Japanese settlers, particularly intellectuals and opinion leaders in Seoul, struggled to adjust their identities from 'magnificent Japanese nationals' to a defeated people during the process of decolonisation (Watt 2015). In an earlier masterful work, Watt reveals how Japan sought to erase its imperial history and wars of aggression by emphasising the hardships that Japanese repatriates experienced on their way home (Watt 2009). Similarly, Yeon-Sik Yi argues that Japan highlighted its people's experiences of detainment and pauperisation, portraying repatriates from the Soviet occupied zones as victims as if to dispel their wartime responsibilities (Yi 2008). Howard Kahm examines the economics of Japanese repatriation, showing how Japanese repatriates created new economic connections between Korea and Japan by smuggling contraband goods through Busan (Kahm 2016). Meanwhile, Tessa Morris-Suzuki focuses on the new regime of border controls between Korea and Japan under the US Occupation, which became the prototype of Japan's current migration and border control system. The US military (re)drew a maritime border between South Korea and Japan and attempted to strictly control the movement of people between the two regions. In this process, Korean repatriates' re-entry to Japan was defined as 'stowing away', and thus had to be suppressed. The Japanese represented Koreans as 'invaders' in an attempt to reset Japanese collective identity in the process of rebuilding Japan as a racially homogenous nation-state (Morris-Suzuki 2006, 2010).

Although these scholars have carefully examined the historical implications of repatriation, infectious diseases and quarantine were not their main concerns. However, these issues do make appearances in some important research which provides insights for considering this subject. For example, Sebastian Conrad examines the process whereby Japan attempted to erase its imperial past during the postwar period and later reconstructed a politically and culturally acceptable narrative. He refers to quarantine procedures in defeated Japan as a rite of passage for repatriates to cleanse the taint of empire (Conrad 2014). Yet there were also some important continuities. As Christopher Aldous and Akihito Suzuki show, some postwar public health organisations and activities in Japan were 'formed around' those of the prewar era, thus explaining their rapid emergence. Another continuity from colonial to postcolonial periods was the tendency to view specific groups or ethnicities as 'carriers of diseases' rather than considering the social factors that caused epidemics (Aldous and Suzuki 2012). In previous work, I have also demonstrated that the racial views of US and Japanese medical officers affected the ways in which they conceived the risks of diseases and quarantine procedures (Kim 2021).

In this article, I pay closer attention to the quarantine procedures implemented in postwar Busan, where the official repatriation program was first implemented. The geographical proximity of Busan and Japan meant that it was potentially easier to evade quarantine procedures and reach Japan by unofficial means. This maritime border was therefore viewed as porous and a site for the movement of 'hazardous elements'. US forces were anxious to prevent the spread of infectious diseases which had the potential to incapacitate occupation forces and create social disorder. Therefore, quarantine and other preventive measures were designed to be particularly exacting and robust. Considering all these factors, this chapter explores quarantining repatriates in Busan during the early period of US military occupation. I argue that the regime of repatriation and quarantine reflects the US's attempt to establish a new order in the occupied regions of Northeast Asia, which included resetting the collective identities of both Koreans and Japanese.

Dismantling the Empire

When Japan surrendered, its government had no plans in place for around 6.9 million Japanese nationals overseas (half of whom were civilians and half members of the armed forces) and over 2 million colonial subjects within Japan (Watt 2009: 61). In Korea alone, there were 700,000–800,000 Japanese civilians while about 240,000 Japanese servicemen were stationed in the country (McWilliams 1988: 10). Just before the termination of hostilities following the Soviet invasion, some Japanese swiftly left Korea for their own safety (ibid., 38). In Japan, too, considerable numbers of Koreans were waiting for the day to return to their homeland. On 15 August 1945, there were about 2 million Koreans in Japan proper, just over half of whom had been coerced into forced labour in private companies, especially coal mines and the Japanese armed forces (Choi 2017). As the number of Japanese people in Korea rushing back to Japan rapidly increased following Japan's surrender, the Japanese government asked General Headquarters (GHQ) in Manila for approval to operate two large- ferries, Kōan Maru (7,100 tons) and Tokuju Maru (3,500 tons), between Busan and Senzaki (in Shimonoseki) and Hakata. The ships began sailing on 31 August and 2 September, respectively (Choi 2017).

During the colonial period, Korea's geographical position made it a strategic bridgehead between Japan and the Asian continent. Busan was particularly important in this respect and was by far the busiest port in Korea. Busan had been designated, to all intents and purposes, as a Japanese imperial city even before Japan became a colonial power in a formal sense.[2] It had been a vital point on the main traffic artery for the Japanese Empire throughout the colonial period and a great volume of traffic flowed through Busan to and from Shimonoseki and other Japanese ports. In 1911, a railway linked Busan to a branch of the South Manchuria Railway via Seoul and Uiju.[3] Hence, repatriating Japanese poured into Busan enroute to their homeland.

Busan was chaotic. The masses of returning Japanese were swelled by a constant influx of Koreans returning from Japan. The SCAP feared that disorganized mass immigration would cause social and political turmoil, and was particularly concerned that repatriates might carry pathogens with them to Japan. During the war, public health had deteriorated due to shortages of medicine and medical personnel. Moreover, many houses and urban facilities, including hospitals, public water supply and the waste collection system, were destroyed by Allied air strikes.[4]

2 Ariyoshi, Akira (1904), 'Kyoryūchi eisei kairyōhi ni kokko hojo wo furuno hitsuyō ni tsuki hikenrinshin no ken (Issue of subsidy from the Japanese government for the sanitary reform in the Japanese Settlement in Busan)', from Japanese Consul Ariyoshi Akira to Foreign Minister Kimura Jutarō, Aug 16 1904, 3-11-5-5, Diplomatic Archives of the Ministry of Foreign Affairs of Japan.

3 Allied Geographical Section SWPA (1945), *Special Report No.111 Pusan Korea*. Date: 31 Aug 1945, WO 252/999, The National Archives of the UK.

4 General Headquarters, Supreme Commander of the Allied Powers (GHQSCAP 1945a), *Summation of Non-Military Activities in Japan and Korea Number 1. September–October 1945*, Tokyo: GHQSCAP.

Many people were without shelter and exposed to unhealthy environmental conditions. Acute communicable diseases such as diphtheria, venereal diseases, typhoid fever and other filth-borne diseases were rampant. From autumn 1943 to 1944, typhus was also prevalent in Hokkaido and the northeastern part of Japan.[5]

The US military preparations to invade the Japanese mainland towards the end of the war utilized military intelligence reports and disease surveillance data for preventive measures. For example, typhus was expected to be rampant in postwar Japan as it appears wherever poverty, crowding, and insanitary conditions prevail, in times of social dislocation – it was also comparatively deadly.[6] The US military therefore stockpiled DDT and typhus vaccine in the Philippines (Sams 1998: 125) before Japan surrendered. Particularly, Korean labourers in Hokkaido's coal mines were seen to be the main spreaders of typhus by the Occupation forces (Rengōgun 1950: 226–227). The US military uncritically accepted Japanese long-standing biases against Koreans rather than considering that social factors made them more susceptible to diseases (Aldous 2006). For example, Korean mining labourers were forced to do hard labour in poor conditions which made them more susceptible to typhus and other diseases (Joo 2017). While the Japanese government and the SCAP were negotiating the terms of the surrender, massive numbers of Koreans rushed to Japanese ports to board ships for Korea. Japanese authorities and US military officers viewed those labourers as carriers of lice and rickettsia and therefore

5 Anonymous (1946), 'Sengo bōeki taisaku no jūten (Major emphasis of preventive measures against diseases in the postwar period)', Nihon iji shinpō (Japanese medical journal), 1175: 3 and 6.

6 Joint Intelligence Study Publishing Board (1944), *Joint Army-Navy Intelligence Study of Southwest Japan:* Kyūshū, Shikoku, and Southwestern Honshū, Washington D.C.: Joint Intelligence Study Publishing Board.

responsible for spreading typhus on the way to the ports (Sams 1998: 85).

Meanwhile, medical systems and sanitary conditions in Korea were even worse than Japan. During the colonial period, about 99% of all drugs and hospital supplies in Korea were imported from Japan. However, during the war it became increasingly difficult to import medicine from the metropole.[7] More importantly, public health infrastructure in colonial Korea was far inferior to Japan. Above all, sanitary administrations and infrastructure had been constructed and operated by the Japanese, primarily for their own needs. Koreans had little role in administering programs and little was done to improve their general health.[8] Due to the poor sanitary environment and inadequate disease control system, typhoid fever and dysentery (amoebic and bacterial) were prevalent and insect-borne diseases such as malaria caused widespread sickness (Simmons 1944–1954: 150).[9] Japanese living conditions in Korea were generally much better than those of Koreans and it was far easier for them to access medical services and public health facilities. By contrast, it was difficult for Koreans to see a doctor due to their chronic poverty. A medical missionary working at Severance Hospital in colonial Korea explained, '[t]he poverty of the Korean people is so great that the cost of proper medical care seems more than they can afford' (Buskirk 1931: 112).

After the war, sanitary conditions were strained in many parts of Korea, and particularly in the port of Busan. A massive number of Japanese flocked to Busan and stayed around the

---

7 The Bureau of the Medical and Surgery, US Military (1911–1946), 'JANIS 75 Chapter XI Health and Sanitation', *Korea (Chosen)*, 470/57/17/E.1014/Box 22. The National Library of Korea (hereafter, TNLK), p. 41.

8 War Department (1945), *TB MED 208, Medical and Sanitary Data on Korea*, Washington D.C.: War Department, p. 6.

9 Ibid., p. 36.

port until boarding. About 11,000 Japanese were present at the port on 31 August 1945 (Choi 2006), only two weeks after the surrender. Busan's sanitary facilities were ill-equipped to deal with such numbers; there were only two public latrines in the port for repatriates.[10] Human waste piled up and the port stank badly; flies swarmed and spread dysentery. Furthermore, there were few Japanese officials to take charge of the crowds; most Japanese police and other local government officials had escaped to Japan before the influx began, and the port was in utter disorder (Nishinihon Toshokan 1980: 27–28).

Military government

The chaotic situation and a surging crowd of Japanese returnees in Busan deepened the US military's worries about occupation. Before they arrived in South Korea, one of the US military's main concerns was the unfamiliar natural environment and 'oriental' diseases which might threaten the troops' safety.[11] This sense of unfamiliarity was heightened by the last-minute nature of preparations for the occupation of Korea. Major-General John R. Hodge of the 24th Corps was appointed the commanding officer of the United States Army Forces in Korea (USAFIK) on short notice, with less than three weeks before they embarked.

Korea was a largely unknown country for the United States. In a short time, the USAFIK had to learn about Korea from a handful of documents. The most useful of these was the Joint Army-Navy Intelligence Study of Korea, the so-called JANIS 75,

10 General Headquarters, Far East Command, Supreme Commander Allied Powers, and United Nations Command (GHQFECSCAPUNC 1945–1948a), *Japanese Repatriation*, RG 554 Records of General Headquarters, Far East Command, Supreme Commander Allied Powers, and United Nations, USAFIK: XXIV Corps, G-2 Historical Section, TNLK.

11 G-2 (1945–1948a), 'Supply and Administration', in *History of United States Army Forces in Korea, Part 1*, . Accessed 17 August 2018.

which was published by the Joint Intelligence Study Publishing Board in April 1945 (Medical Department 1955: 268). This is one of a series of reports which provided intelligence between April 1943 and July 1947 to assist the war-effort and prepare the military for occupation. The reports covered a range of subjects from geography through to economics and politics. The Medical Intelligence Division contributed a medical section to JANIS. The medical intelligence section was created when the US military prepared to enter WWII, and its main concern was the potential impact of local diseases on military populations (Clemente 2005; Harrison 2016). The division collected relevant data and analysed them for military purposes and other strategic goals. This task was similar to the disease surveillance which is currently defined by the US Center for Disease Control and Prevention (CDC) as on-going systematic collection, analysis and interpretation of health-related data needed for planning, implementing, and evaluating public health practices (Krishna 2021).

By the spring of 1944, the attention of those involved in strategic intelligence was shifting to Japan and its overseas possessions since the studies essential to the imminent invasion of North-West Europe had been completed (Medical Department, US Army 1955: 270). The report on Korea presupposes possibilities not only for military operations in the country but also for occupation and domination of the region (Lee 2015). The report has several sections including 'People and Government', 'Oceanography', 'Resources and Trade', 'Gazetteer and Map Appraisal' and 'Health and Sanitation'.[12] The 'Health and Sanitation' section describes the hygienic environment, medical

12 Joint Intelligence Study Publishing Board (1945), *Joint Army-Navy Intelligence Study of Korea, Including Tsushima and Quelpart*, Washington: Joint Intelligence Study Publishing Board.

system, condition of infrastructures and disease risks in Korea. The report contains five categories (A–E) of disease problems in Korea ranked according to their impact on the safety of US troops. Category A: diseases of military importance such as malaria, dysentery, typhus fever, venereal disease, trench foot and frostbite. Category B: diseases of potential military importance including cholera and disease which may be introduced such as plague, Japanese B encephalitis. Category C: diseases of minor military importance such as leptospirosis, rat-bite fever, rabies. Category D: diseases common among the civil population such as diphtheria, smallpox, leprosy, typhoid and paratyphoid fever and so on. Category E: miscellaneous diseases such as anthrax and tetanus.[13] On the basis of the medical intelligence report, the US military prepared preventive measures for diseases. Particularly, suppressive malaria treatment and all precautions required in malarious areas were ordered and special units such as the 216th Malaria Survey Detachment and the 175th Malaria Control Unit landed with the occupation forces (Geukdong munje yeon'guso 1989: 200–208).

General Hodge and the 24th Corps were sent to South Korea from Okinawa where they had landed in March 1945 for the battle of Okinawa. On 8 September, he and his corps arrived in South Korea and the following day the formal surrender of the Government-General and the Japanese armed forces in Korea south of 38th degree of latitude took place at the Government-General building in Seoul. Simultaneously, the USAMGIK was established. On 20 September, the US military government instituted the various bureaus of governance, such as Finance, Education, Justice, Mining & Industry, Communications, Transportation, Public Safety and Agriculture & Commerce, and announced the responsibilities and duties of each organisation.

13 Ibid., pp. 23–25.

Four days later, on 24 September, the Bureau of Public Health was established. The military government enhanced the capabilities of the Bureau of Public Health and all duties, functions, funds, records and property of the public health section of the Police Bureau were transferred to it.[14] During the colonial period, the Government-General had implemented police-centred sanitary administration because the police had control over many aspects of people's lives (Park 2022). The police adopted a coercive method of controlling infectious diseases but the government did little to improve sanitary facilities or living conditions. When epidemics were feared, the police attempted to prevent the spread of the disease by enforcing house-to-house inspection to discover patients in the early stages or those not being attended by physicians. As a result, many cases were concealed by families due to fear of the police. The reporting system for communicable diseases was therefore unreliable and the general public health system was inadequate due to the police's lack of the expertise.[15] With the poor hygienic conditions and inadequate sanitary administration during the colonial period, the US military government had to reform public health promptly.

The Welfare Branch of the Bureau of Public Health and Welfare was established by an ordinance of October 27 to relieve the poor and give relief to refugees from Japan and the Soviet occupational zone.[16] Between September and October 1945, a massive number of Koreans who had been forced to work in factories and mines in Japan returned to Korea. When municipal officers mobilised Koreans to Japan for the war regime, Japanese

14 GHQSCAP (1945a), *Summation of Non-Military Activities in Japan and Korea*.

15 War Department (1945), *TB MED 208 Medical and Sanitary Data on Korea*, p. 5.

16 GHQSCAP (1945b), *Summation of Non-Military Activities in Japan and Korea Number 2. November 1945*, Tokyo: GHQSCAP.

officers had promised high wages and good treatment. However, most of forced labourers had not been paid or otherwise compensated for their work and were provided no travel allowances when they repatriated. These labourers demanded payment from the former Japanese chiefs of municipalities and some took to rioting; they were supported by local Commissars and leftist groups (An 2015: 29; Choi 2021). As communist influence was gradually expanding in many parts of Asia, the US military was determined to suppress social unrest which could result in expanding leftist influence in South Korea. Moreover, the US military intended to demonstrate the superiority and benevolence of the US regime in contrast to the Soviet Union which now occupied the peninsula above the 38th parallel. These circumstances prompted the military government to introduce a welfare system in South Korea (Shin 2000; Hamada 2010).

However, it was difficult to find Koreans trained in public health and welfare to support the US military to carry out these programs. Indeed, there were few Koreans who could support the military government in any capacity because key positions in all levels of colonial government had been filled exclusively by Japanese. Since formally annexing Korea in 1910, the Japanese had made every effort to deprive Korea of the ability to stand alone as an independent country.[17] Thus, it was an urgent matter for the military government to nurture Korean medical professionals and public health experts. They asked the International Health Division of the Rockefeller Foundation to grant ten fellowships to train Korean physicians in the United States.[18]

17 G-2 (1945–1948b), 'Korean Relations', in *History of United States Army Forces in Korea, Part 1*, http://db.history.go.kr/item/level.do?itemId=husa. Accessed September 07, 2018; GHQSCAP (1945a), *Summation of Non-Military Activities in Japan and Korea*.

18 Choi, C.C (1949), 'Public Health in Korea', in Foreign Agricultural Service (ed.), *Foreign trade, insecticides*, RG 166 Records of the Foreign Agricultural

To solve problems immediately at hand, however, the military government attempted to mobilise Japanese manpower in various ways. Initially, General Hodge intended to retain the Japanese Governor-General Abe Nobuyuki and his officers to facilitate administration. The Japanese government also adopted guidelines to encourage as many Japanese residents in Korea as possible to remain settled in Korea. The Government-General of Korea set up the Bureau of Planning on 27 August 1945, to process the end of the war and manage the evacuation of Japanese civilians. The Bureau found that about 650,000 Japanese were hoping to return to Japan and the rest were willing to remain in Korea (Park 2017). However, the US military government's plan caused bewilderment and disappointment among Koreans, who protested not only the retention of former colonial officers but also the continued authority of the hated Japanese police.[19] In the end, the USAMGIK dismissed Governor-General Abe and subsequently discharged key officials of the Government-General on 12 September. Ultimately, the US military government decided with few exceptions to force Japanese to leave Korea as soon as possible, but eviction of the Japanese created a serious shortage of administrative and technical personnel. The military government therefore relied heavily on Korean officers and police who had worked for the colonial regime who shared the US's hostility towards communism and, as a result, these officers achieved power in many fields (Kim 2008; Park 2011). The military government also found itself with little choice but to employ some Japanese personnel for a time, particularly to manage the repatriation.

Service; Record Group, Narrative Reports 1946–1949, TNLK.

19 G-2 (1945–1948c), 'Taking over the Government', in *History of United States Army Forces in Korea, Part I*, . Accessed 174 August 2018.

The beginning of repatriation control

Shortly after the military government was established, the official repatriation program began. On 20 September, SCAP directed USAFIK that the first priority of governance was to disarm the Japanese military and send them to Japan as soon as possible. Repatriation of Japanese civilians was the second priority. Two days later, on 22 September 1945, SCAP issued the Memorandum for the Japanese Government (SCAPIN-48) which required the latter to institute public health measures. The Memorandum had nine sections; the sixth section directed the Japanese government to 'Inaugurate port quarantine control in cooperation with US Naval Forces'.[20] In South Korea, the Displaced Persons Office of the Foreign Affairs Section of the military government took charge of the movement of repatriates to and from ports. The port of Busan was chosen by the US military as the main port for the repatriation program. The 40th Infantry Division and the 160th Infantry Regiment arrived in Busan on 23 September. From that day, daily conferences were held to prepare the repatriation program. They planned for a rate of evacuation of 4,000 per day and, at first, this figure was to consist almost entirely of troops.

On 28 September, the repatriation program began under the formal control of the 40th Division. The 40th Infantry Division guarded and supervised the Japanese Armed Forces and civilians moving to Japan through the port.[21] The specific task of processing and loading Japanese military personnel and civilians from Pier No.1 in the port was assigned to the 160th

---

20 Kōseishō (1949), Eisei gyōsei gyōmu hōkoku: kōseishō hōkokurei Shōwa *21 nen* (Report on public health administration 1946), Tokyo: Kōseishō daijin kambō tōkei jōhōbu, pp. 1–14.

21 Bullit, John M. (1945), *40th Infantry Division: History of Evacuation and Repatriation Through the Port of Pusan: Korea, 28 Sept. 45–15 Nov*, Washington DC: Department of the Army, p. 1.

Infantry Regiment. The standing operating procedures were developed by the 40th Infantry Division in the Philippines as the division took charge of the disarmament and repatriation of the defeated Japanese troops.[22]

The most important part of the repatriation procedures was quarantine. The US military took the view that the 'Orient' was full of pathogens, in much the same way as Japan had viewed its former colonies. Japanese perception of poor hygiene standards in its overseas possessions influenced domestic perceptions of Japanese repatriates (Watt 2009: 15 and 92). The US military was therefore concerned about the possibility of repatriates spreading diseases. When the 40th Infantry Division started processing the repatriates, they saw myriad flies and mosquitoes that fed on years of accumulated filth, which threatened the troops' health and morale.[23] Furthermore, masses of Japanese civilians had to wait around the harbour until the troops were evacuated. Thus, the port and its vicinity were overcrowded and refugee shelters became unsanitary. Some had the comparative good fortune of being able to stay at repatriation camps, but many were forced to sleep in warehouses or on railway platforms. In some cases, they had to wait up to 20 days to get a place on a ship from the port of Busan (Nihonjin Sewakai 1945a). In this situation, maintaining sanitation in an area flooded with repatriates to 'whom cleanliness was no habit' was regarded as an essential task for the US military.[24]

The procedure of Japanese repatriation was as follows. First, quarantine officers deloused Japanese repatriates and their

---

22 Ibid., p. 4.

23 G-2 (1945–1948d), 'Processing of Japanese at Pusan. Interview with 1st Lt. John M. Bullit, XXIV Corps G-3 Section, former Asst. G-2, 40th Inf. Div., 27 May 46', in *History of the United States Army Forces in Korea, Part I*. Accessed August 10, 2018.

24 Bullit (1945), *40th Infantry Division*, p. 29.

baggage with dichlorodiphenyltrichloroethane (DDT). DDT was first synthesized in 1874, but its insecticidal effect was only discovered in 1939 by a Swiss chemist, Paul Müller. Towards the end of the Second World War, DDT became the predominant insecticide for malaria and typhus control (Kinkela 2011). DDT was first introduced to Korea and Japan by the US military as a white disinfectant powder which had psychological as well as biological effects. It represented a technological miracle which epitomized the superiority of the United States, while its application to delouse the Japanese symbolized their defeat and humiliation (Nishinihon Toshokan 1980: 4; Aldous 2006). After delousing with DDT, the repatriates were immunized for smallpox and typhoid where necessary. Certificates of immunization were inspected before boarding ships in compliance with Army Forces Circular No. 32 (subject 'Immunization'). If repatriates were not able to present a certificate, they were not allowed to board.[25] If they had the right certificates, the US military searched the repatriates and their luggage to ensure that they were not violating the strict policies against taking contraband or looted assets. Japanese were only permitted to take up to 1,000 yen and there were strict limits on how much baggage individuals could take.[26] After completing all these procedures, repatriates were permitted to board a ship. The new discipline imposed upon Japanese repatriates by Occupation forces drove home their change in status from rulers to subjects.

To quarantine repatriates in Busan, the US military relied heavily on Japanese personnel, both military and civilian. The US sanitary officers recruited Japanese military men on the dock

---

25 GHQFECSCAPUNC (1945–1948b), *Repatriation Information Book, September 25–December 31 1945*, RG 554 Records of General Headquarters, Far East Command, Supreme Commander Allied Powers, and United Nations Command. USAFIK: XXIV Corps, G-2 Historical Section, TNLK, p. 48.

26 Bullit (1945), *40th Infantry Division*, p. 19.

to clean it whenever necessary. Japanese troops cleaned the pier and its surroundings and sprayed DDT into every corner.[27]

The role of the Japanese Relief Society, the so-called Nihonjin Sewakai (hereafter JRS) was also significant in dealing with repatriation. The JRS was formed in Seoul on 20 August 1945, at the request of the Japanese Government-General in Korea and the Japanese military stationed in Korea by influential Japanese businessmen, scholars and journalists (Rho 2006). The society established twelve branches in the main Japanese residential areas such as Incheon and Busan as well as near the 38th parallel. Later, this society became the only non-official repatriation organization of the Japanese authorized by the US military government.[28] Its main duties were to provide general information about repatriation and to undertake relief work for Japanese refugees from the North. Another important task was publication of a daily bulletin (Keijō Naichijin Sewakai Kaihō, hereafter JRS Bulletin). This bulletin was published from 2 September 1945, providing Japanese residents and refugees (from North Korea and Manchuria) with information about repatriation schedules as well as general conditions in Korea and Japan. The bulletin posted the timetables of repatriation trains to Busan and ships to Japan from the port (*JRS Bulletin* 1945b). It also reported on general conditions in the ports of Hakata (Fukuoka) and Senzaki, which were the major ports receiving Japanese repatriates from Korea (*JRS Bulletin* 1945c). The JRS assisted not only the repatriation procedures but also encouraged Japanese repatriates to recognize Japan's situation as a defeated country and to demonstrate that they were 'internationally minded people' (*JRS Bulletin* 1945d, e).

27 Ibid., p.29; GHQFECSCAPUNC (1945–1948b), *Repatriation Information Book*, pp. 46-48.

28 GHQFECSCAPUNC (1945–1948b), *Repatriation Information Book*, p. 23.

Another duty of the society was to provide information about medical services such as the schedule of immunizations for Japanese residents and refugees (*JRS Bulletin* 1945g). In addition, the society supported the operation of the Medical Relief Union staffed by Japanese doctors, medical students, and nurses. The MRU provided free medical care for repatriates at former Japanese hospitals in South Korea, as well as on repatriation trains and ships. Initially former medical students of Keijo Imperial University volunteered for medical relief activities for Japanese refugees from the North in Seoul. With Japanese doctors' help, they opened the Relief Hospital for war refugees on 1 October 1945. Japanese professors from the medical school of Keijo Imperial University and other medical college members joined the effort. Ten days later, based on the members of the Relief Hospital, the JRS Medical Relief Union was established. This union's activities were supported by the US military government, which authorized the transfer of medical goods and food from the Japanese military in Korea to the union (Nishinihon Toshokan 1980: 7, 22, 25 and 31). The Medical Relief Union provided medical services not only to Japanese refugees from the North and residents in Seoul, but also to Japanese repatriates in Busan, as well as Hakata and Senzaki in Japan.[29] The most critical location for relief and medical care was Busan, since almost all the local Japanese physicians had been evacuated from the city. The Medical Relief Union sent a special detachment to Busan from Seoul, which under American supervision provided treatment for Japanese patients at the port.[30] They also assumed the duties of delousing and immunizing Japanese repatriates in Busan prior to embarkation.[31]

---

29 Ibid., p. 30.

30 GHQFECSCAPUNC (1945–1948a), *Japanese Repatriation*.

31 G-2 (1945–1948e), 'Priorities and Procedures', in *History of United States Army Forces in Korea, Part I*, http://db.history.go.kr/item/level.do?itemId=husa.

In the case of Koreans repatriating from Japan, too, all authorized ships unloaded at the port of Busan. Japanese ships returning Japanese nationals from Busan to Shimonoseki and Hakata carried Koreans from Japan on the return trip.[32] While waiting for ships to Korea, Korean repatriates in the Japanese ports were exposed to abominable conditions. For instance, many Koreans in Shimonoseki were sitting on straw mats near the wharf; they were famished and exhausted, and the sick were neglected by port officials (*Maeilsinbo* 1945). For some time, inspections of the Reception Centres and embarkation ports in Japan revealed that measures in place for the feeding, housing, sanitation, and control of movements of Korean and Chinese repatriates were deplorable.[33]

When Korean returnees arrived in Busan, they were met by a guide group composed of US military personnel and members of local Korean welfare societies. The Korean societies were independent of the Foreign Affairs Section of the USAMGIK in operational matters. Welfare operations were initially concerned mainly with caring for Koreans arriving from Japan and Japanese departing from Korea. Later, the United Refugee Relief Service was established at Busan to coordinate the activities of participating agencies.[34] The US Medical Corps also cooperated with Korean welfare societies and the US military government teams in the diagnosis and treatment of Korean returnees from Japan both at the Busan wharf and on the train from Busan to Seoul.[35] Korean repatriates were marched in groups of 100 from Pier No. 1 to the reception compound where they were dusted with DDT and had

Accessed December 01, 2017.

32 GHQSCAP (1945a), *Summation of Non-Military Activities in Japan and Korea.*

33 GHQSCAP (1945b), *Summation of Non-Military Activities in Japan and Korea.*

34 Ibid.

35 GHQFECSCAPUNC (1945–1948b), *Repatriation Information Book*, pp. 29–32.

their Japanese currency exchanged into Korean currency (500 yen per person); after 25 November 1945, this was increased to 1,000 yen, equivalent to the price of 20 packs of cigarettes at the time (Morris-Suzuki 2010: 65–66). This strict limit left Korean returnees in a serious financial predicament and became one of the main reasons for Korean repatriates to attempt to return from Japan by illegal shipping (Yi 2018).

By 1 December 1945, all remaining Japanese army troops, except the Seoul and Busan Liaison Detachments, personnel in the Busan Military Hospital, and 500 members of the labour corps were evacuated from Busan. Another 10,000 troops had been evacuated from Incheon in mid-October; almost 50,000 troops had been evacuated from Jeju-do by mid-November; and roughly 10,000 Japanese naval personnel had been cleared from Jinhae before 1 December.[36] The 160th Infantry Regiment at the port of Busan, up until 22 February 1946, when its last report was submitted, had processed a total of 1,130,972 persons, of which 710,536 were incoming Koreans, 102,984 were evacuated Japanese soldiers, and 317,452 were evacuated Japanese civilians.[37] Throughout the repatriation process, the Japanese repatriates remained passive, obedient, and generally cooperative in effecting their removal from Korea (GHQFECSCAPUNC 1945–1948a).[38] Lieutenant John M. Bullit of the 40th Infantry Division, at No.1 Pier of Busan port, described a long queue of Japanese repatriates who 'presented

36 G-2 (1945–1948f), 'Processing and Evacuation', in *History of United States Army Forces in Korea, Part 1*, http://db.history.go.kr/item/level.do?itemId=husa. Accessed July 23, 2018.

37 G-2 (1945–1948g), 'The 40th Division Occupies Southeastern Korea', in *History of United States Army Forces in Korea, Part 1*, http://db.history.go.kr/item/level.do?itemId=husa. Accessed 12 August, 2018.

38 GHQFECSCAPUNC (1945–1948a), *Japanese Repatriation.*

a kaleidoscopic panorama of squalor and misery, testimony of the defeat of a nation and the collapse of a conqueror's dream'.[39]

Repatriation quarantine in Japan

When Japanese repatriates reached Japan, they had to go through quarantine. Repatriation quarantine in Japan started later than in Busan but was carried out more rigorously. In accordance with SCAPIN-48, reception centres and quarantine stations attached to the centres were established at all major ports. Quarantine for repatriates in Japan started from October 1945 but was not formally launched until December. The Ministry of Welfare was responsible for operating the centres under the supervision of American health officers (Sams 1998: 89–91). Eleven ports were designated as reception centres for processing returning Japanese and had been set-up to care for a total of 45,500 Japanese returnees per day. Ten of these ports had an estimated daily capacity of 30,500 for processing Koreans and Chinese for repatriation from Japan.[40] By December 1946, 4,662,597 Japanese repatriates (2,328,951 soldiers and 2,355,646 civilians) had returned to Japan and passed through quarantine.[41]

Quarantine procedures in Japan were as follows: Upon arrival, repatriate ships anchored off the coast of a repatriation port and quarantine officers boarded the ship to check certificates issued by quarantine officers at departure ports. Then officers ascertained whether there were any infectious disease patients (including suspected ones) on board. If cases of communicable diseases, such as cholera, typhus, plague, smallpox, etc., were

39 Bullit (1945), *40th Infantry Division*, p. 31.

40 GHQSCAP (1945b), *Summation of Non-Military Activities in Japan and Korea.*

41 Kōseishō (1949), Eisei gyōsei gyōmu hōkoku, pp.1-14.

found, they were removed to isolation hospitals. The remaining repatriates were quarantined onboard for 14 days, or longer if more cases of disease were observed on the ship. At the end of this period, if no additional cases were reported, repatriates were allowed to disembark. However, if further cases were detected, a further 14-days of quarantine was required from the date of the last proven case. As repatriates disembarked, quarantine officers sprayed them and their belongings with DDT to remove fleas and body lice. At the quarantine station, repatriates were required to use medicated baths and receive vaccinations against smallpox and typhus as well as inoculation for typhoid and paratyphoid (Hikiageengochō 1950: 77; Yoshida 1979).

The main purpose of repatriation quarantine was to stop pathogenic elements at the water's edge. For the SCAP, an epidemic posed a serious threat to maintaining order and stability. Epidemic diseases would not only threaten the safety of occupying forces, but also interfere with 'the success of the occupation mission' to reconstruct Japan.[42] Thus, laboratory facilities were established to detect cases of communicable diseases and carriers of pathogens. Returnees were screened not only for quarantinable diseases (cholera, plague, smallpox, typhus and yellow fever), but also for other notifiable diseases (typhoid fever, para-typhus, diphtheria, dysentery, scarlet fever and meningitis) (Yamashita 1975). Japanese returnees, especially those from Korea and Manchuria, also received chest X-rays for tuberculosis and their blood was examined for malarial parasites (Sams 1998: 89–91).

---

42 Public Health and Welfare Section of GHQ/SCAP (1946–1951), 'Public Health and Welfare in Japan', *The name of Series: Reparations and Public Welfare Activities, 1946–51*, Tokyo: PHW, pp.1-5.

Medicalized controls on both sides of the border often hinged on the application of quarantine officers and medical experts' medical knowledge as well as different perceptions of disease (Trubeta et al. 2021: 4). This was evident in the repatriation quarantine in Japan. Some diseases with which the US military and Japanese were particularly concerned were screened, such as venereal diseases (sexually transmitted infections). Also, leprous repatriates were subjected to quarantine even though the disease was not highly contagious (Yamashita 1975). Indeed, American quarantine policies against leprosy were stricter than those imposed in other countries; it was not until 1947 that leprosy was removed from the list of diseases which required a travel permit. The Japanese government also had a policy of isolating patients with leprosy from the early twentieth century. Both the US and Japan adhered to isolation policies for leprosy long after it had been proven to be scientifically unnecessary (Sato and Frantz 2005), and leprous repatriates were segregated when they returned to their homeland.

Illegal shipping

Japanese repatriates were only able to leave for home after completing several stages of quarantine. In the process, they sometimes suffered humiliation, and in some cases were sent to isolation hospitals. Moreover, they were severely limited in how much property they could take to Japan. Therefore, many repatriates sought smugglers in the vicinity of Busan to transport them and their belongings to Japan (Kahm 2016). They used relatively small fishing or trading vessels, which were vulnerable to storms and sea-mines (Guksapyeonchanwiwonhoe 1999: 155–156). By late October 1945, four or five ships had been lost due to mines in the harbour or typhoons. Smuggling ships also fell prey to pirates.[43]

Illegal shipping was seen by the occupying forces as one of the main ways in which diseases spread and a violation of their rules. The JRS bulletin admonished people not to take illegal vessels and stressed that 'illegal shipping was the misery of all Japanese' (*JRS Bulletin* 1945f). Despite the JRS's published statements, though, the US military authorities strongly suspected its Busan branch was 'the central agency responsible for the organisation and coordination of illegal traffic'. However, the authorities did not crack down on the JRS because its other work was so useful;[44] instead, the military tightened its coastal control to suppress illegal shipping. At night, destroyers beamed powerful searchlights across Busan harbour every 15 minutes. Korean relief societies also assisted the US military in controlling illegal transportation from Busan. These societies were independent of the Foreign Affairs section in operational matters, licensed by the city of Busan and operated under municipal supervision. However, the military government governed their policies and directed the distribution of relief supplies and investigated their solicited funds.[45]

Many Korean repatriates also used smugglers to transport goods and unauthorised sums of Japanese currency, which could only be exchanged on the black market, since Korean banks were not authorised to exchange Japanese yen. According to the Korean relief societies, about 48,000 Koreans arrived in

43 G-2 (1945–1948h), *Illegal Shipping*, in *History of the United States Army Forces in Korea, Part I*, http://db.history.go.kr/item/level.do?itemId=husa. Accessed August 12, 2018; GHQFECSCAPUNC (1945–1948c), *Repatriation & Removal of Peoples in Pusan Areas*, RG 554 Records of General Headquarters, Far East Command, Supreme Commander Allied Powers, and United Nations, USAFIK: XXIV Corps. USAFIK: XXIV Corps, G-2 Historical Section, TNLK.

44 G-2 (1945–1948h), *Illegal Shipping*.

45 GHQFECSCAPUNC (1945–1948b), *Repatriation Information Book*, pp.55-57.

the Busan area by illegal means between 27 September and 17 November 1945, and as many as 19,000 had arrived illegally at the nearby port of Masan by 18 December 1945. Koreans who travelled in this manner received no medical processing and were thus regarded as a serious health menace. Therefore, all Koreans found disembarking from unauthorised ships in the Busan area were taken to the compound to be quarantined and immunised against typhoid and smallpox.[46]

Illegal movement happened at the 38th parallel, too. It was estimated that there were 263,435 Japanese in North Korea as of 15 September 1945, and 206,508 Japanese had illegally crossed the border by 28 August 1946.[47] These figures included all the Japanese had walked from Manchuria to North Korea after Japan's defeat. Officially, the Soviets 'banned' the movement of Japanese from their occupational zone to the US occupational area until an agreement was reached between the USSR and the US on 19 December 1946. This agreement was for the return of Japanese nationals from Soviet and Soviet-controlled areas, and of Korean nationals in Japan to their home north of the 38th parallel. Before it was signed, however, the Soviets tolerated Japanese civilians fleeing to the South and, even encouraged many to cross the border, although they detained Japanese troops and skilled workers.[48] In the Spring of 1946, the number of Japanese refugees from the North increased rapidly, travelling largely by rail to the border or in coastal vessels to Busan by stages. The US military presumed that the

46 Ibid., p.70.

47 GHQFECSCAPUNC (1945–1948d), *Orders & Directives: Japanese Surrender and Status of Non-Japanese Controlled Korea*, RG 554 Records of General Headquarters, Far East Command, Supreme Commander Allied Powers, and United Nations Command, USAFIK: XXIV Corps, G-2 Historical Section, TNLK.

48 GHQFECSCAPUNC (1945–1948c), *Repatriation & Removal of Peoples in Pusan Areas*.

Soviets wanted to be rid of as many Japanese as they could, for each was an extra mouth to feed.[49] Although the Soviets were supposed to inoculate Japanese refugees prior to embarkation, often they did not. In fact, the Soviets demanded that Japan supply the necessary medicaments including typhus serum and smallpox vaccine.[50]

The US military believed that this illegal movement overburdened transportation and relief agencies, as well as increasing the spread of diseases. To strengthen public health, on 14 December 1945, the US military began to vaccinate refugees from the North against smallpox and delouse them with DDT. They employed about 4,000 Koreans to carry out these tasks.[51] The Americans briefly tried turning back Japanese at the 38th parallel, but the Soviets refused to accept them. The US military concluded it was better to accept the Japanese refugees who crossed the border and send them to the quarantine station since they would attempt to cross the 38th parallel by any means and by-pass quarantine, thus increasing the spread of contagious diseases (Pacific Stars and Stripes 1946).[52] Nevertheless, many Japanese illicitly crossed the border or sailed to ports in the northern part of South Korea. Some died enroute. For example, on 22 September 1946, two ships arrived in Incheon illegally from North Korea and Manchuria. There were 524 Japanese aboard the ship from North Korea, and two of them died. Another ship from Manchuria carried 842 Japanese among which five died

49 GHQFECSCAPUNC (1945–1948e), *Repatriation of Displaced Persons & Regulations regarding Repatriates*, RG 554 Records of General Headquarters, Far East Command, Supreme Commander Allied Powers, and United Nations Command. USAFIK: XXIV Corps, G-2 Historical Section, TNLK.

50 GHQFECSCAPUNC (1945–1948a), *Japanese Repatriation.*

51 GHQSCAP (1945c), *Summation of Non-Military Activities in Japan and Korea Number 3. December 1945*, Tokyo: GHQSCAP.

52 GHQFECSCAPUNC (1945–1948d), *Orders & Directives.*

from malnutrition and dehydration. They had sailed for ten days to Incheon without food and little water.[53]

From early 1946, the number of Koreans' travelling illegally to Japan increased rapidly. Most had been previously repatriated from Japan, and had found that the social and economic conditions in Korea were much worse than in Japan. They also found widespread political unrest over the division of the peninsula. Many struggled to find work and were suffering extreme poverty. For those who had returned with little money and few belongings, the situation seemed hopeless. In February 1946, about 200,000 Korean repatriates were residing in Busan causing shortages of accommodation and food, price inflation and spreading infectious diseases (*Joseonilbo* 1946). Moreover, many Korean repatriates had left their families in Japan in the hope that they would either be able to bring their family to Korea or return to them in Japan. In the postwar period, special provisions were made in some countries to allow the reunion of families divided by new postcolonial borders. The SCAP, however, issued a series of ordinances prohibiting cross-border movement between South Korea and Japan without its express permission (Morris-Suzuki 2006).

In June 1946, the Korean Coast Guard was established by the US military government. Its main duties were to suppress piracy in Korean coastal waters and illegal shipping between Korea and China and Korea and Japan (Guksapyeonchanwiwonhoe 1999). Subsequently, many Korean stowaways were arrested near Busan (*Busansinmu*n 1946a; *Yeongnamilbo*1946). However, many Koreans still crossed illegally, and the policing of smuggling along the coast of Japan was strengthened. From July, the British Commonwealth Occupation fleets also began to patrol Japanese coastal areas for illegal ships (*Jung'angsinmu*n 1946a).

53 GHQFECSCAPUNC (1945–1948a), *Japanese Repatriation*.

Table 8.1: Result of quarantining Korean illegal entrants, 1946

		Senzaki	Hakata	Sasebo	Karatsu	Total
Smallpox	Case	1	–	1	–	2
	Death	–	–	–	–	–
Cholera	Case	31	1	150	2	184
	Death	9	1	31	–	41
Cholera Bacilli Carriers		51	–	162	–	213

Ref: Yamashita (1975).

In July alone, 7,378 illegal Korean entrants were arrested in the coastal areas of Japan (*Busansinmun* 1946b). This influx of illegal Koreans was blamed for spreading infectious diseases in Japan, especially cholera.[54]

The cholera outbreak

On 17 August 1946, in the Lower House of Japan, Shiikuma Saburō of the Nihon Progressive Party raised the issue of illegal Korean entrants. He claimed that tens of thousands of Koreans had entered Kyushu and San'in illegally, accusing them of spreading cholera and causing economic turmoil by stoking the black market. He demanded stronger border controls to prevent Koreans from illegally entering Japan, expressing his belief that Korean stowaways were an 'indescribable threat to residential life' (Shūgiiin 1946). Indeed, there were cholera cases as well as bacilli carriers among the Koreans who were arrested in Japanese coastal areas (Table 8.1).

However, Shiikuma failed to mention that cholera had appeared in Japan before Korea. A repatriation ship from Guangdong, China, had arrived in Uraga on 5 April 1946 with

54 GHQSCAP (1946a), *Summation of Non-Military Activities in Korea Number 11. August 1946*, Tokyo: GHQSCAP.

three corpses who had died of cholera and seventeen passengers showing symptoms of the disease. Subsequently, many repatriation ships from Guangdong, Xiamen, Hanoi and other parts of Asia carried cholera to Uraga and other repatriation ports in Japan (Kōseishō Kōshūeiseikyoku 1980: 78–79). Soon, cholera was prevalent in Japan. Moreover, the cholera outbreak in Japan was a direct result of the US military's mistakes and negligence. There had been serious outbreaks of cholera in India and China in November 1945, and the US military was well-aware that the movement of millions of displaced people would create suitable conditions for the spread of cholera to Japan and Korea if they did not rigorously impose quarantine.[55] Nevertheless, the chief US medical officer in China failed to properly effect quarantine processing, and cholera spread to Japan (Sams 1998: 89–91).

Meanwhile, the USAFIK issued 'Quarantine Procedures for Cholera in Repatriates' on 13 April in response to cholera having been reported aboard repatriation vessels entering Japan from China. The procedures indicated that prior to any individual disembarking from a repatriation ship from China, a medical officer would have to board the vessel and thoroughly investigate whether there were any cases of cholera or not. If there were cases, the patients had to be removed to a hospital in the port's vicinity capable of strictly enforcing isolation and which had been approved for such by the military government.[56]

Eventually, cholera was reported on a repatriation ship with 3,100 Korean returnees from Guangdong which entered the port of Busan on 1 May 1946. As of 7 May there were twelve cholera cases and eleven deaths among the passengers of

55 GHQFECSCAPUNC (1945–1948f), *Public Health & Welfare: Health of Troops*, RG 554 Records of General Headquarters, Far East Command, Supreme Commander Allied Powers, and United Nations Command. USAFIK: XXIV Corps, G-2 Historical Section, TNLK.

56 Ibid.

the ship. Because there were no proper isolation hospitals in Busan, quarantine officers removed only the corpses while cholera patients (including suspected ones) were isolated onboard the ship. To compound the challenges, several passengers were suffering from other infectious diseases such as paratyphoid and malaria. The other passengers were thus exposed to numerous risks and pleaded to be allowed to disembark (*Busansinmun* 1946c; *Jung'angsinmun* 1946b). On 8 May the infected passengers were moved to an isolation hospital near the port (*Minjujungbo* 1946).

As cases and deaths from cholera increased on the ship, Korean public health officers and doctors planned to vaccinate essential staff for quarantine (*Yeongnamsinmun* 1946). The Department of Public Health and Welfare of South Gyeongsang Province determined that the acute infectious disease on the ship was cholera. However, US military medical officers were sceptical about the Korean public health officers' judgement. In mid-May, a medical officer of the USAFIK officially stated that the repatriation ship was being investigated and cholera bacilli had not been identified. He commented that only seven people had died of the twenty-six patients who were suffering from severe diarrhoea and he disagreed with the Korean officers' diagnosis (*Busansinmun* 1946d).

Soon, cholera cases were being reported among Busan citizens who lived near the port. Some Korean returnees who arrived in Busan on 15 May from Shanghai fell ill when they reached Daejeon and Incheon (*Busansinmun* 1946e). After disembarking in Busan, they took a train with other repatriates and headed to their hometowns (*Jayusinmun* 1946). Eventually, US military and Korean public health officers prepared to impose quarantine against cholera at the port of Busan. On 26 May 1946, a former Japanese hospital ship began to be used as a quarantine ship (*Jung'angsinmun* 1946c). Quarantine for rail passengers started three days later. At the beginning of June, maritime quarantine against cholera began in earnest in all the main ports. However, cholera had by then already spread throughout South Korea, including Seoul. In July, cases were reported in Pyongyang, Wonsan and along the railway line to Pyongyang in North Korea.[57]

On 16 July 1946, the Commander of USAFIK informed SCAP that the cholera situation in Busan was under control, with quarantine lifted in most areas of the city and only ten new cases reported in the previous six days. Meanwhile, the port of Incheon was jammed, with 'at present a thirty-day backlog in the harbour'. The port of Busan was reopened on 1 August (Choi 2006). Around that time, the US military ordered that Japanese repatriation be completed soon and that, except for a handful of staff, Japanese personnel engaged in repatriation work in South Korea were to leave the country (Nishinihon Toshokan 1980, 35). Soon afterwards, sixty men of the Korean Constabulary took over repatriation work at Busan from the US Army. In the Autumn, cholera gradually subsided, with a total of 15,481 cases and 10,043 deaths reported by 28 October.[58]

Despite the fact that cholera had spread to Japan before Korea, and that the negligence of the US military was a significant contributor to the scale of the cholera epidemic, the Japanese blamed it on the Koreans. Nor was there any acknowledgement that the unprecedented movement of repatriates and the spread of cholera throughout Asia were direct results of Japan's imperial expansion and wars of aggression. Showing no sign of remorse, they perceived their former colonial subjects as an external threat from the outside. The SCAP shared this view

57 GHQFECSCAPUNC (1945–1948a), *Japanese Repatriation.*

58 GHQSCAP (1946b), *Summation of Non-Military Activities in Korea Number 13. October 1946*, Tokyo: GHQSCAP.

and tightened control of the maritime border between Korea and Japan, using cholera as an excuse. On 18 August, SCAP announced that the influx of Koreans threatened the health of the Occupation and the Japanese people through the spread of cholera and typhus. Even after cholera had mostly disappeared from Japan and Korea, on 13 December 1946, SCAP issued further orders to the Japanese Government "to stop the illegal entry of Koreans, potential carriers of cholera into Japan" (Conde 1947).

During the age of imperialism, the Japanese consistently blamed their imperial subjects, particularly Koreans, for a host of diseases rather than recognizing endemic vectors within their own country or the role of social conditions in generating epidemics (Aldous and Suzuki 2012: 90–91). Similarly, in postwar Japan, Koreans (both illegal entrants and residents in Japan) were seen by the Japanese and SCAP as subversives – both pathogenically and ideologically – who were deeply intertwined with communism. The League of Koreans in Japan, established in October 1945, organized and joined political and social movements, including May Day for food supply in 1946, often with the Japanese Communist Party. They also protested for Japanese employers to pay overdue wages for Korean labourers forced to work in Japan during the war. More generally, Korean residents in Japan provided support to other Koreans seeking to illegally re-enter and settle in Japan.

Initially Koreans in Japan were treated as members of 'liberated nations' by SCAP. However, SCAP gradually came to view Koreans in Japan as a disruptive and lawless minority. Among other things, Koreans were blamed for the black market, despite the fact that the black market in Japan had flourished during the war. After the war, many ex-military officers, bureaucrats and conglomerates were engaged in the black market which was contributing to inflation in postwar Japan (Conde 1947; Griffiths 2002). Despite this, Koreans were regarded as the main culprits, as well as being involved in smuggling and the increase in crime more generally. Gradually, SCAP's anti-Korean sentiment emerged into the open and orders (such as application of jurisdiction, preparation of registered lists and forced repatriation of illegal immigrants) were issued to Koreans in Japan as emergency measures (Ricketts 2000; Morris-Suzuki 2006; Choi 2021). Moreover, South Korea was seen by the US Occupation forces as fertile ground for the establishment of communism (Cummings 1997: 198). From the Spring of 1946, when the first US-Soviet Joint Commission broke down and negotiations were indefinitely adjourned, the US military gradually strengthened its oppression of left-wing groups (or divided them) including the Communist Party of Korea, which enjoyed great support among the Korean people. The US military suppressed left-wing media outlets by suspending their publications, raiding the offices of left-wing organisations, and arresting key persons of the Communist Party of Korea (Park 1991; Park 2017). In this situation, Korean stowaways as well as Korean residents in Japan were regarded as dangerous threats to Japanese society who posed an obstacle to transforming Japan into a healthy democracy sympathetic to US geopolitical strategies. Hence, SCAP tended to 'pathologize' Koreans, as public health provided a convenient rationale to monitor and suppress them both at the border and within Japan.

Conclusion

Following Japan's defeat in WWII, the Japanese empire was dismantled and a new Cold War system gradually formed in the Asia-Pacific region. The US and the USSR were engaged in global competition which shaped international relations (Wallerstein 1993). The Korean peninsula was divided into North and South at the 38th parallel. The Soviets occupied North Korea while South

Korea and Japan were placed under US military occupation. For the US military, stabilizing the occupied regions and establishing a new political order was essential. To this end, it was necessary to repatriate several millions Japanese and their former colonial subjects expeditiously and methodically, although the massive migration of repatriates was a major threat to the public health and security of the US occupying forces as well as their newly subject populations in Japan and Korea.

It was therefore deemed necessary to control pathogens, both to protect US troops and reduce the sources of social unrest in the occupied regions. The US military quarantined repatriates at all major ports. Busan was the main repatriation port in South Korea because it was a crucial point on the main transit route between Korea and Japan and its harbour was well-equipped. At the Busan quarantine station, Japanese repatriates were screened both for pathogens and contraband. Further preventive measures (e.g. delousing with DDT and immunization) were imposed to prevent the spread of diseases to Japan. Before boarding, repatriates had to be purified according to standards set by the US military through quarantine procedures.

Quarantine is a long-standing and visible border control method and thus an obvious expression of the power of the state over individuals or groups (Harrison 2016: 251). At the turn of the twentieth century, Japan, as a new imperial power, utilized maritime quarantine in the port of Busan, not only to keep diseases in check but to consolidate its imperial territory through screening potentially harmful agents. Hence, quarantine measures often exceeded what was required to prevent the spread of diseases across the region (Kim 2013). Under the US military's surveillance system, Japanese repatriates had to pass through quarantine procedures both to screen for disease and to cleanse the taint of their imperial past. Repatriation quarantine procedures conducted by the Americans impressed on the Japanese that they were citizens of a defeated country. When returning to their home country, Korean repatriates were also subjected to dusting with DDT powder and quarantine under the US military. As well as protecting against disease, these procedures may also have been intended as disciplinary measures by which Koreans would become familiar with their new social order. In practice, as well as metaphorically, the US military attempted to stamp its authority on Korea and Japan as key battlegrounds for the opposing ideologies of the Cold War. For many, quarantine and disinfection were the first manifestations of a new reality.

In this new regime, illegal entrants were regarded as a public threat on account of their potential to destabilize society through disease, criminal activity and political activism. Geographical proximity and improved transport between Busan and Japan facilitated the movement of pathogens and other perceived 'harmful elements'. The Occupation forces consequently cracked down on stowaways between Busan and Japan. This was particularly evident from the spring of 1946, when cholera spread to Japan and later to Busan by repatriation ships, becoming prevalent in both countries. The Japanese authorities refused to acknowledge any culpability for these outbreaks and scapegoated Korean stowaways, who were blamed for the spread of cholera and other diseases in Japan. Even after the quarantine for cholera was lifted in Busan, and the epidemic receded in Japan and Korea, cholera was used to justify strengthening border controls between Korea and Japan to stop 'subversive Koreans' from infecting Japanese society. This tendency was accompanied by growing concern over the expansion of communist forces in South Korea and Japan. In this regard, the border controls implemented by the US Occupation forces revealed their insecurities, as competition between the two super-powers became more intense.

References

Aldous, Christopher (2006), 'Typhus in Occupied Japan (1945–1946): An Epidemiological Study'. *Japanese Studies* 26(3): 317–333.

Aldous, Christopher and Suzuki, Akihito (2012), *Reforming public health in Occupied Japan, 1945–52: Alien prescriptions?*, Abingdon, Oxon, Routledge.

Anonymous (1946), 'Sengo bōeki taisaku no jūten (Major emphasis of preventive measures against diseases in the postwar period)', Nihon iji shinpō (Japanese medical journal), 1175: 3 and 6.

An, Jong-Cheol (2015), *Haebanghu Sahoeundong* (Social movement in liberated Korea), Yangpyeong: Saenggakswimpyo.

Araragi, Shinzō (2017), 'The collapse of the Japanese empire and the great migrations: Repatriation, assimilation, and remaining behind', in Barak Kushner and Sherzod Muminov (eds), *The Dismantling of Japan's Empire in East Asia: Deimperilization, postwar legitimation and imperial afterlife*, London and New York: Routledge.

Augustine, Matthew R. (2017), 'The Limits of Decolonization: American Occupiers and the "Korean Problem" in Japan, 1945–1948', *International Journal of Korean History*, 22(1): 43–75.

Bullit, John M. (1945), *40th Infantry Division: History of Evacuation and Repatriation Through the Port of Pusan: Korea, 28 Sept. 45–15 Nov. 45*, Washington DC: Department of the Army.

Busansinmun (1946a), 'Ilboneuro gujikhaeng (Leave for Japan to find a job)', *Busansinmun*, 12 June.

Busansinmun (1946b), 'Ilbone milhang gyeokjeung, 7 wôljung'e man-myeong irago (Rapid increase in stowaways, 10,000 in July)', *Busansinmun*, 20 August.

Busansinmun (1946c), 'Samcheonmyeong saui gongpo (3,000 people in fear of death)', *Busansinmun*, 5 May.

Busansinmun (1946d), 'Kolera gyuneun balgeyon andoetda (Cholera bacilli have not been found)', *Busansinmun*, 17 May.

Busansinmun (1946e), 'Incheone hoyeolja (Cholera in Incheon)', *Busansinmun*, 22 May.

Buskirk, James Dale Van (1931), *Korea, Land of the Dawn*, New York: Missionary Education Movement of the United States and Canada.

Chapman, David (2016), 'Identifying and Defining Self in a Changing Japan', in S. R. Nagy (ed.), *Japan's demographic revival: Rethinking migration, identity and sociocultural norms*, New Jersey: World Scientific.

Choi, Deokyo (2021), 'The Empire Strikes Back from Within: Colonial liberation and the Korean minority question at the birth of postwar Japan, 1945–47', *American Historical Review*, 126(2): 555–584.

Choi, Youngho (2006), 'Ilbon'e paejeon gwa bugwanyeonrakseon: Bugwanhangroe gwihwanjadeul (Defeat of Japan and the Busan-Shimonoseki cross-channel liner: Repatriates on this channel liner)', *Hanil Minjok Munje Yeongu* (The journal of Korean-Japanese national studies), 11: 243–287.

Choi, Youngho (2017), 'Institutionalizing Japan's Relief System for Repatriates: Koreans and Japanese at Hakata Port in 1945', *International Journal of Korean History*, 22(2): 155–182.

Clemente, Jonathan D. (2005), 'The Fate of an Orphan: The Hawley Board and the debates over the postwar organization of medical intelligence', *Intelligence and National Security*, 20(2): 264–287.

Conde, David (1947), 'The Korean Minority in Japan', *Far Eastern Survey*, 16(4): 41–45.

Conrad, Sebastian (2014), 'The Dialectics of Remembrance: Memories of Empire in Cold War Japan', *Comparative Studies in Society and History*, 56(1): 4–33.

Cumings, Bruce (1997), *Korea's Place in the Sun: A Modern History*, New York: Norton.

Dai kyūjū teikokugikai shūgiin honkaigi dai sanjūgō, (90th Plenary Session of the House of Representatives of the Imperial Diet) 17 Aug, 1946, https://teikokugikai-i.ndl.go.jp/simple/detail?minId=009013242X03019460817&spkNum=11.

Geukdong munje yeon'guso (1989), *Jibang migunjeong jaryojib* (Data on local administration of the US military government), Seoul: Gyeong'in Mumhwasa.

Griffiths, Owen (2002), 'Need, Greed, and Protest in Japan's Black Market, 1938–1949', *Journal of Social History*, 35 (4): 825–858.

Guksapyeonchanwiwonhoe (1999), 'The Secretary of Navy (July 22, 1946)', *Hanguk Hyeondaesa Jaryojipseong 46: Juhan Migunsagomundan Munseo* (Documents of USAFIK), Gwacheon: Guksapyeonchanwiwonhoe.

Guthrie-Shimizu, Sayuri (2010), 'Japan, the United States, and the Cold War, 1945–1960', in M. P. Leffler and O. A. Westad (eds), *The Cambridge History of the Cold War*, Cambridge: Cambridge University Press, pp. 244–265.

Hamada, Yasunori (2010), 'Beigunseiki no minami chosen kyūgoseisaku ni kansuru ikkōsatu: kyūgo gyōsei no saihensei wo chūshinni (A study of South Korea relief policy during the US military government)', Shitennoji daigaku daigakuin kenkyūronshū, 5: 81–101.

Harrison, Mark (2016), 'Afterword', in Alison Bashford (ed.), *Quarantine: Local & Global Histories*, London: Palgrave Macmillan, pp. 251–257.

Harrison, Mark (2017), 'Pandemics', in Mark Jackson (ed.), *The Routledge History of Disease*, Abingdon: Routledge, pp. 129–146.

Hikiageengochō (1950), *Hikiageengo no kiroku* (Records on aids to repatriates), Tokyo: Hikiagechō.

Jayusinmun (1946), 'Guihwan dongposeoneso hoyeok chimip (Cholera brought by a Korean repatriation ship)', *Jayusinmun*, 23 May.

Joo, Young-min (2017), 'Bukhaedo gorakgareul tonghaebon gangjedongwon (Compulsory mobilization seen from Bunkae-do Gorak-ga)', *Yeoksagyoyuknonjib* (The Society of History Education), 64: 239–275.

Joseonilbo (1946), 'Jeonjae gwihwan dongpo 20 man, busan janryu (200,000 Korean returnees remain in Busan)', *Joseonilbo*, 11 February.

JRS Bulletin (1945a), 'Fusan kyūshin (Express message from Busan), *JRS Bulletin*, 28, 4 October.

JRS Bulletin (1945b), 'Hikiage no jijō wa kaudesu (This is the situation of repatriation)', *JRS Bulletin*, 54, 7 November.

JRS Bulletin (1945c), 'Fuzan to Fukuoka no jōkyō (Situation of Busan and Fukuoka)', *JRS Bulletin*, 19, 25 September.

JRS Bulletin (1945d), 'Fujinyo fukusōni ki o tsukemaseu (Ladies, watch your clothes)', *JRS Bulletin*, 24, 30 September.

JRS Bulletin (1945e), 'Yobōchusha nit suite (About preventive shot)', *JRS Bulletin*, 37, 16 October.

JRS Bulletin (1945f), 'Nihonh eno mikkō o tomeyo (Stop smuggling to Japan)', *JRS Bulletin*, 43, 24 October.

Jung'angsinmun (1946a), 'Daeil milhangja juui, yeonggukhamdaega chuldong gyeonggye (Stringent British Navy precautions against Korean stowaway)', *Jung'angsinmun*, 20 July.

Jung'angsinmun (1946b), 'Busanhang'e hoyeolja! (Cholera in the port of Busan)', *Jung'angsinmun*, 7 May.

Jung'angsinmun (1946c), 'Guihwanseone geomyeok (Quarantine against repatriation ships)', *Jung'angsinmun*, 26 May.

Kahm, Howard (2016), 'Between Empire and Nation: A micro-historical approach to Japanese repatriation and the Korean economy during the US occupation of Korea, 1944–6', *Journal of Contemporary History*, 51(1): 124–144.

Kim, Jeong-Ran (2013), 'The Borderline of "Empire": Japanese maritime quarantine in Busan c. 1876–1910', *Medical History*, 57(2): 226–248.

Kim, Jeong-Ran (2021), 'Jegukui henjeok jiugi: paejeon hu ilboneseoui guihwanja geomyeok (Erase the taint of empire)', in Choi Hae-Byeol (ed.), *Jilbyeong Gwanriui Sahoemunhwasa: Ilsangsaenghwaleseo Gukga Jeongchaekggaji* (Social history of disease control), Seoul: Ehwa Woman's University Press, pp. 291–321.

Kim, Jung Hai (2008), 'Mi gunjeong'giui haengjeonggwa jeongchaekbyeonhwaui teukseong (A study of public administration and policy during the United States military administration era)', *Haengjeong Nonchong* (Korean journal of public administration), 46(3): 145–172.

Kōseishō Kōshūeiseikyoku (1980), *Kein'ekiseidohyakunenshi* (One hundred years history of quarantine), Tokyo: Gyōsei.

Kinkela, David (2011), *DDT and the American Century: Global Health, Environmental Politics, and the Pesticide That Changed the World*, Chapel Hill: University of North Carolina Press.

Krishna, Bhuvana (2021), 'Disease Surveillance: The bedrock for control and prevention, *Indian Journal of Critical Care Medicine*, 25 (7): 745–746.

Lee, Han-Jung (2007), 'Geundaehwawa mobang: [chiine sarang] e natana seoyang pungjo (Modernization and imitation)', *Ileo Ilmunhak Yeongu* (The Japanese language and literature association of Korea), 62: 71–89.

Lee, Seung-Ook (2015), 'Trevor Barnes and Joel Wainwright, Mapping Human Terrain in the Joint Army-Navy Intelligence Study of Korea (1945)', *The Professional Geographer*, 67 (4): 663–675.

Lee, Steven Hugh (1995), *Outposts of Empire: Korea, Vietnam and the origins of the Cold War in Asia, 1949–1954*, Montréal and Buffalo: McGill-Queen's University Press.

Maeilsinbo (1945), 'Joseonijaedongpogujehoe ilbon guhoban sachal sogam (The impression of the Korean Relief Union's investigation in Japan)', *Maeilsinbo*. 27 September.

McWilliams, Wayne C. (1988), *Homeward Bound: Repatriation of Japanese from Korea after World War II*, Hong Kong: Asian Research Service.

Medical Department, United States Army (1955), *Preventive Medicine in World War II, Vol. 3, Personal Health Measures and Immunization*, Washington, D.C.: The Surgeon General Department of the Army.

Minjujungbo (1946), 'Bangyeok Uiyongdae Jojik (Volunteer army for quarantine)', *Minjujungbo*, 9 May.

Morris-Suzuki, Tessa (2006), 'Invisible Immigrants: Undocumented migration and border controls in early postwar Japan', *The Journal of Japanese Studies*, 32 (1): 119–153.

Morris-Suzuki, Tessa (2010), *Borderline Japan: Foreigners and Frontier Controls in the Postwar Era*, New York: Cambridge University Press.

Nishinihon Toshokan Konsarutanto Kyōkai (1980), Aru sengoshi no joshō: MRU hikiage iryō no kiroku (The prologue of postwar history: Record of the Medical Relief Union for repatriation), Fukuoka: Nishinihon Toshokan Konsarutanto Kyōkai.

Pacific Stars and Stripes (1946), 'USSR is Silent on 2 American Korea Protest: General Hodge Cites Mass Japanese Exodus into Southern Korea', *Pacific Stars and Stripes*, 23 August.

Park, Ji-young (2022), 'Colonial Research on Public Hygiene and its Postcolonial Legacy: Focusing on Hygiene Laboratory in Colonial Korea', *Korean Journal of Medical History*, 31(2): 429–466.

Park, Kyeongmin (2017), '1945 nyeon paejeon hu Jaejoilbonin'e gwigyeol: gyeongseong ilbonin sehwahoe'ui jaesan munjewa sikminji jibae insik'eul jungsimeuro (The conclusion of Japanese residents in Korea after defeat in the war)', *Ilbon Gonggan* (Japan Space), 21: 103–127.

Park, Su-Hyon (2011), 'Hanguk minjuhwawa chinilcheongsan munje (Korea's democratization and punishing pro-Japanese)', *Gieok-gwa Jeonmang* (Memory and prospect), 24: 130–160, 359.

Park, Sun-Sup (2017), '"Dongnipsinmun" ui jwagyeonghwae daehan gaenyeomsajeok jeopgeun (A conceptual historic approach for the left-leaning of the Independence News)', *Yeoksayeongu* (Journal of history), 32: 115–148.

Park, Tae-Gyun (1991), '1945–1946 nyeon migunjeong'e jeongchiseryeok jaepyeon gyehoekgwa namhan jeongchigudoe byeonhwa (The US military government's planning for reorganization of politicians and changing the political aspect in South Korea ranging from 1945 to 1946)', *Hanguksa yeongu* (The journal of Korean history), 74: 109–160.

Rengōgun sōshireibu hen, Kyōdō tsushinsha shōgaibu yaku (translator) (1950), Nihon senryōki no shimei to Seika (The mission and the achievements of the US military occupation), Tokyo: Itagaki Shoten.

Ricketts, Robert (2000), 'Senryōkiniokeru chiikishakaito zainichi chōsenjin (Local community and Koreans in Japan in postwar Japan)', *Tōzainanboku* (Bulletin of the Wako Institute of Social and Cultural Sciences), 01(01): 4–15.

Rho, Ki-Young (2006), 'Haebang hu ilbonin'e gwihwan gwa jungangilhanhyeophoe (Japanese repatriation and 'The Central Japanese-Korean Association' after the liberation of Korea)', *Hanil Minjok Munje Yeongu* (The journal of Korean-Japanese national studies), 10: 125–159.

Sams, F. Crawford. (1998), *'Medic': The Mission of an American Military Doctor in Occupied Japan and Wartorn Korea*, Armonk, N.Y. and London: M.E. Sharpe.

Sato, Hajime and Frantz, Janet E. (2005), 'Termination of the leprosy isolation policy in the US and Japan: Science, policy changes, and the garbage can model', *BMC International Health and Human Rights*, 5(3): 1–16.

Shin, Jwa-Seop (2000), 'Gunjeonggiui Bogeonuiryojeongchaek (The policy of the United States Army military government in Korea toward public health and medicine in occupied South Korea)', *Uisahak* (Korean journal of medical history), 9(2): 212–232.

Simmons, James Stevens (1944–1954), *Global Epidemiology: A Geography of Disease and Sanitation Vol 1*, Philadelphia: J.B. Lippincott.

Trubeta, Sevasti, Promitzer, Christian, and Weindling, Paul (eds.), (2021), *Medicalising Borders: Selection, containment and quarantine since 1800*, Manchester: Manchester University Press.

Watt, Lori (2009), *When Empire Comes Home: Repatriation and Reintegration in Postwar Japan*, Cambridge and London: Harvard University Press.

Watt, Lori (2015), 'Embracing Defeat in Seoul: Rethinking Decolonization in Korea, 1945', *The Journal of Asian Studies*, 74(1): 153–174.

Wallerstein, Immanuel (1993), 'The World-System After the Cold War', *Journal of Peace Research*, 30(1): 1–6.

WHO, Public Health Surveillance, http://www.who.int/topics/public_health_surveillance/en/.

Yamashita, Yoshiaki (1975), 'Shōwa nijūnendai no ken'ekishi (History of quarantine in the Showa 20s)', Igakushi kenkyū (Studium historiae medicae), 44: 1–10.

Yeongnamilbo (1946), 'Ilbonmilhangja eomjungcheobeol (Severe punishment against stowaways to Japan)', *Yeongnamilbo*, 30 June.

Yeongnamsinmun (1946) 'Busane Hoyeolja Chimip (Cholera invaded Busan)', *Yeongnamsinmun*, 9 May.

Yi, Yeon-Sik (2008), 'Haebang jikhu 38 ibuk ilbonin'e georyuhwangeyong byeonhwa: 'Jeonjaengpihaejaron'e daehan bipanjeok gochal (The change of circumstances of the Japanese residents in North Korea just after liberation)', *Hanil Minjok Munje Yeongu* (The journal of Korean-Japanese national studies), 14: 163–230.

Yi, Yeon-Sik (2018), 'Haebang jikhu namhan guihwanjae haeoe jaeiju hyeonsang'e gwanhan yeongu (A study on the migration phenomena of Korean repatriates just after liberation)', *Hanil Minjok Munje Yeongu* (The journal of Korean-Japanese national studies), 34: 77–124.

Yoshida, Jusaburō (1979), 'Hikiage Ken'ekishi no koto (About the history of repatriation quarantine)', *Igakushi kenkyū* (Studium historiae medicae), 4: 43–45.

Index